All Clear 3

Teacher's Book

Philip Wood

Macmillan Education
4 Crinan Street, London N1 9XW, UK
A division of Macmillan Publishers Limited

Companies and representatives throughout the world

ISBN 978-0-230-46726-2

Written by Philip Wood

First published 2015

Designed by emc design limited
Cover design by Designers Collective

Back cover images by: Nature Publishing Group, Studio8, Thinkstock.

Student's Book credits
Text, design and illustration © Macmillan Publishers Limited 2015
Designed by emc design limited

Illustrated by Humberto Blanco (Sylivie Poggio Artists Agency) pp5, 33; Susanna Spelta (Sylvie Poggio Artists Agency) p32; Rory Walker pp12, 46, 90, 61

Picture research by Penelope Bowden, Proudfoot Pictures

The authors and publishers would like to thank the following for permission to reproduce their photographs: **Alamy**/age fotostock Spain p66(7), Alamy/AGF Srl p56(4), Alamy/All Canada Photos p72(ml), Alamy/Alliance p86(9), Alamy/amana Images Inc p38(tl), Alamy/colin anderson p87(b), Alamy/Art Directors and TRIP p13(br), Alamy/David Ball p108(tl), Alamy/Patrick Batchelder p4(3), Alamy/Robin Beckham p6(1), Alamy/Caspar Benson p76(14), Alamy/David Bleeker – London p72(bl), Alamy/Blend Images p108(br), Alamy/Eric Constantini p67(r), Alamy/Craig Holmes Premium p52(7), Alamy/Lev Dolgachov p37, Alamy/Chris Dorney p52(6), Alamy/Paul Doyle p72(tr), Alamy/Elizabeth Whiting & Associates p18(14), Alamy/Dirk Ercken p96(3), Alamy/eye35.pix p47(br), Alamy/fashionpix p102, Alamy/Stuart Forster p96(10), Alamy/Elly Godfroy p18(11), Alamy/James Hardy/PhotoAlto p86(1), Alamy/Hemis p42(12), Alamy/Heritage Image Partnership Ltd p93(t), Alamy/Hero Images Inc. p8(6), Alamy/Wesley Hitt p38(tennis), Alamy/Andrew Holt p43(m), Alamy/Chris Howarth/France p29(a), Alamy/D. Hurst pp40, 78(laptop, 108(laptop), Alamy/IDREAMSTOCK p18(4), Alamy/Image Source p11, Alamy/Brian Jannsen pp42(9), 96(4), Alamy/Darren Jew p42(2), Alamy/JHPhoto p96(14), Alamy/Juice Images p86(7), Alamy/jvphoto p18(5), Alamy/Evgeny Karandaev p23(br), Alamy/kolvenbach pp40(br), 41(l), Alamy/Raimund Kutter/ImageBROKER p72(c), Alamy/J Marshall – Tribaleye Images p62(7), Corbis/145/Brian Lawrence p42(5), Alamy/oliver leedham p106(mr), Alamy/Don Mason p22(13), Alamy/MBI pp52(2), 56(3), Alamy/Tatiana Morozova p75(bcl), Alamy/Eric Nathan p66(6), Alamy/NorthScape p97(l), Alamy/OJO Images Ltd p8(8), Alamy/David Pearson p96(13), Alamy/Photoalto p81(l), Alamy/Jeffrey Pickthall p49(t), Alamy/Pictorial Press Ltd p76(4), Alamy/Picture Partners p106(ml), Alamy/James Quine p76(2), Alamy/Radius Images pp8(11), 86(4), 106(tcr), Alamy/Robert Harding World Imagery p48(b), Alamy/Alex Segre p43(b), Alamy/StampCollection p76(10), Alamy/Neil Tingle p41(tl), Alamy/Peter Titmuss p62(3), Alamy/Derek Trask p40(bcr), Alamy/Travelscape Images p62(12), Alamy/Andrew Watson p71, Alamy/Michael Weber/ImageBROKER p62(4), Alamy/Edward Westmacott p109(br), Alamy/Jan Wlodarczyk p38(c), Alamy/YAY Media AS p87(t); **Corbis** pp72(tcr), 86(12), Corbis/Aflo/Splash News p77(t), Corbis/Yuri Arcurs/Tetra Images p8(5), Corbis/FACUNDO ARRIZABALAGA/epa p40(London), Corbis/Bettmann p25(l), Corbis/Jamie Budge p76(1), Corbis/Michael Cole p15(l), Corbis/dondoc-foto/F1 Online p25(r), Corbis/Carolina Faruolo/Lebrecht Music p106(tcl), Corbis/Tia Gille p106(br), Corbis/Leon Harris p38(lm), Corbis/Rune Hellestad p108(blc, laptop), Corbis/Hero Images p28(7), Corbis/Image Source p77(b), Corbis/Ch'ien Lee/Minden Pictures p42(8), Corbis/Simon Marcus p38(rm), Corbis/Mika p62(1), Corbis/Jose Luis Pelaez, Inc. p72(tcl), Corbis/Alessia Pierdomenico/Reuters p52(1), Corbis/Psihoyos p76(11), Corbis/Radius Images p72(tm), Corbis/Rubberball p38(tm), Corbis/Anup Shah p28(2), Corbis/Jordan Siemens p38(br), Corbis/Splash/US Fund for UNICEF/Splash News p56(b), Corbis/Ant Strack p106(bcr), Corbis/Brad Swonetz p97(7), Corbis/Uwe Umstätter/Westend61 p38(tr), Corbis/Underwood & Underwood pp35(t), 83(l), Corbis/Steve Vidler p74(bcr), Corbis/Visionhaus p15(tr), Corbis/Wavebreak Media Ltd p79, Corbis/Ben Welsh pp91(tr,bl), Corbis/Debby Wong p76(7); By kind permission of **Carlo Crippa** p63(t); **Fotolibra**/Olaf Protze p4(4); By kind permission of **Fresh Films**/Ricci Reinbold p80(m,b); **Getty Images** pp40(bcl,laptop), 72(br), Getty Images/AFP/Stringer p49(l), Getty Images/H. Armstrong Roberts p25(c), Getty Images/Ascent Xmedia p28(1), Getty Images/Allan Baxter p42(6), Getty Images/Elizabeth Beard p45, Getty Images/Peter Beavis p96(5), Getty Images/Al Bello p41(tr), Getty Images/bilderlounge p8(13), Getty Images/Blend Images – KidStock p8(9), Getty Images/Ivan Bliznetsov p97(r), Getty Images/Blue Magic Photography p100, Getty Images/Blue Jean Images p62(8), Getty Images/Steve Bly p62(2), Getty Images/Jon Bower at Apexphotos p46(r), Getty Images/Paul Bradbury pp8(14), 14, 18(12), Getty Images/C Brandon p101(br), Getty Images/Peter Cade 22(9), Getty Images/Ryerson Clark p66(4), Getty Images/Comstock p72(tl), Getty Images/Comstock Images p8(1), Getty Images/Valerie Crafter p42(10), Getty Images/Crocodile Images p18(9), Getty Images/Eileen Darby p21, Getty Images/Winston Davidian p34, Getty Images/Peter Dazeley pp22(8), 22(14), Getty Images/Steve Debenport p92, Getty Images/Mitch Diamond p42(1), Getty Images/Digital Vision pp22(5), 96(1), Getty Images/Digitaler Lumpensammler p42(3), Getty Images/Kevork Djansezian p99(b), Getty Images/Jim Dyson p108(tr), Getty Images/Topher Donahue p28(5), Getty Images/Richard Drury p66(9), Getty Images/Wayne Eastep p75(br), Getty Images/Europa Press pp76(13), 106(tm), Getty Images/Lauree Feldman Calculate p46(m), Getty Images/Sue Flood p31, Getty Images/Floridapfe from S.Korea Kim in cherl p66(5), Getty Images/FREDERICK FLORIN p76(9), Getty Images/Jim Frazee p28(12), Getty Images/Fuse p41(bcr), Getty Images/Frank Gaglione p109(bcl), Getty Images/Pawel Gaul p48(t), Getty Images/Ian Gavan p109(cr), Getty Images/Paul Gilham p41(br), Getty Images/mauro grigollo p27, Getty Images/Charles Gullung p86(10), Getty Images/Izabela Habur p68, Getty Images/Jeffrey Hamilton p18(1), Getty Images/hana/Datacraft p96(6), Getty Images/Richard Heathcote p40(bl), Getty Images/Hero Images p17, Getty Images/Ralf Hettler p35(b), Getty Images/Hola Images p86(8), Getty Images/Jason Homa p62(5), Getty Images/Nancy Honey p106(cm), Getty Images/Hulton Archive p69(b), Getty Images/Images Etc Ltd p62(11), Getty Images/Edwin Jimenez p66(8), Getty Images/Anna Kallberg p7(l), Getty Images/Renee Keith p106(bl), Getty Images/Mike Kemp p86(11), Getty Images/KidStock p75(bcr), Getty Images/Jeff Kravitz p99(t), Getty Images/Bernhard Lang p33(r), Getty Images/Markus Lange p28(9), Getty Images/Kevin Landwer-Johan p62(9), Getty Images/David Leayh p66(1), Getty Images/Rich Legg p8(7), Getty Images/Loop Delay p106(tl), Getty Images/Lorado p62(10), Getty Images/Ghislain & Marie David de Lossy p86(6), Getty Images/MarcelTB p56(1), Getty Images/Ryan McVay p96(8), Getty Images/Michael Ochs Archives p109(cr), Getty Images/Ricky John Molloy p86(2), Getty Images/Pamela Moore p56(5), Getty Images/Tara Moore p18(7), Getty Images/Tim Newman p52(8), Getty Images/Nikada p52(9), Getty Images/Dimitri Otis p57(tl), Getty Images/Pictfolio p18(10), Getty Images/Popperfoto p59(r), Getty Images/Print Collector p59(l), Getty Images/Michael Putland p108(tc), Getty Images/J.Carlos Roldan p44(r), Getty Images/Marc Romanelli p75(cr), Getty Images/Andy Ryan p4(2), Getty Images/Chris Ryan p89, Getty Images/Oli Scarff p66(b), Getty Images/Justin Setterfield p15(br), Getty Images/Jueren & Christine Sohns p28(3), Getty Images/Jamie Squire p40(tr), Getty Images/STOCK4B-RF p86(13), Getty Images/Manuel Sulzer p28(6), Getty Images/Alexey Tkachenko p18(3), Getty Images/UpperCut Images p55, Getty Images/Annemarie van den Berg p29(br), Getty Images/Betsie Van der Meer p22(7), Getty Images/Guy Vanderelst p103(l), Getty Images/Benedicte Vanderreydt p8(4), Getty Images/Venturelli p76(8), Getty Images/David Vernon p18(8), Getty Images/Visit Britain/Britain on view p42(4), Getty Images/VM p8(12), Getty Images/VSD Software Piotr Jaczewski p51, Getty Images/Theo Wargo p109(bl), Getty Images/Westend1 p18(13), Getty Images/Juliet White p108(bl), Getty Images/Adrianna Williams p44(l), Getty Images/Windsor & Wiehahn p28(4), Getty Images/Kevin Winter p96(9), Getty Images/Heinz Wohner p28(10), Getty Images/WPA Pool p49(r), Getty Images/Yellow Dog Productions p52(10), Getty Images/Zero Creatives p86(5); **Glow Images**/Aflo Sport p41(bl), Glow Images/Benis Arapovic p41(bcl), Glow Images/Elena Elisseeva p96(2), Glow Images/Hero Images pp22(11), 101(tc), Glow Images/Roger Richter/Corbis p22(1), Glow Images/Timelapse Library Ltd p40(tl), Glow Images/West Coast Surfer p52(4), Glow Images/H. & D. Zielske p103(r); **The Kobal Collection**/UMBILICAL PRODUCCIONS/TV3/TVE/CANAL+/ICEC/ICAA p63(b); By kind permission of **Patrick McConlogue** p19(tl,tc); **Photocusine**/Fondacci/Markezana p65; **Photodisc** p75(tl, tr); **Plainpicture**/fStop p108(bcr); **Rex Features**/Everett Collection pp74(blc, laptop), 101(mr), Rex Features/Jonathan Hordle p76(3), Rex Features/MediaPunch p101(bl), Rex Features/Moviestore p82, Rex Features/Moviestore Collection pp74(t), 83(r), Rex Features/David Rowland p101(ml), Rex Features/BILL ZYGMANT p93(b); **Thinkstock**/amanalang p101(tr), Thinkstock/anilsam p33(l), Thinkstock/Anja Peternelj p105, Thinkstock/Apple Tree House p28(8), Thinkstock/BananaStock p6(2), Thinkstock/bangkaewphoto p91(tl), Thinkstock/Micha? Bednarek p28(11), Thinkstock/Jani Bryson pp7(r), 101(tl), Thinkstock/Jui-Chi Chan p4(5), Thinkstock/Samer Chand p47(tl), Thinkstock/István Csák p29(b), Thinkstock/Songquan Deng p46(l), Thinkstock/George Doyle p76(6), Thinkstock/fatchoi p56(2), Thinkstock/funstock p106(tr), Thinkstock/f9photos p42(11), Thinkstock/IgorKovalchuk p96(2), Thinkstock/IPGGutenbergUKLtd p23(tr), Thinkstock/Itos p43(t), Thinkstock/jfollby p62(6), Thinkstock/KevinAlexanderGeorge p47(bl), Thinkstock/kkgas/iStock Editorial p4(1), Thinkstock/leszekglasner p76(12), Thinkstock/lisafx p22c(3), Thinkstock/Lukas_zb p91(br), Thinkstock/Petr Malyshev p38(bl), Thinkstock/Oleksiy Mark p23(bl), Thinkstock/Monkey Business Images Ltd pp23(tl), 52(5), Thinkstock/moodboard p22(6), Thinkstock/Amy Myers p6(3), Thinkstock/Photick/Laurence Mouton p47(tr), Thinkstock/Purestock p8(7), Thinkstock/RolfSt p66(2), Thinkstock/rommma p23(bcr), Thinkstock/Howard Sayer p22(10), Thinkstock/sumnersgraphicsinc p96(11), Thinkstock/Claudia Gabriela Tapuleasa p22(4), Thinkstock/tashka2000 p13(bl), Thinkstock/tetmc p57(tr), Thinkstock/Vstock LLC p38(bc), Thinkstock/Wavebreakmedia Ltd pp22(12), 58, 74(bl), Thinkstock/whitetag p18(6), Thinkstock/XiXinXing p8(3), Thinkstock/Cathy Yeulet p22(2), Thinkstock/Linda Yolanda pp13(tl,tr), 67(l), 81(r), Thinkstock/Feng Yu p18(2), Thinkstock/ZHARATE p42(7); **Superstock** p74(br), Superstock/age fotostock p66(3), Superstock/Belinda Images p72(swim), Superstock/Gallo Images p24, Superstock/imageBROKER P8(10), Superstock/Mauritius Images p86(3), Superstock/Stock Connection p76(5), Superstock/Tetra Images pp52(3), 80(t), Superstock/Underwood Photo Archives p69(t); By Kind permission of **Felicity van Steenbergen** p53(b,t).

Material curricular para la Educación Secundaria Obligatoria del área de Lengua Extranjera: Inglés, que corresponde al proyecto presentado para su supervisión y/o aprobación / homologación / registro en las Entidades de Educación de las Comunidades Autónomas.

All Clear conforms to the objectives set by the Common European Framework of Reference and its recommendations for the evaluation of language competence.

Printed and bound in Spain by Impresos Izquierdo
2019 2018 2017 2016 2015
10 9 8 7 6 5 4 3 2 1

Contents

Introducing All Clear

All Clear is a four-level ESO course which contains a wide range of up-to-date, real-world material of genuine interest to teenagers. Its step-by-step approach and careful recycling of grammar and vocabulary through easy-to-follow learning outcomes provide your students with a clear path towards achieving key language and communication skills. While All Clear is designed to guide your students to develop their language competence, it also teaches invaluable life skills for lifelong learning and prepares learners to successfully pass their exams.

Linguistic content

Vocabulary

All Clear approaches **vocabulary** in a practical way, introducing new lexis with ample visual support and systematic contextualized exposure throughout the unit. Vocabulary sets are recorded on the Class Audio CDs and can be downloaded from the Digital Resource Centre so students can practise pronunciation. The Workbook has a picture dictionary of the target vocabulary.

Grammar

Fully comprehensive **grammar** tables in the grammar section guide students through the exercises while additional schematic grammar tables are provided in the Language Reference. Authentic-style texts and dialogues provide the context essential for understanding the unit grammar.

Skills

All Clear provides achievable coverage of all four skills which helps to improve students' ability to communicate effectively in real-world contexts. **Receptive** skills are developed through authentic reading texts and engaging listening activities. The topical link continues with the **production** of model dialogues and texts with **interaction** between students being guided through carefully crafted speaking and writing tasks.

Reading

All Clear contains different genres of reading text to capture students' interest and at the same time also present essential grammar and vocabulary from the unit.

Writing

All Clear takes a highly scaffolded approach to written interactions and production with **Model Texts**, **All Clear Tips** and a three-step **Writing Task** which shows students how to plan, write and check their own work.

Listening

Clear recordings and graded exercises provide students with the opportunity to hear in context the target grammar and vocabulary they have learned.

Speaking

All Clear repeats the well-structured formula used for Writing for spoken interaction and production. **Model Dialogues** with a three-step **Speaking Task** guide students through production and practice of their own dialogues.

Lifelong learning skills

Life skills

Students are encouraged to develop life skills with the **Culture Reading** pages in each Student's Book unit which present lifestyles in Britain and other countries, a **Cultural Awareness** quiz and video documentary in the Student's Book Revision Units, and with additional life skills analysed in the **Macmillan Life Skills Collaborative Projects** in the Workbook in which students are invited to reflect on how they put into practice their personal life skills in a team as well as the team's life skills as a whole.

Digital competence

All Clear treats digital competence transversally with digital learning outcomes in skills work and the use of online tools for production and interaction in the **Digital Competence** pages in the Student's Book and the **collaborative projects** in the Workbook. The **Digital Competence** worksheets in the Teacher's Resource File provide an opportunity to review and learn new digital skills in an English language environment while the Teacher's Book teaching notes indicate websites where students can learn more about the topics in the Student's Book.

Self-study

The **Workbook** offers the perfect tool for self-study and helps to foster learner autonomy by encouraging students to take an active role in their own learning. The Workbook contains revision of grammar and vocabulary, and an extensive colour section including reference material, extra practice, wordlists and collaborative projects.

Self-evaluation

Students can check their progress in the Workbook through the **My Progress** charts at the end of each Workbook unit and the self- and group evaluation in the **Macmillan Life Skills Collaborative Projects**.

Cultural awareness

The **Culture Reading** pages in the Student's Book feature a whole range of teenage-focused culturally relevant topics from sport to film-makers while the **Cultural Awareness** pages in the term **Revision** sections can be supplemented with **Culture videos** and **worksheets** from the Digital Resource Centre.

Cross-curricular content

All Clear provides ample transversal practice in the Student's Book of other school subjects including geography, biology, science, language and literature, arts and drama as well as physical education, with additional practice in the **Content-based Learning** section of the Teacher's Resource File.

Mixed ability and accessibility

Macmillan cooperates with the ONCE in the preparation of Braille versions of students' material and is committed to providing accessibility for visually-impaired students.

Council of Europe and Key Competences

All Clear follows the guidelines of the Foreign Languages Area of the Council of Europe which mark the way not only to learn a language but also how to communicate through it in carefully graded steps.
All Clear provides practice of the key competences set out in the Common European Framework of Reference (CEFR) for Foreign Languages and uses these to create learning objectives to assess students' competence in productive, receptive and interactive activities and strategies.

Key Competences

CLC	Competence in linguistic communication
CMST	Competence in mathematics, science and technology
DC	Digital competence
L2L	Learning to learn
SCC	Social and civic competence
SIE	Sense of initiative and entrepreneurship
CAE	Cultural awareness and expression

Support and solutions for teachers

All Clear includes a full range of print and digital components which provide teachers with the support they need and solutions for all types of learning environments:

- Teacher's Book
- Class Audio CDs
- Teacher's Presentation Kit
- Teacher's Resource File
- Tests and Exams Pack
- Student's Digital Material

Teacher's Book

Class Audio CDs

Digital Resource Centre
- Teacher's Presentation Kit
- Editable Teacher's Resources
- Culture videos and worksheets

Teacher's Resource File

Tests and Exams Pack with CEFR Skills Exam Generator

Student's Digital Material

Overview of components

Student's Book

The Student's Book includes:

- a Starter Unit (4 pages)
- nine units (10 pages each)
- three revision sections (4 pages each)
- an access code to All Clear Student's Digital Resources

The downloadable Teacher's Presentation Kit is also available at www.allclear.macmillan.es

Vocabulary

Vocabulary sets are presented using photographs and are recycled and practised in context throughout the unit. They are recorded on the Class Audio CD for pronunciation practice.

Dialogues give students the opportunity to talk about their own world following a clear example.

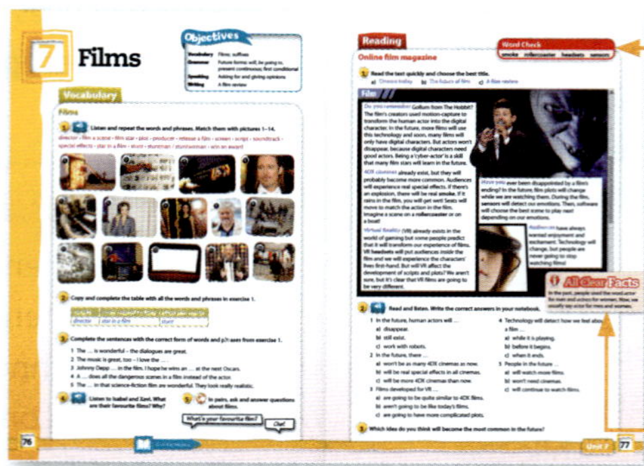

Reading

All Clear uses print and digital genres, from magazine articles to social messaging and wikis, with teen-focused topics presenting the unit language in context.

To help understanding, the **Word Check** pre-teaches some vocabulary items.

The **All Clear Facts** provides interesting additional information.

Reading texts are recorded on the Class Audio CD.

Grammar

Grammar tables lead students through carefully staged practice exercises.

All Clear Rules guide students through the more difficult grammar points.

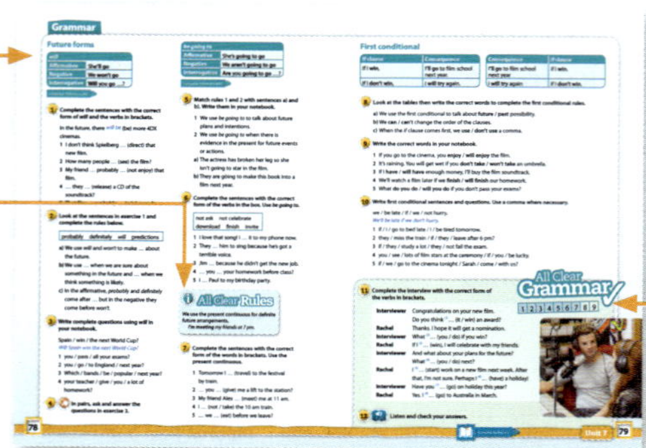

Each two-page grammar section concludes with a cumulative **All Clear Grammar** dialogue or text which contextualizes the new structures and recycles structures from previous units in realistic situations which are familiar to students.

Vocabulary and Listening

This page provides a second lexical set with ample visual support.

Clear listening texts with simple straightforward tasks give students the confidence to extract the main ideas and details of radio programmes, advertisements and conversations.

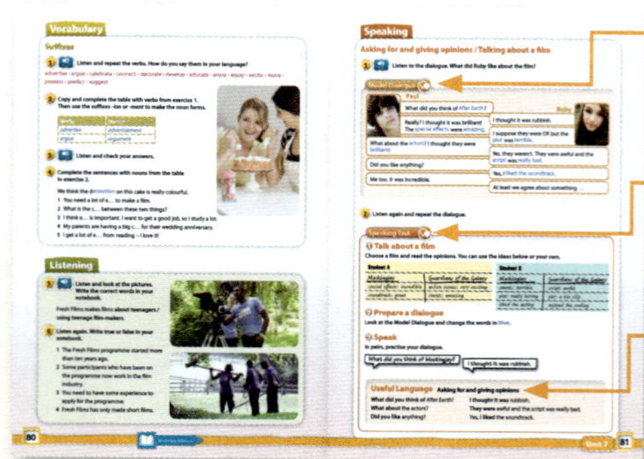

Speaking

Teen-centred **Model Dialogues** for students to follow everyday formal and informal conversations.

The **Speaking Task** guides students through the preparation and production of their own dialogue.

Useful Language highlights key functional structures.

Conversation strategies such as basic rules of courtesy are presented.

Writing

Model Texts use a variety of different print and digital text types.
All Clear Tips highlight and practise specific language points from the Model Text.
The **Writing Task** guides students through the preparation and production of their own texts.

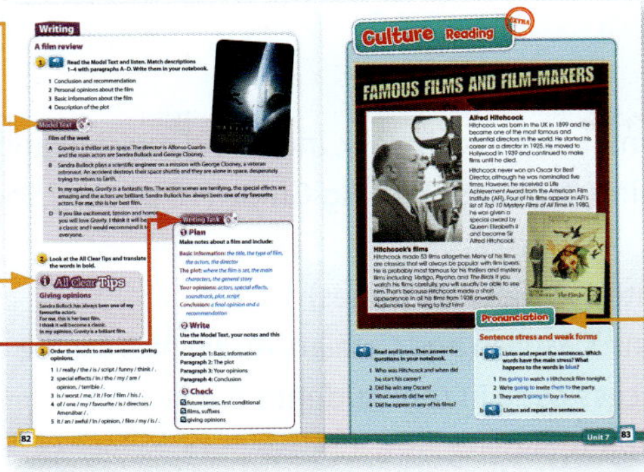

Culture Reading

A second reading text with information about diverse cultural topics provides further context for students to review the unit grammar and vocabulary.
Pronunciation examples are taken from the context of the Culture Reading text.

Language Reference

The **vocabulary** sets are repeated here to aid learning.
Simple **grammar tables** provide at-a-glance support.
Functional Language from the Speaking pages is provided for easy reference.

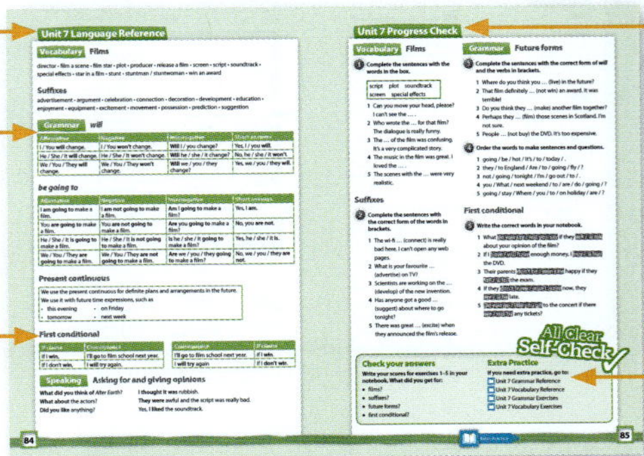

Progress Check

The **Progress Check** provides a manageable **evaluation** of all vocabulary sets and the main grammar points from the unit. Students check their answers to see if they need further practice.
References to material with extra support are given.

Revision: Vocabulary

Revision of vocabulary from the three previous units is provided as a game.

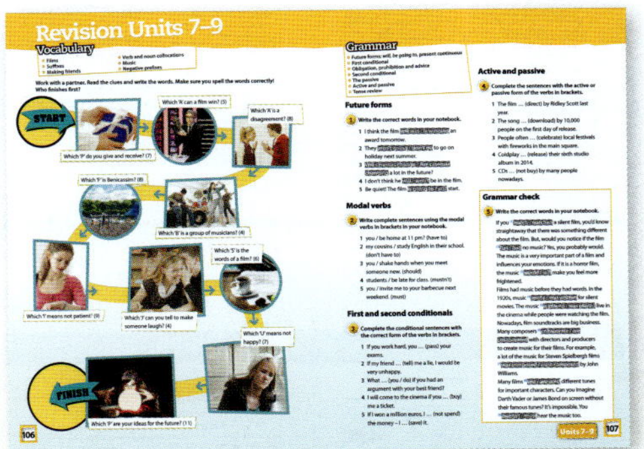

Revision: Grammar

Revision of grammar from the three previous units is provided.

Cultural Awareness

This multimedia page appears in each revision unit.
The fun **quiz** with thought-provoking questions tests students' knowledge of an aspect of life in Britain.
There is a related **Culture video** in the Teacher's Presentation Kit and in the Digital Resource Centre. An accompanying worksheet is available in the Teacher's Resource File.

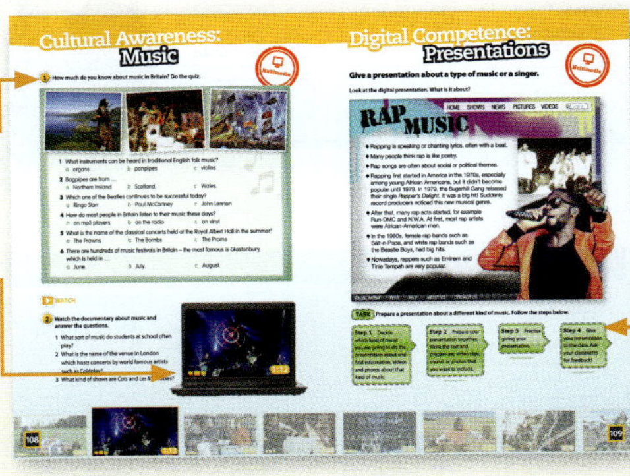

Digital Competence

This Multimedia page appears in each revision unit and covers useful digital learning objectives.
A model digital project created with easy-to-use web tools is presented.
Step-by-step instructions help students improve their digital competence and create their own digital project.

Workbook

The Workbook includes:

- a Starter Unit (4 pages)
- nine units (6 pages each) with grammar and vocabulary, including revision and extension
- full colour Culture: Reading & Listening (9 pages), Writing Guide (18 pages), Speaking (9 pages) and Wordlist (9 pages) sections
- three Macmillan Life Skills Collaborative Projects (6 pages)

The Workbook is available in two editions: Castilian and Catalan. Audio files can be downloaded from www.allclear.macmillan.es using the access code in the Student's Book.

Vocabulary

Contents link to the full-colour Reference and Skills sections. Ample practice of all the vocabulary sets in the Student's Book is provided.

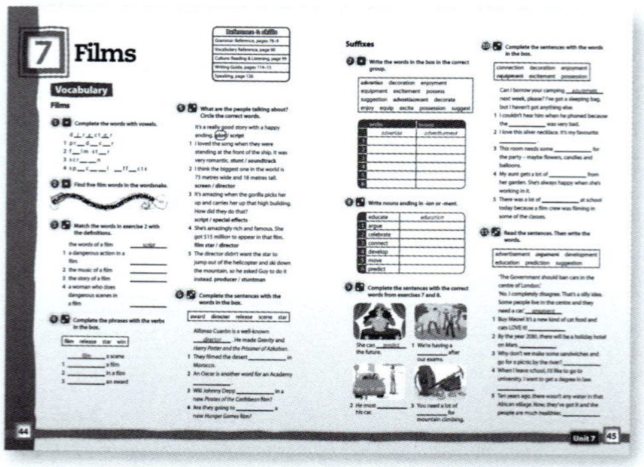

Fun activities motivate self-study. The easy-to-follow exercises are graded with one, two or three stars to indicate level of difficulty.

Grammar

Practice of all the grammar from the Student's Book is given in easy-to-follow exercises graded with one, two or three stars to indicate level of difficulty.
Grammar practice is contextualized.

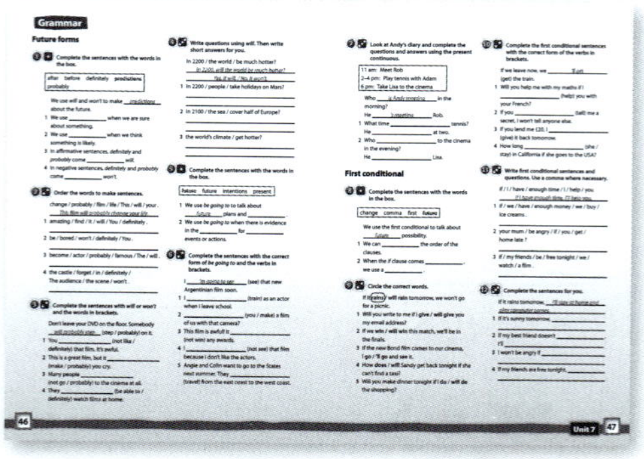

Revision

Dictation reinforces spelling, vocabulary and structures.
Common mistakes are presented in the **Error Correction** section.
More reinforcement of vocabulary and structures is provided in the **Translation** section.
The **Unit Grammar Check** provides consolidation of grammar.

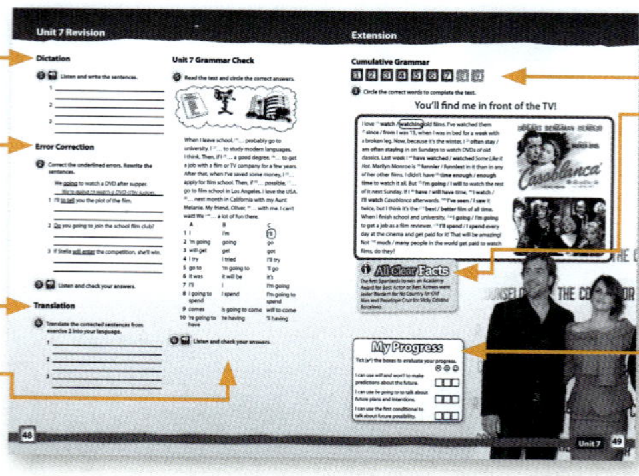

Extension

A **Cumulative Grammar** text gives more ambitious grammar practice.
All Clear Facts give fun and interesting additional information about the topic.
My Progress encourages self-evaluation of progress made with the grammar in the unit.

Grammar Reference

A complete reference guide of all the grammar in the Student's Book is provided.
Grammar usage is explained in either Castilian or Catalan.
Clear examples of usage are provided.

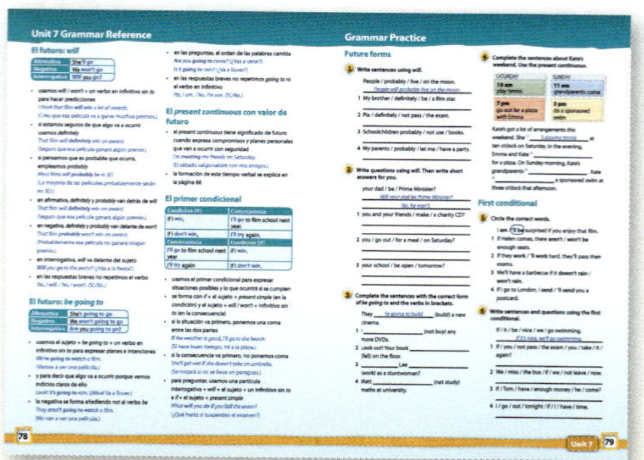

Grammar Practice

Grammar exercises face the Grammar reference pages to provide further reinforcement.

Vocabulary Reference

A **picture dictionary** of the vocabulary sets is provided. Vocabulary activities give more revision.

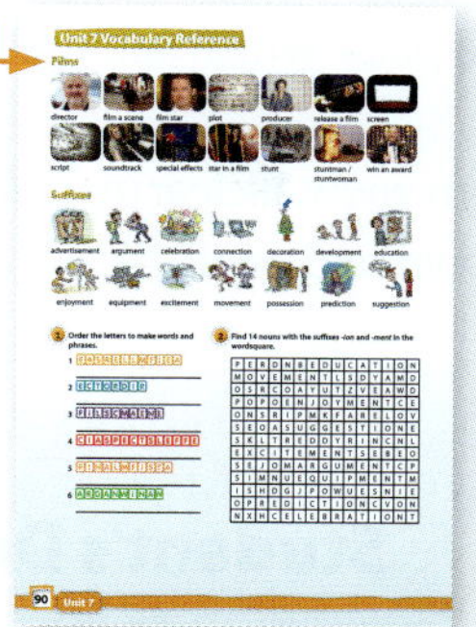

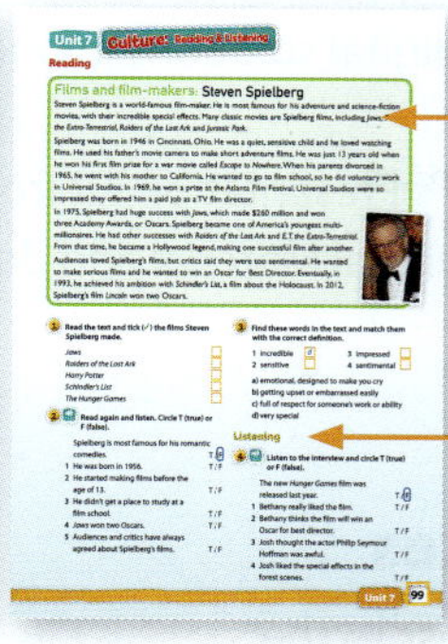

Culture: Reading & Listening

A **reading text** increases cultural awareness.

A **listening exercise** extends the cultural topic in the reading text.

Writing Guide

The step-by-step writing guide has **Tasks** with a variety of different writing outcomes.

A **Model Text** provides an example of what students will write.

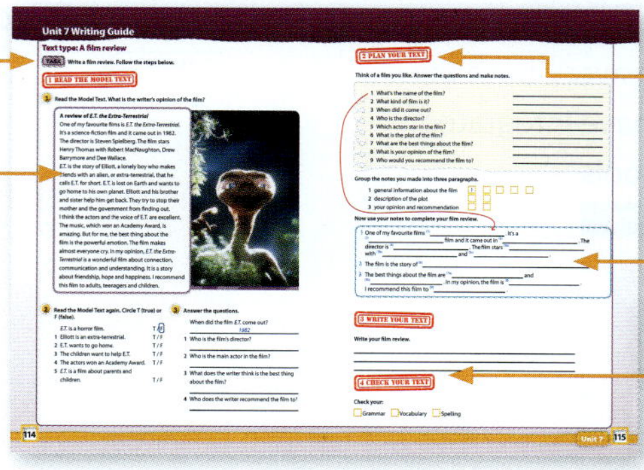

Questions and answers provide a **Plan** for the students' text.

Students use the answers provided to complete a **Draft Text** followed by their own text.

Students are given a reminder to check the text for grammar, vocabulary and spelling.

Speaking

Extra speaking practice is provided to prepare for oral presentations and exams.

Stimulating photos help engage students.

A **Tip** gives practical suggestions for improving speaking.

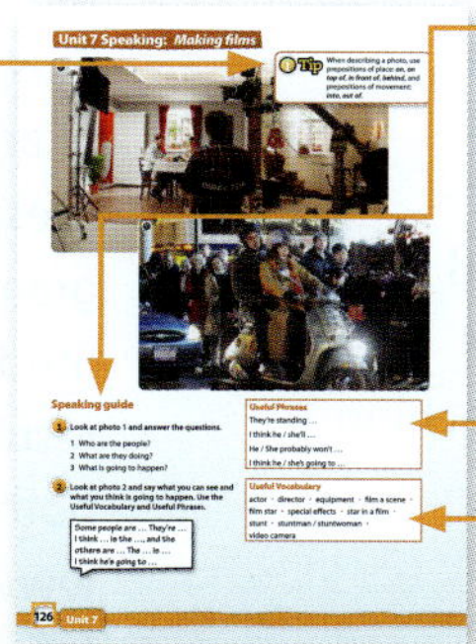

A **Speaking Guide** with questions about photo 1 shows what students can describe in photo 2.

Useful Phrases for describing photos and **Useful Vocabulary** from the unit are provided for easy reference.

Macmillan Life Skills Collaborative Projects

The **Task** has a clearly defined learning outcome.

Clear steps help students work together on a project.

Charts are provided for self and group assessment of **Life Skills** used during the project.

More life skills stimulate social and civic awareness.

Digital Resource Centre

The Digital Resource Centre provides digital solutions in one place which suit the technology available in all teaching environments.

- Teachers can download the Teacher's Presentation Kit from www.allclear.macmillan.es
- Students can access the Student's Digital Material and download audio files for the Workbook.

For teachers

Teacher's Digital Resources

The Digital Resource Centre gives access to the:

- **Teacher's Presentation Kit.** The Student's Book in the Teacher's Presentation Kit includes interactive activities with one-by-one or 'show all' answers. The Workbook includes 'show all' answers. Both the Student's Book and the Workbook have integrated audio links and a full range of IWB tools.

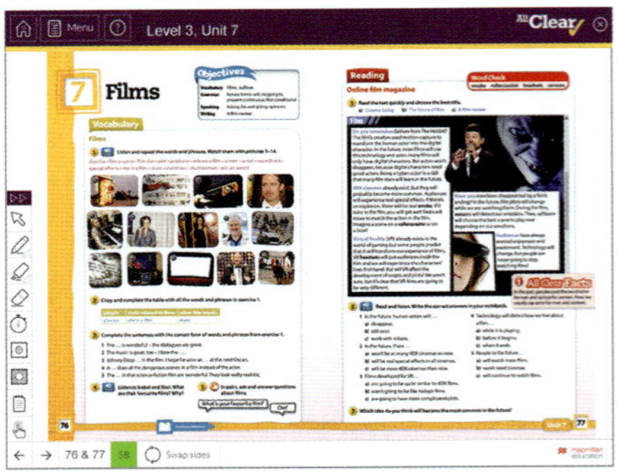

- **Teacher's Resource File** including editable worksheets and corresponding audio files.
- **Workbook audio** in downloadable files.
- **Culture Watch website**, with material designed to enrich students' linguistic and socio-cultural competence, including videos, worksheets, teaching notes at two levels and video transcripts.
- **Students' Digital Material** and **Gradebook**.

For students

Student's Digital Resources

Students who buy the Student's Book obtain an access code for:

- **Student's Digital Material** providing extra practice material and a **Gradebook**.

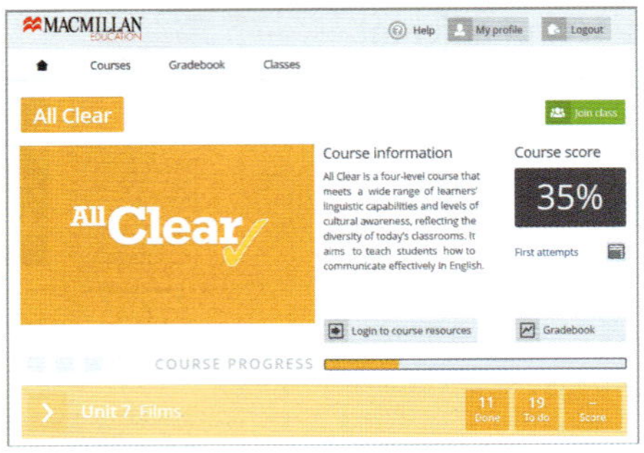

- downloadable audio files for the Workbook.

Additional resources for students

- **Macmillan Secondary Student Website**
  This website provides learners with hundreds of additional activities to practise the language presented in the Student's Book. These cover grammar, vocabulary, reading, writing and listening. Students can work at home or at school, and their results will always be recorded. The website allows both students and teachers to monitor online work.
  www.macmillansecondary.com

- **Macmillan Dictionary Online**
  The Macmillan Dictionary Online is an online dictionary and thesaurus in one and offers free tools and resources. With just one click of a button, users can consult definitions, synonyms, grammar information, example sentences, common phrases, British and American pronunciations and much more.
  www.macmillandictionary.com

All Clear Resources for teachers

Teacher's Book

The **Teacher's Book** is designed to help you make the most of the All Clear components and improve your students' results. The unit **Overview** spread provides a quick guide to the contents and objectives and is followed by page-by-page **teaching notes** and **answer keys**. There are **warmers** and **extra activities** as well as **cultural background information** and **web information** to help engage students' interest. **Mixed-ability solutions** suggest special activities for students who need extra help and for fast finishers. The Teacher's Book includes the complete **Student's Book**, including audioscripts and the Workbook **answer key**.

Class Audio CDs

All the audio recordings from the Student's Book are included on two audio CDs.

Teacher's Resource File

The **Teacher's Resource File** is an invaluable source of photocopiable worksheets and resources. It contains a **Multi-level Materials Bank** which recycles and practises grammar and vocabulary for classroom diversity as well as innovative **Language Excellence** worksheets to extend grammar practice and a **Lifelong Learning** section which develops digital competence and study skills as well as worksheets to accompany the Culture Watch video website. **Evaluation and Key Competences** are covered by evaluation rubrics and key competences worksheets while the **Content-based Learning** section features CLIL worksheets which link to other areas of the curriculum as well as Macmillan Readers worksheets. Editable files and all the audio files for the listening activities can be downloaded from the Teacher's Resource Centre.

Tests and Exams Pack

Tests and Exams

The Tests and Exams disk provides PDF and editable tests and exams. The material includes:

- a Placement Test and Key Competences Diagnostic Test which can be used to assess the language level of students
- tests available at three levels: basic, standard and extra. Each level has:
  - nine progress tests
  - three end-of-term tests
  - one end-of-year test
- answer keys, audio files and audioscripts for all the tests and exams

CEFR Skills Exam Generator

The CEFR Skills Exam Generator disk provides teachers with a tool to generate their own skills-based exams. Covering CEFR levels A1+ to B1, the material includes a range of reading, writing, listening and speaking tasks typical of external exams.

Teacher's Book

The wide range of different features and tasks in the Teacher's Book helps teachers make the best use of the All Clear materials.

Each unit in the Teacher's Book starts with two complete **Overview** pages which cover the following categories: **Unit objectives and key competences**

Linguistic content: grammar, vocabulary, functional language and pronunciation

Skills: learning outcomes: reading, listening, speaking and writing

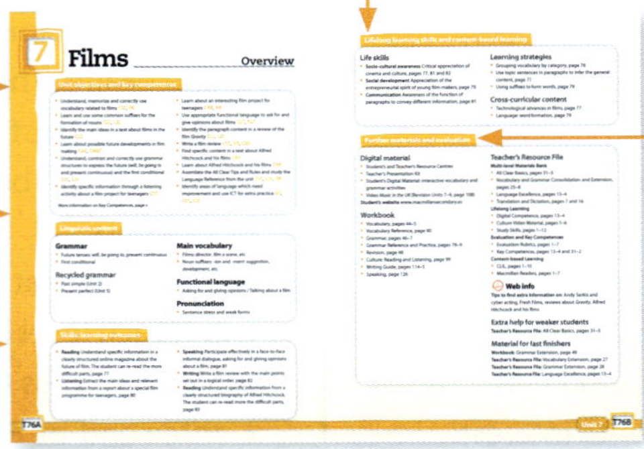

Lifelong learning skills and content-based learning: life skills, learning strategies, cross-curricular content

Further materials and evaluation: digital material, Workbook, Teacher's Resource File, evaluation material, web info, extra help for weaker students and material for fast finishers

Clear **Lesson Aims** summarize the work that will be covered.

Optional **Warmer** tasks are short and practical.

Extra activities are included for consolidation or extension.

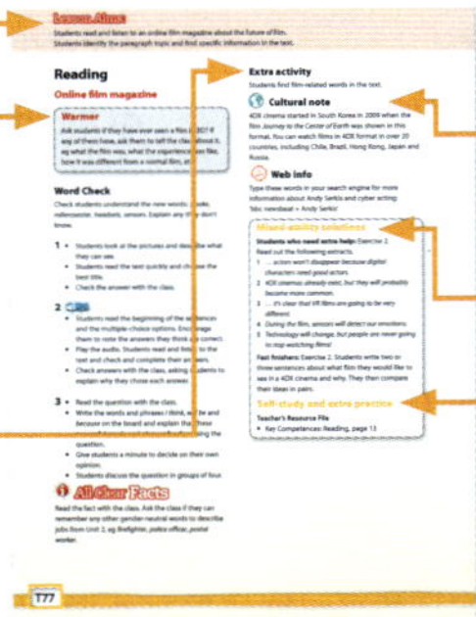

Cultural notes provide interesting background information to the topic.

Mixed-ability solutions give ideas for students who need extra help as well as fast finishers.

Web info guides teachers to useful topic-related websites.

Teacher's Resource File

The Teacher's Resource File contains 264 pages of photocopiable material, answer keys and audioscripts – all the worksheets and extra materials your class needs to fully exploit the contents of All Clear. It is divided into 11 sub-sections arranged into four main sections, ensuring easy navigation. The relevant answer key is located at the end of each section.

Multi-level Materials Bank

Basics

All Clear Basics worksheets are aimed at students who need extra help, making them an ideal solution to classroom diversity. They feature revision of key vocabulary and grammar in the Student's Book and a language reference section.

Vocabulary and Grammar

Two **Vocabulary Consolidation and Extension** worksheets and two **Grammar Consolidation and Extension** worksheets per unit provide revision and extended practice of all the vocabulary and grammar in the Student's Book.

Language Excellence

The **Language Excellence** worksheets feature extended grammar practice within real-life contexts to enhance students' linguistic and communication skills.

Translation and Dictation

The **Translation** and **Dictation** worksheets are linked to each unit. Audio files of the dictation exercises are available in the Digital Resource Centre.

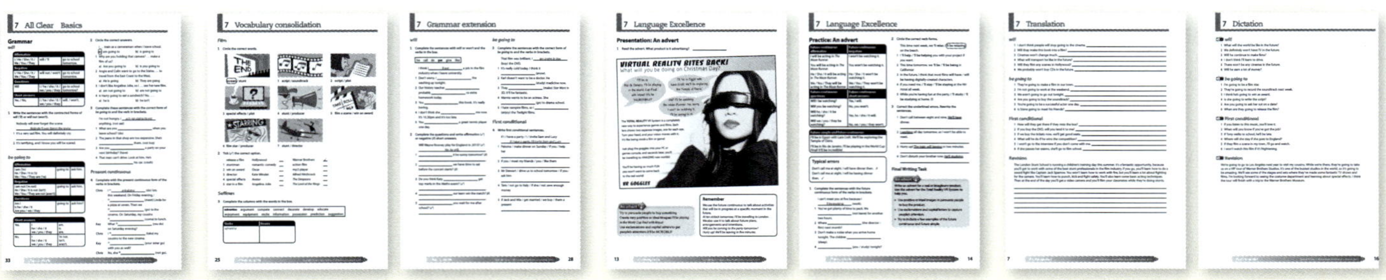

Lifelong Learning

Digital Competence

The **Digital Competence** worksheets train both teachers and students to use free web tools to improve their life skills. Students can learn English and improve their digital competence through projects such as infographics and web-based image-editing tools. Each worksheet comes with Teaching Notes which provide more information about the web tools and explain how to make the most of the worksheets in class.

Culture Video Material

Each **Cultural Awareness** page in the term Revision sections of the Student's Book is linked to a related **Culture video** in the Teacher's Presentation Kit with engaging footage of real life in English-speaking countries. The Teacher's Resource File provides worksheets which test students' comprehension of the audiovisual material during and after watching the videos, Teaching Notes and Audioscripts.

Study Skills

The **Study Skills** worksheets provide students with tips and activities to help them reflect on their learning process and develop their study skills, such as using a dictionary.

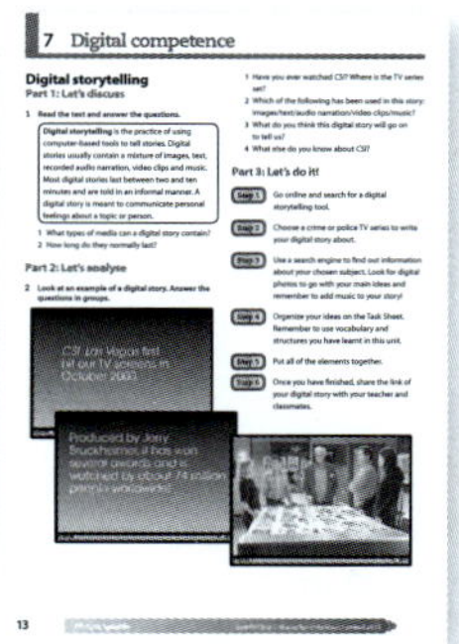
7 Digital competence

Digital storytelling

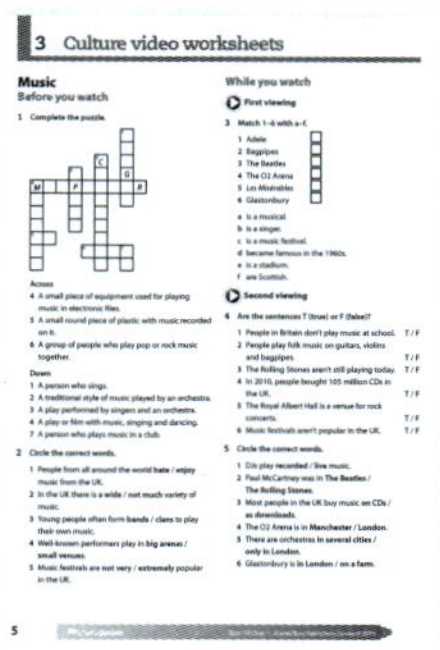
3 Culture video worksheets

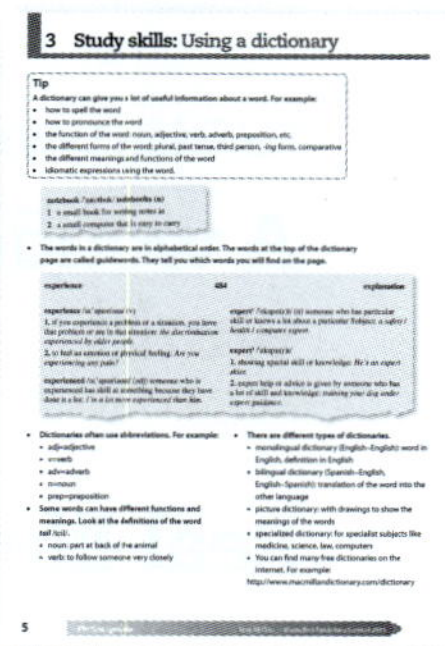
3 Study skills: Using a dictionary

Evaluation and Key Competences

Evaluation Rubrics

The **Evaluation Rubrics** can be used to assess student's reading, writing, listening and speaking skills and their progress throughout the year. They focus on specific learning outcomes covered in class, such as writing a formal letter or giving a presentation, and include evaluation criteria which show what students are achieving successfully.

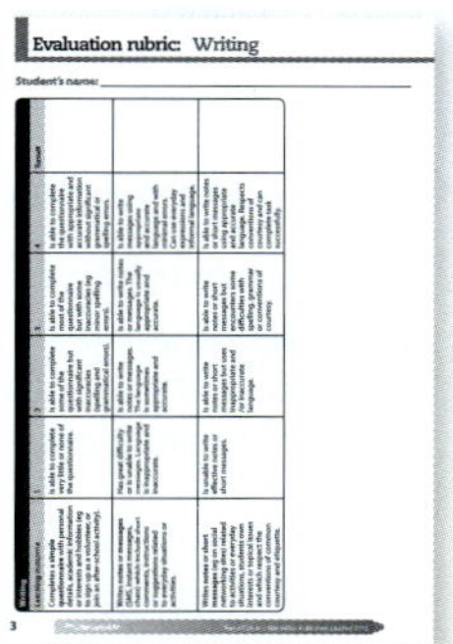
Evaluation rubric: Writing

Key Competences

The **Key Competences** worksheets provide further work on skills with reading, writing, listening and speaking pairwork activities. Relevant competences are clearly indicated on each worksheet.

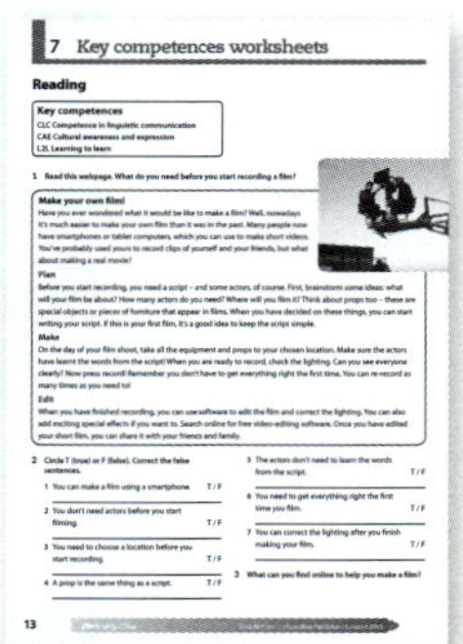
7 Key competences worksheets

Content-based Learning

CLIL

CLIL worksheets link cultural topics with other areas of the school curriculum. Teaching Notes provide ideas for using the material in class.

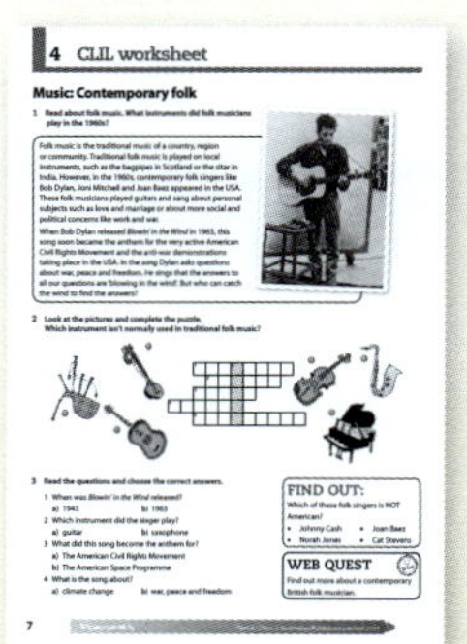
4 CLIL worksheet

Macmillan Readers

Macmillan Readers worksheets are provided to accompany a series of Macmillan graded readers.

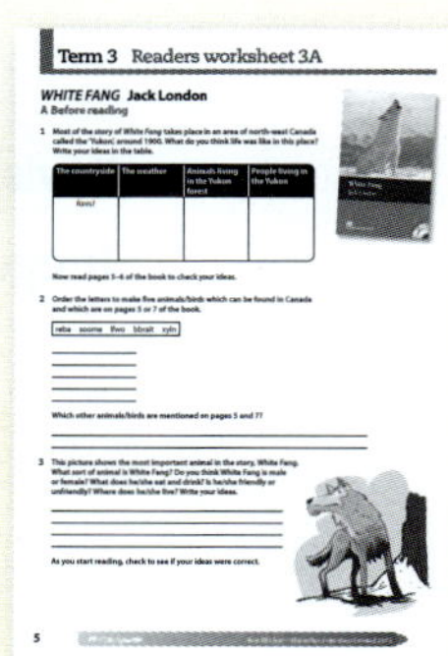
Term 3 Readers worksheet 3A

Writing	Listening	Speaking	Culture Pronunciation	Key competences	Language Excellence
Questions and answers • Present continuous for future arrangements • Introductions • Talking about school					
• A personal profile • Joining ideas	• Celebrity hobbies	• Making suggestions / An evening at home	**Reading:** Famous sporting events **Pronunciation:** /ɒ/ /ɔː/ /əʊ/	CAE CLC DC L2L SCC SIE	• A personal profile • Gerunds
• A thank you letter • Thank you letters	• A miracle – thanks to technology	• Making requests and offers (1) / Shopping for electronic gadgets	**Reading:** Famous inventions and inventors **Pronunciation:** Word stress	CAE CLC CMST DC L2L SCC SIE	• A magazine article • *used to*
• A description of an accident • Time expressions	• Tree couple get home safely	• Telling anecdotes / Talking with friends	**Reading:** Famous writers and books **Pronunciation:** Sentence stress	CAE CLC DC L2L SCC SIE	• A news report • Past perfect simple
Digital competence A digital wall					
• A travel guide entry • Qualifiers	• A trip to New York	• Describing your weekend / A day out	**Reading:** Famous places **Pronunciation:** /ɑː/ /eɪ/ /uː/	CAE CLC DC L2L SCC SIE	• A social media post • Exclamatory sentences
• A magazine article • Connectors of purpose: *to* + infinitive	• Selena Gomez, Goodwill Ambassador	• Making requests and offers (2) / A fundraising event	**Reading:** Famous heroes and heroines **Pronunciation:** Contractions	CAE CLC DC L2L SCC SIE	• A blog • Present perfect simple with *just*, *yet* and *already*
• A description of a journey • Linkers	• Solo sailor	• Talking about a journey / At the station	**Reading:** American History online **Pronunciation:** /ɜː/ /iː/ /ʌ/	CAE CLC DC L2L SCC SIE	• A fictional story • Quantity
Digital competence Blog posts					
• A film review • Giving opinions	• Teenage film-makers	• Asking for and giving opinions / Talking about a film	**Reading:** Famous films and film-makers **Pronunciation:** Sentence stress and weak forms	CAE CLC CMST DC L2L SCC SIE	• An advert • Future continuous
• A formal letter • Linkers of addition and contrast	• Relationship advice	• Describing people / A party	**Reading:** Famous friendships **Pronunciation:** /aɪ/ /ɪ/ /ʊ/ /ɔɪ/	CAE CLC DC L2L SCC SIE	• A forum • Modals of possibility, probability and permission
• A description of a musical hero • Time expressions	• A new trend in the music world	• Agreeing and disagreeing / A concert	**Reading:** Famous music venues **Pronunciation:** Sentence stress and /ə/	CAE CLC DC L2L SCC SIE	• A factual text • The passive with reporting verbs
Digital competence Presentations					• A chat • Reported speech ➜ Go to the Student Resource Centre

CAE Cultural awareness and expression • **CLC** Competence in linguistic communication • **CMST** Competence in mathematics, science and technology • **DC** Digital competence • **L2L** Learning to learn • **SCC** Social and civic competences • **SIE** Sense of initiative and entrepreneurship

S Starter unit

Vocabulary

Exercise 1
1 market
2 art gallery
3 monument
4 fishing port
5 aquarium

Revision

1 1.01 **Listen and repeat the words. Match some of them with pictures 1–5.**

aquarium • art gallery • campsite • castle • cathedral • fishing port • market • monument • safari park • statue • town square • water park

1 

2 

3 

4 

Exercise 2
1 miss a turn
2 chat show
3 temperature
4 build
5 screen

2 **Choose the odd one out.**

1 leave home get a job miss a turn get married
2 chat show electrician surgeon lifeguard
3 keyboard temperature mouse webcam
4 cruel build loyal brave
5 tired screen pleased bored

5 

Exercise 3
Students' own answers

3 **Add one more word to each group in exercise 2.**

Classroom language

Exercise 4
1 c
2 e
3 d
4 b
5 a

4 **Match questions 1–5 with answers a–e in your notebook.**

1 How do you say *respuesta* in English?
2 What does *stamp* mean?
3 How do you spell it?
4 Can you lend me a pencil, please?
5 How do you pronounce *Wales*?

a) /weɪlz/
b) Yes, of course.
c) Answer.
d) T-H-E-R-E.
e) You put a stamp on a letter before you post it.

Lesson Aims:

Students revise places in a town.
Students identify vocabulary relating to life events, jobs, computer equipment, adjectives of personality and adjectives describing feelings.
Students revise classroom language.

Vocabulary

Revision

Warmer

If this is the first time that you have taught the class, introduce yourself and ask some students their names. If the students already know each other, you could also ask them to introduce themselves and the person next to them.

1 1.01

- Books closed. Ask students what places in a town they can think of. Write them on the board.
- Play the audio. Students listen and repeat the words. Check that they are saying the words with the correct stress.
- Elicit the translation of the words.
- Students match some of the words with the pictures.
- Check answers with the class.

2
- Explain to students that they need to find the word that doesn't belong to the same vocabulary set as the others.
- Do the first question with the class as an example.
- Students find the odd one out for the remaining sets of words. Explain any vocabulary that they don't remember.
- Check answers with the class.

3
- Students add one more word to each group in exercise 2.
- Elicit a few examples for each group from the class.

Classroom language

4
- Elicit from students some useful expressions for communicating in English in class. Give prompts if necessary, eg *spell*, *repeat*, *mean*, etc.
- Students match the questions with the answers.
- Check answers with the class.

Extra activity

Students ask and answer the questions in pairs.

Self-study and extra practice

Workbook
- pages 4–5

Lesson Aims:

Students briefly revise *be*, the present simple, *have got*, countable and uncountable nouns, *there is / there are*, *some / any*, *can*, *be going to*, the present continuous, the past simple and questions and answers.

Grammar

Present tenses

Warmer

On the board write present simple and present continuous. Ask students to work in pairs to invent three statements for each tense – one affirmative, one negative, one interrogative. Collate the statements on the board and ask students to correct them if necessary.

1 • Correct the first sentence (*Dan and Megan are friends.*) with the class as an example.
- Students correct the other sentences.
- Check answers with the class.
- Clarify any grammar points, as necessary.

Expressions of quantity

2 • Elicit some countable and uncountable nouns from the class.
- Students classify the countable and uncountable nouns.
- Check answers with the class.

3 • In pairs, students think of five more words for each group in exercise 2.
- Students tell you some of their words.

4 • Revise *there is / there are* and *some / any* by asking students to describe what they can see in the classroom.
- Look at the example with the class.
- Students complete the sentences with *is / isn't* or *are / aren't*.
- Check answers with the class.

Questions and answers

5 • Revise question words briefly.
- Students choose the correct words to complete the questions.
- Check answers with the class.

Extra activity

Practise the pronunciation of the questions and encourage the correct intonation. Demonstrate how the voice falls at the end of *Wh-* questions.
Students ask and answer the questions in pairs.

6 • Order the words to make the first question (*Can you swim?*) with the class as an example.
- Students order the words to make the rest of the questions.
- Check answers with the class.
- Clarify any problems with question formation.

7
- Practise the pronunciation of the questions in exercises 5 and 6. Encourage students to stress the content words – verbs, nouns, adjectives.
- Discuss the possible short answers needed to answer each question in exercise 6: eg *Yes, I can.*; *Yes, he does.*, etc.
- Students ask and answer the questions in pairs.

Students who need extra help: Exercise 1. Tell students which word in each sentence needs to be changed.

Fast finishers: Exercise 4. Books closed. Write on the board: *bananas, apples, water, milk, grapes* and *coffee*. Students describe what is and isn't in the picture from memory.

Self-study and extra practice

Workbook
- pages 5–6

Grammar

Present tenses

1 **Correct the sentences. Write them in your notebook.**

1 Dan and Megan is friends.
2 Rita's favourite sport are swimming.
3 Megan live with her parents in Reading.
4 Rita don't like tennis.
5 Dan and Rita don't going to the same school.
6 Do Dan like playing football?
7 Has got Megan any brothers and sisters?
8 Beth are Dan's best friend.

Exercise 1
1 ~~is~~ are
2 ~~are~~ is
3 ~~live~~ lives
4 ~~don't~~ doesn't
5 ~~going~~ go
6 ~~Do~~ Does
7 ~~Has got Megan~~ Has Megan got
8 ~~are~~ is

Expressions of quantity

2 **Copy the table in your notebook and classify the words.**

apple • bread • chocolate • fruit • grape • juice • milk • money • tomato • water

Countable	Uncountable
...	...

Exercise 2
Countable: apple, grape, tomato
Uncountable: bread, chocolate, fruit, juice, milk, money, water

3 **Add five more words to each group in exercise 2.**

Exercise 3
Students' own answers

4 **Look at the picture. Copy and complete the sentences in your notebook with *is* / *isn't* or *are* / *aren't*.**

There *is* some fruit.
1 There … any apples.
2 There … any milk.
3 There … some bread.
4 There … any chocolate.
5 There … some grapes.

Exercise 4
1 aren't
2 isn't
3 is
4 isn't
5 are

Questions and answers

5 **Write the correct words in your notebook.**

1 **How** / **What** is your name?
2 **How** / **What** old are you?
3 **Where** / **When** do you live?
4 **What** / **Why** do you like skateboarding?
5 **Why** / **Who** is your best friend?

Exercise 5
1 What
2 How
3 Where
4 Why
5 Who

6 **Order the words to make questions.**

1 you / Can / swim / ?
2 your best friend / like / Does / chocolate / ?
3 Have / got / you / any pets / ?
4 there / Is / a computer / in your bedroom / ?
5 there / any good shops / where you live / Are / ?
6 you / go / going / shopping / at the weekend / Are / to / ?
7 studying / English / we / Are / at the moment / ?
8 go to school / yesterday / Did / you / ?

7 **In pairs, ask and answer the questions in exercises 5 and 6.**

Can you swim?
Yes, I can.

Exercise 6
1 Can you swim?
2 Does your best friend like chocolate?
3 Have you got any pets?
4 Is there a computer in your bedroom?
5 Are there any good shops where you live?
6 Are you going to go shopping at the weekend?
7 Are we studying English at the moment?
8 Did you go to school yesterday?

Grammar

Present continuous for future arrangements

8 It's Monday. Look at Amy's calendar and complete the sentences with the correct form of the verbs in brackets.

1 On Tuesday evening she … (do) her homework.
2 On Wednesday she … (play) football.
3 On Friday evening she … (watch) DVDs at Sara's house.
4 On Saturday she … (go) to the beach.
5 On Sunday Amy … (visit) her grandparents.

Exercise 8
1 's doing
2 's playing
3 's watching
4 's going
5 's visiting

Listening

1 1.02 Listen to Mia, Max and Ruby introducing themselves. Match pictures 1–3 with the people.

Exercise 1
1 Max
2 Ruby
3 Mia

2 Listen again and copy and complete the profiles.

	Age	Lives	Likes	Doesn't like
Mia	*15*	*London*		
Max				
Ruby				

Exercise 2
See Extended answers on T6

Lesson Aims:

Students briefly revise the present continuous for future arrangements.
Students listen to three people introducing themselves and identify general and specific information.

Grammar

8 • Revise the use of the present continuous to talk about future arrangements by asking students about their plans for tonight, the weekend, etc.
- Look at Amy's calendar with the class.
- Students complete the sentences with the correct form of the verbs in brackets.
- Check answers with the class.

Extra activity

Students complete a calendar like Amy's and then ask each other about their plans in pairs.

Listening

1 1.02

- Students look at the pictures.
- Play the audio. Students listen to three people introducing themselves and match the pictures with the people.
- Check answers with the class.

2 • Students copy the table.
- Play the audio again. Students listen again and complete the profiles.
- Check answers with the class.

Extended answers
Exercise 2

	Age	Lives	Likes	Doesn't like
Mia	15 (example)	London (example)	going to the cinema science-fiction films watching cartoons on TV	horror films
Max	14	Scotland	watching films at home on DVD fantasy films watching reality shows on TV	going to the cinema romantic comedies
Ruby	14	Manchester	downloading films watching films on her laptop adventure films watching sports programmes on TV	animated films

Extra activity

Students write another line in the table with information about themselves. They then use this to give a short personal presentation in groups of three.

Self-study and extra practice

Workbook
- pages 5–6

Lesson Aims:

Students learn and practise functional language to introduce themselves and talk about school.

Speaking

Introductions / Talking about school

Warmer

Ask students if they like school and what their favourite subjects are.

Model Dialogue

1 1.03

- Students read the question.
- Play the audio. Students read and listen to the dialogue to find out what Sophia's favourite school subjects are.
- Check the answer with the class.

2
- Play the audio again. Students listen again and this time repeat the dialogue.
- Focus on and explain the expressions *Are you lost?*; *Can you tell me where … is?*; *What do you think of … ?*; *What are your favourite subjects?*; *Can you … ?*; *Would you like to … ?*. Get the class to pay attention to intonation, both of questions and answers.

Speaking Task

1 Talk about school

Students choose a place in school, some school subjects and some instruments from the information given or use their own ideas.

2 Prepare a dialogue

Students look at the Model Dialogue and change the words in blue to make their own dialogue.

3 Speak

Students practise their dialogues in pairs.

Mixed-ability solutions

Students who need extra help: Speaking Task. Students write out their dialogue before they do step 3.

Fast finishers: Speaking Task. Students imagine they are someone famous when they were young and act out another dialogue using different ideas. If possible, they do this without looking at the Model Dialogue.

Self-study and extra practice

Workbook
- page 7

Exercise 1
English and maths

Speaking

Introductions / Talking about school

1 1.03 **Listen to the dialogue. What are Sophia's favourite school subjects?**

Model Dialogue

Sophia: Hi, I'm Sophia.

Leo: Hi, I'm Leo.

Sophia: Are you lost?

Leo: Yes, I am. This is my first day. Can you tell me where the music room is?

Sophia: Yes, of course. Come with me. So, what do you think of the school?

Leo: It looks OK, but it's a bit big. Do you like it?

Sophia: Yes, I do. It's great but we get a lot of homework.

Leo: What are your favourite subjects?

Sophia: English and maths. And yours?

Leo: English, history and music.

Sophia: Can you play the guitar?

Leo: Yes. I play in a band. We're looking for a singer at the moment.

Sophia: Really? I can sing!

Leo: Seriously? Would you like to do an audition?

Sophia: Yes, fantastic!

2 **Listen again and repeat the dialogue.**

Speaking Task

1 Talk about school

Use the ideas below or your own ideas.

Places in school	Subjects	Instruments
basketball court school cafeteria science lab	art geography history ICT literature music PE science	drums / drummer keyboards / keyboardist trumpet / trumpet player violin / violin player

2 Prepare a dialogue

Look at the Model Dialogue and change the words in blue.

3 Speak

In pairs, practise your dialogue.

Are you lost?

Yes, I am. This is my first day. Can you tell me where the science lab is?

Useful Language

Talking about school

Are you lost?
Can you tell me where the music room **is?**
What do you think of the school?
What are your favourite subjects?
Can you play the guitar?
Would you like to do an audition?

1 My interests

Overview

Unit objectives and key competences

- Understand, memorize and correctly use vocabulary related to free-time activities and for describing character CLC
- Identify the general content and extract specific information from a magazine article about an online video project about teenagers and their bedrooms CLC
- Understand, contrast and correctly use grammar structures related to the present CLC, L2L
- Correctly use the gerund after preference verbs and prepositions CLC
- Identify specific information through a listening activity about celebrity hobbies CLC
- Use appropriate functional language to make suggestions CLC, SCC
- Write a personal profile CLC, SIE, CAE
- Identify specific information from a text about the Wimbledon tennis championships CLC
- Learn about a sociologically interesting project CAE
- Learn about the Wimbledon tennis championships CAE
- Assimilate the All Clear Tips and Rules and study the Language Reference from the unit CLC, L2L, SIE
- Identify areas of language which need improvement and use ICT for extra practice DC, CLC, L2L

More information on Key Competences, page v

Linguistic content

Grammar

- Present simple
- Adverbs of frequency
- Present continuous
- Time expressions
- Gerunds

Main vocabulary

- Free-time activities: *chat online*, *do voluntary work*, etc
- Character adjectives: *adventurous*, *cautious*, etc

Functional language

- Making suggestions / An evening at home

Pronunciation

- The /ɒ/ /ɔː/ and /əʊ/ sounds

Skills: learning outcomes

- **Reading** Understand specific information in a clearly structured magazine article about an online video project about teenagers and their bedrooms. The student can re-read the more difficult parts, page 9
- **Listening** Understand a programme about celebrity hobbies. Delivered slowly and with clarity, page 12
- **Speaking** Participate effectively in a face-to-face informal dialogue, suggesting and deciding what to do, page 13
- **Writing** Write a personal profile with simple and relevant descriptions of personal details and activities, page 14
- **Reading** Understand specific information in a clearly structured article about the Wimbledon tennis championships. The student can re-read the more difficult parts, page 15

Lifelong learning skills and content-based learning

Life skills

- **Self knowledge** Reflecting on one's character, page 12
- **Communication** Overcoming disagreement to reach a compromise, page 13
- **Socio-cultural awareness** Learning about a traditional cultural and sporting event in another country, page 15
- **Communication** Coming to a joint decision on how to spend free time: learning to compromise, agree, disagree, page 13

Learning strategies

- Predicting the topic of a text from the title, page 9
- Examining a text for examples of a particular grammar structure, page 10

Cross-curricular content

- PE: sports and outdoor activities, sporting events, page 15
- Language: conventions for writing a personal profile, page 14

Further materials and evaluation

Digital material

- Student's and Teacher's Resource Centres
- Teacher's Presentation Kit
- Student's Digital Material: interactive vocabulary and grammar activities
- Video *Sport* (Revision Units 1–3, page 40)

Student's website www.macmillansecondary.es

Workbook

- Vocabulary, pages 8–9
- Vocabulary Reference, page 84
- Grammar, pages 10–1
- Grammar Reference and Practice, pages 66–7
- Revision, page 12
- Culture: Reading and Listening, page 93
- Writing Guide, pages 102–3
- Speaking, page 120

Teacher's Resource File

Multi-level Materials Bank

- All Clear Basics, pages 1–5
- Vocabulary and Grammar Consolidation and Extension, pages 1–4
- Language Excellence, pages 1–2
- Translation and Dictation, pages 1 and 10

Lifelong Learning

- Digital Competence, pages 1–2
- Culture Video Material, pages 1–2
- Study Skills, pages 1–12

Evaluation and Key Competences

- Evaluation Rubrics, pages 1–7
- Key Competences, pages 1–2 and 19–20

Content-based Learning

- CLIL, pages 1–10
- Macmillan Readers, pages 1–7

Evaluation material

- Unit 1 end-of-unit test: Basic, Standard and Extra
- CEFR Skills Exam Generator

Web info

Tips to find extra information on: celebrities and their hobbies, the Wimbledon tennis championships, the rules of tennis

Extra help for weaker students

Teacher's Resource File: All Clear Basics, pages 1–5

Material for fast finishers

Workbook: Grammar Extension, page 13
Teacher's Resource File: Vocabulary Extension, page 3
Teacher's Resource File: Grammar Extension, page 4
Teacher's Resource File: Language Excellence, pages 1–2

1 My interests

Objectives

Vocabulary	Free-time activities; character adjectives
Grammar	Present simple; adverbs of frequency; present continuous; time expressions; gerunds
Speaking	Making suggestions
Writing	A personal profile

Vocabulary

Free-time activities

1 1.04 **Listen and repeat the words. Match them with pictures 1–14.**

chat online • do voluntary work • draw cartoons • go dancing • go out for a meal • go to the cinema • go to the gym • go to a youth centre • learn a language • make models • play computer games • play an instrument • play tennis • relax

Exercise 1

1 go to a youth centre
2 go to the cinema
3 learn a language
4 play tennis
5 play an instrument
6 make models
7 go out for a meal
8 chat online
9 do voluntary work
10 draw cartoons
11 go to the gym
12 play computer games
13 relax
14 go dancing

2 **Copy and complete the sentences with free-time activities from exercise 1.**

1 I … . I go to Spanish classes twice a week.
2 I like making things with my hands. I … of planes.
3 I do a lot of sport and exercise. I often … or … .
4 I … once a week. I visit people in hospital.
5 I sometimes … with my friends. We love pizza!
6 I love using technology. I often … or … .

Exercise 2

1 learn a language
2 make models
3 go to the gym; play tennis (in either order)
4 do voluntary work
5 go out for a meal
6 chat online; play computer games (in either order)

3 1.05 **Listen to Emma and Danny. What is Emma's favourite free-time activity?**

Exercise 3

Emma's favourite free-time activity is going to the youth centre.

4 **In pairs, ask and answer questions about your free-time activities.**

What are your favourite free-time activities?

I like playing tennis, chatting online and going dancing.

Vocabulary Reference

Lesson Aims:

Students revise some expressions related to free-time activities and learn some new expressions related to this area.
Students listen to and practise a dialogue about free-time activities.

Vocabulary

Free-time activities

Warmer

With books closed, brainstorm some free-time activities students do or would like to do and write them on the board, supplying the translation when needed.

1 1.04

- Play the audio. Students listen and repeat the words.
- Practise the stress in some of them, eg go to a youth centre, play computer games, etc.
- Students match the words with the pictures.
- Check answers with the class.

2

- Students complete the sentences with free-time activities from exercise 1.
- Check answers with the class.

3 1.05

- Students read the question.
- Play the audio. Students listen and identify Emma's favourite free-time activity.
- Check the answer with the class.

4

- Practise the question and answer with the class, paying attention to stress and intonation.
- Highlight or elicit the use of the gerund after *like*.
- Students ask and answer the question in pairs.

Extra activity

Books closed. Ask students if they can remember all the free-time activities that use *go*. Then ask them if they can think of more expressions with *go* followed by the gerund, like *go dancing*, and followed by *to*, like *go to the cinema*.

Mixed-ability solutions

Students who need extra help: Exercise 4. Students write their answer before they start the activity.

Fast finishers: Exercise 4. Students write about the similarities and differences between what they and their partner like doing in their free time.

Self-study and extra practice

Workbook

- Vocabulary, page 8
- Vocabulary Reference, page 84

Teacher's Resource File

- All Clear Basics, page 1
- Vocabulary Consolidation, page 1
- Vocabulary Extension, page 3

Lesson Aims:

Students read a magazine article about an online video-documentary project about teenagers and their favourite spaces. Students use the title to predict the content, and find specific information.

Reading

A magazine article

Warmer

Ask students if they ever watch videos made by teenagers on the internet. Investigate further, asking which sites they visit and what type of videos they watch.

1 • Tell students to look just at the title of the article. Brainstorm with the class what it might be about. Point out to the class that often the title gives us a good indication of the content to follow.

Word Check

Check students understand the new words: *bloggers*, *interview*, *post*. Explain any they don't know.

2 1.06

• Play the audio. Students read and listen to the text and check their predictions.

3 • Read through the statements with the class, making sure they understand what each one means.
• Students read the text again and decide if each statement is true or false. They write the text that supports their answers.
• Check answers with the class.

4 • Students read the text and answer the questions.
• Check answers with the class.

All Clear Facts

Read the fact with the class. Ask students if they've ever watched a vlog or heard of any vloggers.

Web info

Type these words in your search engine for more information about the ideas described in the article: 'influential vloggers'

Mixed-ability solutions

Students who need extra help: Exercise 3. Tell students the paragraph in which to find the relevant information.

1 *paragraph 2*
2 *paragraph 3*
3 *paragraph 5*
4 *paragraph 6*

Self-study and extra practice

Teacher's Resource File

• Key Competences: Reading, page 1

Reading

A magazine article

Word Check
bloggers interview post

My Favourite Space

Every teen has a favourite space – a place to play an instrument, chat online or simply relax. But do all teenagers have the same favourite space? Let's find out more from two young bloggers who are asking the question, 'What's your favourite space?'

Jamie and Ellie Nelson are a brother and sister from Liverpool. They are the co-founders of a video blog called *My Favourite Space*. In the blog, Jamie and Ellie talk about their hobbies and their favourite spaces. They also **interview** their friends on video for the blog.

Jamie and Ellie usually film the videos in their local area, but every summer they interview their cousins in Spain when they go there on holiday. They work together as a team. Jamie interviews their friends and Ellie films and edits the videos. They **post** a new blog entry every week.

Are you using your computer now? Check out My Favourite Space!

We asked Jamie some questions. Let's see what he says.

'Ellie and I have different hobbies and different favourite spaces. Ellie draws cartoons and makes models in her free time. At the moment, she's drawing a cartoon of me! It's very funny. Her favourite space is the living room because she edits her films there, but my favourite space is the park. I enjoy playing football there. When I'm not interviewing friends for the blog or playing football, I often play computer games in my bedroom.'

Security is very important. They never give the addresses or surnames of the teenagers in the videos. People under 18 also need permission from their parents to participate.

i All Clear Facts

A video blog is also known as a vlog. Someone who posts a vlog is often called a vlogger.

1 Look at the title of the text. What do you think the text is about?

Exercise 1
Students' own answers

2 1.06 Read and listen. Check your answer to exercise 1.

3 Write true or false in your notebook. Copy the text that shows your answers.

1 Jamie and Ellie don't talk about their free-time activities in My Favourite Space.
2 The website only has videos of teenagers in Liverpool.
3 Jamie and Ellie do similar things in their free time.
4 The website protects its users' identities.

Exercise 3
1 false – In the blog, Jamie and Ellie talk about their hobbies and their favourite spaces.
2 false – … every summer they interview their cousins in Spain when they go there on holiday.
3 false – Ellie and I have different hobbies …
4 true – Security is very important. They never gives the addresses or surnames of the teenagers in the videos.

4 Answer the questions in your notebook.

1 What does Jamie do for the blog?
2 How often do they post a new blog entry?
3 What does Ellie do in her free time?
4 What's Jamie's favourite space?

Exercise 4
1 Jamie interviews their friends for the blog.
2 They post a new blog entry every week.
3 Ellie draws cartoons and makes models in her free time.
4 Jamie's favourite space is the park.

Grammar

Present simple

Affirmative	She **plays**
Negative	We **don't play**
Interrogative	**Do** you **play** …?

Language Reference p16

1 Look at the table. Find examples of the present simple in the text on page 9.

2 Write the correct words in your notebook to complete the rule.

We use the present simple for **actions happening now / habits and routines**.

Adverbs of frequency

100%	I'm **always** energetic at the weekend.
	He **usually** plays computer games in the evening.
	We **often** go to a youth centre at the weekend.
	She **sometimes** draws cartoons.
	You **hardly ever** chat online during the week.
0%	They are **never** dishonest.

3 Complete the sentences with adverbs of frequency and the correct form of the verbs in brackets.

I *often do* sports. (do / often)

1 She … her friends at the weekend. (meet / usually)
2 They … bored. (be / sometimes)
3 We … to the cinema. (go / hardly ever)
4 He … dancing. (go / never)
5 You … a car to work. (drive / always)
6 I … voluntary work. (do / often)

i All Clear Rules

Adverbs of frequency go before the main verb but after the verb *be*.

Present continuous

Affirmative	**She's drawing**
Negative	We **aren't drawing**
Interrogative	**Are** you **drawing** …?

Language Reference p16

4 Look at the examples in the table and write the correct words in your notebook to complete the rule.

We use the present continuous for **actions happening now / habits and routines**.

5 Complete the sentences with the correct form of the verbs in brackets.

1 I … (chat) online to my best friend at the moment.
2 Ben … (play) computer games right now.
3 They … (go) to the cinema now.
4 I … (play) tennis now. I … (lose) the game!
5 Eva … (draw) cartoons by hand at the moment. She's really good!
6 My parents … (relax) on the sofa. They're really tired!

Time expressions

6 Copy and complete the table with the time expressions in the box.

always at the moment every day now often this week twice a week usually

Present simple	Present continuous
every day	

7 Complete the sentences with the correct form of the verbs in brackets. Use the present simple or the present continuous.

1 I … (play) computer games every day.
2 She usually … (do) voluntary work once a week.
3 At the moment, we … (draw) cartoons.
4 I … (chat) online now.
5 They often … (go) to the cinema at the weekend.

Exercise 1
Paragraph 1: has, have, 's
Paragraph 2: are, are, talk, interview
Paragraph 3: film, interview, go, work, interviews, films, edits, post
Paragraph 4: says
Paragraph 5: have, draws, makes, 's, is, edits, is, enjoy, play
Paragraph 6: is, give, need

Exercise 2
habits and routines

Exercise 3
1 usually meets
2 're sometimes
3 hardly ever go
4 never goes
5 always drive
6 often do

Exercise 4
actions happening now

Exercise 5
1 'm chatting
2 's playing
3 're going
4 'm playing; 'm losing
5 's drawing
6 are relaxing

Exercise 6
Present simple: always, every day (example), often, twice a week, usually
Present continuous: at the moment, now, this week

Exercise 7
1 play
2 does
3 're drawing
4 'm chatting
5 go

Lesson Aims:

Students revise the present simple for routines and habits with adverbs of frequency.
Students revise the present continuous for actions happening now with time expressions.
Students contrast the use of the present simple and the present continuous. (Continues on page 11.)

Grammar

Present simple

Warmer

Write on the board *I do* and *I don't*. Then say some sentences about yourself, using expressions from page 8, eg *chat online*, *do voluntary work*, etc. Then elicit sentences from students about what they do and don't do of the expressions on page 8. Finally, ask them what tense they have been using.

1
- Students look at the grammar table. Elicit affirmative, negative and interrogative sentences and short answers using the other pronouns. Ask why *he*, *she* and *it* are special.
- You may want to revise the basic spelling rules for the third person singular.
  1 Verbs ending in *-o*, *-ch*, *-sh*, *-ss*, *-x* and *-z*, add *-es*.
  2 Verbs ending in consonant + *y*, remove the *y* and add *-ies*.
  3 Verbs ending in vowel + *y*, add *-s*.
- Students find examples of the present simple in the text on page 9.
- Check answers with the class.

2
- Ask why the present simple is used so often in the text on page 9.
- Elicit the correct option to complete the rule.

Adverbs of frequency

All Clear Rules

Write the scale from 100% to 0% on the board and write *always* at the top. Elicit the missing adverbs, prompting as necessary. Check the meaning of the adverbs by asking students to translate them.
Refer students to the example sentences in the box and read through the All Clear Rules with the class. Ask them to find two examples of each rule in the box.

3
- Read through the example with the class. Make it clear that students need to decide where to put the adverb and to put the verb in the correct form.
- Students complete the sentences.
- Check answers with the class.

Present continuous

4
- Mime some actions and elicit from student what you are doing, eg playing football, etc.
- Then write one of the actions on the board, eg *I'm playing football.* Ask what tense it is and why.
- Students look at the grammar table. Elicit affirmative, negative and interrogative sentences and short answers using the other pronouns.
- You may want to revise the spelling rules for the *-ing* form.
  1 Most verbs add *-ing* to the end of the verb.
  2 Verbs ending in *-e*, remove the *-e* and add *-ing*.
  3 One-syllable verbs ending in consonant + vowel + consonant, double the final consonant and add *-ing* (unless the consonant is *w*, *x* or *y*).
  4 Two-syllable verbs ending in consonant + vowel + consonant, double the final consonant when the stress is on the first syllable.
  5 Verbs ending in *-ie*, change the *-ie* to *-ying*.
- Elicit the correct option to complete the rule.

5
- Explain that all the sentences describe actions that are happening now. Make it clear that for this reason they need to use the present continuous form of the verbs.
- Students complete the sentences.
- Check answers with the class.

Time expressions

6
- Write two example sentences on the board, eg *My sister usually studies at Salamanca University. At the moment she's studying in the UK.*
- Elicit which tense is used in each sentence and why.
- Explain that certain time expressions are often used with the present simple while others are often used with the present continuous.
- Students copy the table and write the time expressions under the correct heading.
- Check answers with the class.

7
- Tell students to pay particular attention to the time expression as it help them to determine which tense to use.
- Students complete the sentences.
- Check answers with the class.

Lesson Aims:

Students contrast the use of the present simple and the present continuous. (Continued from page 10.)
Students learn and practise using the gerund after preference verbs and prepositions.
Students practise all the grammar they have seen in the unit in a single text.

Grammar

8 • This exercise is similar to exercise 7 and gives students another chance to practise the difference in use between the two tenses.
- Read through the example with the class.
- Students complete the sentences with the correct form of the verbs in brackets.
- Check answers with the class.

9 • With weaker classes, you may want to do the first question with the class as an example.
- Students write questions using the present simple or the present continuous.
- Check answers with the class.

10
- Practise the questions from exercise 9, paying attention to stress and intonation.
- Students ask and answer the questions with a partner.

Gerunds

Warmer

Ask different students in the class questions with *Do you like … ?* with the gerund, eg *playing football, watching TV, doing homework*, etc. Elicit the response *Yes, I do.* or *No, I don't.* Then get students to ask each other in open pairs across the class.

11 • Students read the sentences in the grammar table. They will probably find it helpful if you translate the sentences or elicit them from the class. Make sure the class understands that the gerund form is the same as the present continuous form, but without *be*.
- Explain that certain verbs expressing preference are followed by the gerund. Explain that we use gerunds after prepositions, too.
- Read through the example with the class, emphasizing that students need to put the first verb in the correct form as well as using the gerund form of the second verb.
- Students write sentences using the correct form of the verbs and gerunds.
- Check answers with the class.

12 • Students write questions using gerunds and answers that are true for them. With weaker classes, you may want to write the first question with the class as an example and point out that the answer can be *Yes, I do.* or *No, I don't.*
- Check the questions with the class and elicit some answers from students.

All Clear Grammar

13 • Tell students that this is a cumulative check of the grammar in this unit.
- As this exercise is quite challenging, you may want students to do it in pairs.
- Students choose the correct words to complete the text.

14 1.07
- Play the audio. Students listen and check their answers.
- Check answers with the class. This is a good moment to check they have understood the new grammar.

Mixed-ability solutions

Students who need extra help:
Exercise 10. Students write their answers first.
Exercise 12. Tell students that the question form of each verb is formed using *do you …* or *are you …* .

Fast finishers: Exercise 12. Write the following sentence stems on the board and ask students to complete them with something that is true for them.
My mum enjoys … ; At the weekend I like … ; In the evening I love … ; I'm not keen on … ; My dad is interested in … .

Self-study and extra practice

Workbook
- Grammar, pages 10–1
- Grammar Reference and Practice, pages 66–7

Teacher's Resource File
- All Clear Basics, pages 3–4
- Grammar Consolidation, page 2
- Grammar Extension, page 4
- Language Excellence, pages 1–2

Digital Activities
- Student's Digital Material

8 **Complete the sentences with the correct form of the verbs in brackets. Use the present simple or the present continuous.**

Simon *isn't talking* (not talk) about his free-time activities now.

1 At the moment, Karen … (learn) French. She … (not study) Spanish.
2 He … (not usually play) an instrument, but he often … (go) to the gym.
3 They … (not do) anything at the moment. They … (relax).
4 I … (not meet) my friends every day. I usually … (see) them at the weekend.
5 We … (not study) today. We … (play) tennis.

Exercise 8
1 is learning; isn't studying
2 doesn't usually play; goes
3 aren't doing; 're relaxing
4 don't meet; see
5 aren't studying; 're playing

9 **Write complete questions in your notebook. Use the present simple or the present continuous.**

1 What / you / usually / do / at the weekend?
2 How / often / you / watch films?
3 What / you / do / now?
4 Where / you / usually / meet your friends?
5 you / listen to music / now?

Exercise 9
1 What do you usually do at the weekend?
2 How often do you watch films?
3 What are you doing now?
4 Where do you usually meet your friends?
5 Are you listening to music now?

10 **In pairs, ask and answer the questions in exercise 9.**

Gerunds

After preference verbs
He **likes** reading.
She **hates** dancing.
Do you **enjoy** making videos?
After prepositions
I'm (not) **keen on** drawing cartoons.
They're (not) **interested in** going to the gym.
Is he **good** / **bad at** playing the piano.

11 **Write complete sentences using gerunds in your notebook.**

Peter / like / play tennis.
Peter likes playing tennis.

1 Kate / be / good at / draw cartoons.
2 They / enjoy / meet their friends.
3 He / hate / travel.
4 You / be / not interested in / go to the cinema.
5 I / be / keen on / play computer games.

Exercise 11
1 Kate is good at drawing cartoons.
2 They enjoy meeting their friends.
3 He hates travelling.
4 You aren't interested in going to the cinema.
5 I'm keen on playing computer games.

12 **Write complete questions using gerunds in your notebook. Then answer them so they are true for you.**

1 you / enjoy / listen to music?
2 you / like / do sports / at the weekend?
3 What / you / love / do on Saturdays?
4 you / be / keen on / do voluntary work?
5 you / be / interested in / make models?

Exercise 12
1 Do you enjoy listening to music?
2 Do you like doing sports at the weekend?
3 What do you love doing on Saturdays?
4 Are you keen on doing voluntary work?
5 Are you interested in making models?
Students' own aswers

All Clear Grammar

1 2 3 4 5 6 7 8 9

13 **Write the correct words in your notebook.**

I'm English, but I (1)**don't live / doesn't live** in England, I live in France. I (2)**go / 'm going** to secondary school in my town. At the moment, I (3)**study / 'm studying** for exams. What (4)**do I usually / do usually I** do in my free time? Well, I (5)**go / 'm going** swimming once a week. I love (6)**meet / meeting** my friends at the weekend. I really enjoy (7)**draw / drawing** cartoons and I'm good (8)**in / at** making models.

Exercise 13
1 don't live
2 go
3 'm studying
4 do I usually
5 go
6 meeting
7 drawing
8 at

14 1.07 **Listen and check your answers.**

Grammar Reference

Vocabulary

Character adjectives

Exercise 1
Students' own answers

Exercise 2
1 adventurous
2 talkative
3 friendly
4 generous
5 energetic
6 funny
7 shy
8 honest

Exercise 3
1 adventurous
2 friendly
3 generous
4 selfish
5 talkative
6 confident
7 funny

Exercise 4
Students' own answers

Exercise 5
The hobbies are mentioned in this order: play the piano, do magic, play bingo, collect *Star Wars* figures, sing karaoke

Exercise 6
1 Robert Pattinson
2 Cristiano Ronaldo
3 Penelope Cruz
4 Leonardo DiCaprio
5 Fernando Alonso

1 1.08 **Listen and repeat the words. How do you say them in your language?**

adventurous • cautious • confident • dishonest • energetic • friendly • funny • generous • honest • lazy • quiet • selfish • serious • shy • talkative • unsociable

2 **Match pictures 1–8 with character adjectives from exercise 1.**

3 **Complete the text with words from exercise 1.**

My brother Alex has got lots of energy – he's very *energetic*. He's (1)… and he loves exploring places like the Amazon. He's got lots of friends because he's very (2)… . He often gives them presents because he's very (3)… . He always thinks about others because he isn't (4)… . Sometimes he doesn't stop talking. He's very (5)… . He isn't shy like me. He's very (6)…, and he can make people laugh because he's (7)… .

4 **Which of the adjectives in exercise 1 describe you?**

I'm adventurous, but I'm not very funny.

Listening

5 1.09 **Copy the hobbies in the box. Listen to the report and number the hobbies in the order you hear them.**

collect *Star Wars* figures	do magic	play bingo	play the piano	sing karaoke

6 **Listen again and complete the sentences with the celebrities in your notebook.**

1 … sometimes uses his hobby in his films.
2 … thinks his hobby is exciting.
3 … does her hobby to relax.
4 … has a collection of toy action figures.
5 … does his hobby for his friends.

Vocabulary Reference

Lesson Aims:

Students revise character adjectives and learn and practise some new ones.
Students listen to a report about celebrity hobbies and identify specific information.

Vocabulary

Character adjectives

Warmer

Books closed. Students think of an adjective which describes their character. Give help with vocabulary as needed. Ask students to tell you their adjective. Write the adjectives they suggest on the board.

1 1.08

- Play the audio. Students listen and repeat the words.
- Students translate the adjectives into their language.
- Practise all the words, highlighting the stressed syllables.

Language note: *funny / fun*

Write these two pairs of sentences on the board.
It's a funny film. You laugh a lot when you watch it.
I like making models. It's a fun activity.
Explain that *funny* describes something or someone who makes you laugh whereas *fun* describes something or someone that you think is interesting.
Ask students to translate both sentence pairs.

2
- Students look at the pictures and say what is happening in each.
- Students match the pictures with adjectives from exercise 1.
- Check answers with the class.

3
- Read the first sentence of the text with the class.
- Students complete the text with words from exercise 1. Make it clear that they will need to use the meaning of the text to help them.
- Check answers with the class.

4

- Tell students to write down three adjectives which describe them and three which don't.
- Read the example sentence in the speech bubble with the class.
- Students say similar sentences to their partner using the adjectives they have chosen.
- Ask some students to tell the class about their partner.

Extra activity

Students use the adjectives to write sentences about their family. They should give an example, eg *My mum's very energetic. She goes to the gym every day.*

Listening

Warmer

Ask students to imagine what they would do in their free time if they were rich and famous.

5 1.09

- Read through the hobbies with the class. Make sure that they understand what they mean.
- Students write the hobbies in their notebooks.
- Play the audio. Students listen and number the hobbies in the order they hear them.
- Check the answer with the class.

6
- Students read the sentences.
- Play the audio again. Students listen again and complete the sentences with the celebrities.
- Check answers with the class.

Web info

Type these words in your search engine for more information about celebrities and their hobbies: 'celebrity hobbies surprise you'

Mixed-ability solutions

Students who need extra help: Exercise 3. Write two options on the board for each gap.

Fast finishers: Exercise 3. Students re-read the text and decide on two or three things that Alex has in common with them.

Self-study and extra practice

Workbook
- Vocabulary, page 9
- Vocabulary Reference, page 84

Teacher's Resource File
- All Clear Basics, page 2
- Vocabulary Consolidation, page 1
- Vocabulary Extension, page 3
- Key Competences: Listening, page 2

Digital Activities
- Student's Digital Material

Lesson Aims:

Students learn and practise functional language to make suggestions for what to do for an evening at home.

Speaking

Making suggestions / An evening at home

Warmer

In pairs, ask students to write a list of five things that they like doing when they're on holiday. Encourage them to use their imagination. Ask different pairs to read out their lists. Help with vocabulary when necessary.

Model Dialogue

1 1.10

- Students read the question.
- Play the audio. Students listen to and read the dialogue to find the answer to the question.
- Check the answer with the class.

2
- Play the audio again. Students listen again and this time repeat the dialogue.
- Focus on and explain the following expressions: *Do you fancy* + gerund?; *Let's get ...* ; *Do you feel like* + gerund?; *Good idea*; *instead*. Also highlight *I'll phone* (not ~~*I phone*~~).

Speaking Task

1 Talk about an evening at home

Students look at the information and choose an activity and some food. They can use the suggestions in the Student's Book or their own ideas.

2 Prepare a dialogue

Students look at the Model Dialogue and change the words in blue to make their own dialogue.

3 Speak

Students practise their dialogues in pairs.

Mixed-ability solutions

Students who need extra help: Speaking Task. Students write out their dialogue before doing step 3.

Fast finishers: Speaking Task. Students act out another dialogue using different activities and food. If possible, they do this without looking at the Model Dialogue.

Self-study and extra practice

Workbook
- Speaking, page 120

Teacher's Resource File
- Key Competences: Speaking, pages 19–20

Digital Activities
- Student's Digital Material

> **Exercise 1**
> They decide to have a pizza.

Speaking

Making suggestions / An evening at home

1 1.10 **Listen to the dialogue. What do Holly and Emma decide to eat?**

Model Dialogue

Holly: Do you fancy playing computer games?

Emma: No, that's boring. Let's watch a film instead.

Holly: OK. What do you want to watch? I've got *The Hunger Games*, *Breakout* and *The Hobbit*.

Emma: Oh, *The Hunger Games*, definitely.

Holly: Let's get some food too.

Emma: OK. Good idea. Do you feel like having a curry?

Holly: No, let's have a pizza instead.

Emma: OK.

Holly: Let's invite Rachel too.

Emma: Yeah, cool. I'll phone her now.

2 **Listen again and repeat the dialogue.**

Speaking Task

1 Talk about an evening at home

Choose an activity and some food. Use the ideas below or your own ideas.

Food
ice cream / pizza / popcorn / sandwich

Activities
play computer games
watch a film
watch football / tennis / basketball

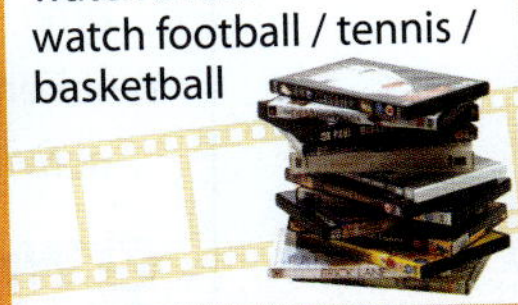

2 Prepare a dialogue

Look at the Model Dialogue and change the words in blue.

3 Speak

In pairs, practise your dialogue.

> Do you fancy watching football?
>
> No, that's boring. Let's watch a film instead.

Useful Language

Making suggestions

Do you fancy playing computer games?
No, that's boring.
Let's get some food too.
OK. **Good idea.**
Do you feel like having a curry?
No, let's have a pizza **instead.**

Writing

A personal profile

Exercise 1
1 He lives in Manchester.
2 Because he's got his GCSE exams.
3 He has guitar lessons and he does voluntary work at a centre for old people.
4 He usually meets his friends. They listen to music, play computer games and often go to parties.

1 1.11 **Read the Model Text and listen. Answer the questions in your notebook.**

1 Where does Will live?
2 Why is Will studying a lot this year?
3 What activities does Will do during the week?
4 What activities does he do at the weekend?

Model Text

This is me!

My name's Will Davis. I'm 16 and I live in Manchester with my parents and my sister. I'm friendly, energetic and talkative!

I don't often go out during the week because I'm usually busy with homework. This year, I've got my GCSE exams, so I'm studying a lot. I'm learning the guitar and I have lessons on Mondays. Once a week, I do voluntary work at a centre for old people. It's hard work, although I enjoy talking to them.

At the weekend, I usually meet my friends. We love listening to music or playing computer games and we often go to parties. I'm never bored!

Exercise 2
Students' own answers
I don't often go out during the week **because** I'm usually busy with homework.
This year I've got my GCSE exams, **so** I'm studying a lot.
It's hard work, **although** I enjoy talking to them.

2 **Look at the All Clear Tips and translate the words in bold. Find examples in the Model Text.**

All Clear Tips

Joining ideas

I'm having guitar lessons ***because*** *I want to be a guitarist.*
I want to be a guitarist, ***so*** *I'm having guitar lessons.*
I want to be a guitarist, ***although*** *I'm not very musical.*

Exercise 3
1 so
2 although
3 because
4 because
5 although

3 **Rewrite the sentences with *so*, *because* or *although* in your notebook.**

We usually go for pizza *because* it's cheap.

1 I'm very sociable, … I love going out and meeting new people.
2 I'm learning the piano, … I'm not very good yet!
3 I'm practising the piano a lot … I've got a concert next week.
4 I do a lot of sport … I'm very energetic.
5 I like sports, … I don't often play them.

Writing Task

1 Plan

Make notes about yourself and include:

Personal details: *your name, age, family, town / city, character*
Activities during the week: *school work, after-school activities*
Weekend activities: *hobbies and free-time activities*

2 Write

Use the Model Text, your notes and this structure:

Paragraph 1: Personal details
Paragraph 2: Activities during the week
Paragraph 3: Weekend activities

3 Check

☑ present simple, present continuous, adverbs of frequency, time expressions, gerunds
☑ free-time activities, character adjectives
☑ joining ideas: *because*, *so* and *although*

Lesson Aims:

Students practise using different linkers to join their ideas.
Students write a personal profile.

Writing

A personal profile

Warmer

Tell students that they are going to write a personal profile to describe the main things about them. Elicit the type of information they might include. Write their ideas on the board, eg name, age, personality, hobbies, etc.

1 1.11

- Students look at the picture and to tell you what they can deduce about the person from it.
- Students read the questions.
- Play the audio. Students read and listen to the profile and answer the questions about Will.
- Check answers with the class.

Extra activity

Students re-read the third paragraph. They identify all the examples of the present simple and the present continuous and say why they are used in each case.

Cultural note

GCSE stands for General Certificate of Secondary Education. It is an academic qualification in a particular subject (French, maths, etc). Students in England and Wales usually do GCSE exams in 8–10 subjects at the age of 15 or 16. In England and Wales, secondary education is compulsory until the age of 17 and from September 2015 this will rise to 18.

All Clear Tips

2
- Read the All Clear Tips with the class.
- Students translate the linkers in bold.
- Students find examples of *because*, *so* and *although* in the text.

3
- Look at the example with the class. Discuss with them why it is not possible to use either *so* or *although* in the sentence.
- Students complete the other sentences with the correct linkers. You may prefer them to do this in pairs as this is a relatively demanding exercise.
- Check answers with the class.

Writing Task

1 Plan

Read the notes with the class. Students make notes about themselves using the headings given.

2 Write

Look at the structure with the class. Students use their notes to write their own personal profile.
Tell them to use some of the linkers they have just practised to join ideas.

3 Check

Encourage students to check their work, paying particular attention to the points mentioned.

Web info

Type these words in your search engine to read a profile of the singer Adele: 'aceshowbiz + adele profile'

Mixed-ability solutions

Students who need extra help: Writing Task. Students do not write the full profile. They just write the notes in step 1.

Fast finishers: Writing Task. Students exchange their text with a partner and look for similarities and differences.

Self-study and extra practice

Workbook
- Writing Guide, pages 102–3

Teacher's Resource File
- Key Competences: Writing, page 2

Lesson Aims:

Students learn about the Wimbledon tennis championships.
Students practice the /ɒ/ /ɔː/ and /əʊ/ sounds.

Culture Reading

Famous sporting events

Warmer

Write the following places on the board. Students tell you which sport each one is associated with. (Answers in brackets.)
Anfield (football)
Les Deux Alpes (skiing)
Monza (Formula 1 motor racing)
Roland Garros (tennis)
Madison Square Garden (basketball and boxing)
Jerez (motorbike racing)
Augusta (golf)
Twickenham (rugby)

1.12

- Students look at the pictures. Ask them if they recognize the sporting event. Ask them what they know about Wimbledon.
- Students read the questions.
- Play the audio. Students read and listen to the text and answer the first question.
- Discuss question 2 with the class.
- For question 3, students work in pairs to discuss famous sporting events in their country.
- Ask a few different pairs to tell the class about an event in their country.

Extra activity

Write the following jumbled tennis words on the board. (Answers in brackets.) Students tell you what the words are and what they mean.
tearck (racket)
tocru (court)
ent (net)
evers (serve)
purime (umpire)

Pronunciation

/ɒ/ /ɔː/ /əʊ/

a 1.13

- Before playing the audio, practise the three vowel sounds, showing students the correct mouth position.
- Play the audio. Students listen and repeat the words.
- Elicit more words with the same sounds, eg *not, from, geography; four, more, walk; no, throw, hotel,* and practise them.

b 1.14

- Play the audio. Students listen and repeat the sentences chorally and individually. Play the audio several times if necessary.

Web info

Type these words in your search engine for more information about

- the Wimbledon tennis championships: 'Wimbledon.com'
- the rules of tennis (video): 'youtube + tennis guide rules of tennis'

Mixed-ability solutions

Students who need extra help: Reading text. Pre-teach the following words and expressions: *take place, watch … live, around the world, court, pass an exam, fit.*

Fast finishers: Reading text. Students read the text again carefully. They then close their books and write down everything they can remember.

Self-study and extra practice

Workbook

- Culture: Reading and Listening, page 93

EXTRA

Culture Reading

FAMOUS SPORTING EVENTS

WIMBLEDON

Wimbledon tennis championship takes place every year in London in the last week of June and the first week of July. All of the world's top tennis players compete.

Spectators

Half a million spectators watch the matches live. The spectators eat 112,000 boxes of strawberries and drink 17,000 bottles of champagne. Around the world, more than 500 million people watch the competition in 185 different countries.

Ball boys and ball girls

On court with the players are ball boys and ball girls. There are 250 in total and they all come from local schools. They start training in February and have to pass an exam and be fit. They are usually 15 years old.

History and famous players

Wimbledon started in 1877 and it's the oldest tennis championship in the world. Famous champions include Serena and Venus Williams (America), Rafael Nadal (Spain) and Roger Federer (Switzerland). In 2013, Andy Murray was the first British man to win Wimbledon for 77 years!

1.12 **Read and listen. Then answer the questions in your notebook.**

1 What is Wimbledon? When and where is it?
2 What fact do you find most surprising about Wimbledon?
3 Are there any famous sporting events in your country? What do you know about them?

Pronunciation

/ɒ/ /ɔː/ /əʊ/

a 1.13 **Listen and repeat.**

/ɒ/ boxes, bottles, watch
/ɔː/ ball, sport, draw
/əʊ/ local, total, oldest

b 1.14 **Listen and repeat the sentences.**

Reading text exercise

1 Wimbledon is a tennis competition. It takes place in the last week of June and the first week of July in London.
2 Students' own answers
3 Students' own answers

Unit 1 Language Reference

Vocabulary Free-time activities

chat online • do voluntary work • draw cartoons • go dancing • go out for a meal • go to the cinema • go to the gym • go to a youth centre • learn a language • make models • play computer games • play an instrument • play tennis • relax

Character adjectives

adventurous • cautious • confident • dishonest • energetic • friendly • funny • generous • honest • lazy • quiet • selfish • serious • shy • talkative • unsociable

Grammar Present simple

Affirmative	Negative	Interrogative	Short answers
I / You **make** models.	I / You **do not make** models.	**Do** I / you **make** models?	Yes, I / you **do**.
He / She / It **makes** models.	He / She / It **does not make** models.	**Does** he / she / it **make** models?	No, he / she / it **does not**.
We / You / They **make** models.	We / You / They **do not make** models.	**Do** we / you / they **make** models?	Yes, we / you / they **do**.

Adverbs of frequency

never	hardly ever	sometimes	often	usually	always
0%	→				100%

Time expressions

now	every day
at the moment	twice a week
at the weekend	this week

Present continuous

Affirmative	Negative	Interrogative	Short answers
I **am** watch**ing** TV.	I **am not** watch**ing** TV.	**Am** I watch**ing** TV?	Yes, I **am**.
You **are** watch**ing** TV.	You **are not** watch**ing** TV.	**Are** you watch**ing** TV?	No, you **are not**.
He / She / It **is** watch**ing** TV.	He / She / It **is not** watch**ing** TV.	**Is** he / she / it watch**ing** TV?	Yes, he / she / it **is**.
We / You / They **are** watch**ing** TV.	We / You / They **are not** watch**ing** TV.	**Are** we / you / they watch**ing** TV?	No, we / you / they **are not**.

Gerunds

After preference verbs	After prepositions
He **likes** play**ing** tennis.	I'm (not) **keen on** draw**ing** cartoons.
She **hates** go**ing** to the gym.	They're (not) **interested in** read**ing** books.
	He's **good** / **bad at** play**ing** the piano.

Speaking Making suggestions

Do you fancy play**ing** computer games?
Let's get some food too.
Do you feel like hav**ing** a curry?

No, that's boring.
OK. **Good idea**.
No, let's have a pizza **instead**.

Unit 1 Progress Check

Vocabulary Free-time activities

1 In your notebook, match 1–5 with a–e to make activities.

1 learn
2 do
3 chat
4 draw
5 make

a) models
b) online
c) cartoons
d) voluntary work
e) a language

Exercise 1
1 e
2 d
3 b
4 c
5 a

Character adjectives

2 Complete the sentences with the words in the box.

cautious	funny	generous
lazy	talkative	

1 Paul's … – he often gives money to charities.
2 Kevin is … – he doesn't like trying new activities.
3 Kate always makes me laugh, she's very … .
4 They're always on the telephone, they're very … .
5 He never wants to help at home – he's very … .

Exercise 2
1 generous
2 cautious
3 funny
4 talkative
5 lazy

Grammar Present simple and present continuous

3 Write complete sentences using the present simple or the present continuous.

1 Sally / use the computer / every day.
2 Jamie / chat online / at the moment.
3 I / not relax / now.
4 She / not play / the guitar / on Fridays.
5 We / study English / three times a week.

Exercise 3
1 Sally uses the computer every day.
2 Jamie is chatting online at the moment.
3 I'm not relaxing now.
4 She doesn't play the guitar on Friday.
5 We study English three times a week.

4 Complete the questions with the present simple or the present continuous form of the verbs in brackets.

1 How often … you … (go) shopping?
2 … you … (watch) TV at the moment?
3 What … your friends … (do) now?
4 … you always … (do) your homework in your bedroom?
5 … your friend … (play) basketball at the weekend?

Exercise 4
1 do (you) go
2 Are (you) watching
3 are (your friends) doing
4 Do (you always) do
5 Does (your friend) play

Gerunds

5 Write complete sentences and questions using gerunds.

1 Simon / like / play computer games?
2 Oliver and Ella / enjoy / watch TV.
3 Maggie / be not keen on / play tennis.
4 Tim and Sue / hate / go shopping.
5 Pete / good at / draw cartoons?

Exercise 5
1 Does Simon like playing computer games?
2 Oliver and Ella enjoy watching TV.
3 Maggie isn't keen on playing tennis.
4 Tim and Sue hate going shopping.
5 Is Pete good at drawing cartoons?

All Clear Self-C

Correct the activities with the class. Students who need extra revision and practice can go to:

Workbook
- Unit 1 Revision, page 12
- Grammar Reference and Practice, pages 66–7
- Vocabulary Reference, page 84

Student's Digital Material
www.allclear.macmillan.es

Check your answers

Write your scores for exercises 1–5 in your notebook. What did you get for:
- free-time activities?
- character adjectives?
- present simple and present continuous?
- gerunds?

Extra Practice

If you need extra practice, go to:
- Unit 1 Grammar Reference
- Unit 1 Vocabulary Reference
- Unit 1 Grammar Exercises
- Unit 1 Vocabulary Exercises

2 Connected Overview

Unit objectives and key competences

- Understand, memorize and correctly use vocabulary related to IT activities and jobs CLC, DC
- Read a news report about someone who overcame adversity to be successful SIE
- Identify the main ideas in a news report about a homeless man who became an entrepreneur CLC
- Understand, contrast and correctly use grammar structures related to the past CLC, L2L
- Listen to a text about advances in medical science CMST
- Identify specific information through a listening activity about someone who had their blindness cured thanks to advances in technology CLC
- Use appropriate functional language in the specific social context of shopping CLC, SCC
- Write a thank you letter using appropriate expressions CLC, SIE, CAE
- Identify specific content in a text about a famous inventor CLC
- Learn about the inventor of the telephone CAE
- Assimilate the All Clear Tips and Rules and study the Language Reference from the unit CLC, L2L, SIE
- Identify areas of language which need improvement and use ICT for extra practice DC, CLC, L2L

More information on Key Competences, page v

Linguistic content

Grammar

- Past simple
- Past continuous

Recycled grammar

- Present simple (Unit 1)
- Present continuous (Unit 1)

Main vocabulary

- IT activities: *charge a mobile phone*, *download a video clip*, etc
- Jobs: *actor*, *artist*, etc

Functional language

- Making requests and offers (1) / Shopping for electronic gadgets

Pronunciation

- Word stress

Skills: learning outcomes

- **Reading** Get the main idea from a news report about a homeless man who became an entrepreneur. Students are guided by pictures to aid understanding, page 19
- **Listening** Understand a news report which describes how medical advances cured someone's blindness. Delivered slowly and clearly, page 22
- **Speaking** Participate effectively in a face-to-face informal dialogue in a shop, page 23
- **Writing** Write a thank you letter with the main points set out in a logical order, page 24
- **Reading** Understand specific information in a clearly structured article about a famous inventor. The student can re-read the more difficult parts, page 25

Lifelong learning skills and content-based learning

Life skills

- **Social development** Empowerment of people through training and initiative, page 19
- **Socio-cultural awareness** The history of mobile phones, page 20
- **Communication** The importance of expressing thanks, page 24
- **Socio-cultural awareness** A famous British inventor, page 25

Learning strategies

- Examining words with the same root, page 22
- Classifying vocabulary, page 24

Cross-curricular content

- IT activities, page 18
- The use of technology for medical applications, page 22
- Language: conventions for opening and closing letters, page 24
- History: Alexander Graham Bell, page 25

Further materials and evaluation

Digital material

- Student's and Teacher's Resource Centres
- Teacher's Presentation Kit
- Student's Digital Material: interactive vocabulary and grammar activities
- Video *Sport* (Revision Units 1–3, page 40)

Student's website www.macmillansecondary.es

Workbook

- Vocabulary, pages 14–5
- Vocabulary Reference, page 85
- Grammar, pages 16–7
- Grammar Reference and Practice, pages 68–9
- Revision, page 18
- Culture: Reading and Listening, page 94
- Writing Guide, pages 104–5
- Speaking, page 121

Teacher's Resource File

Multi-level Materials Bank

- All Clear Basics, pages 6–10
- Vocabulary and Grammar Consolidation and Extension, pages 5–8
- Language Excellence, pages 3–4
- Translation and Dictation, pages 2 and 11

Lifelong Learning

- Digital Competence, pages 3–4
- Culture Video Material, pages 1–2
- Study Skills, pages 1–12

Evaluation and Key Competences

- Evaluation Rubrics, pages 1–7
- Key Competences, pages 3–4 and 21–2

Content-based Learning

- CLIL, pages 1–10
- Macmillan Readers, pages 1–7

Evaluation material

- Unit 2 end-of-unit test: Basic, Standard and Extra
- CEFR Skills Exam Generator

Web info

Tips to find extra information on: a homeless man who designed an app, how Summly condenses news on smartphones, a man whose blindness was cured by advances in technology, thank you notes written by famous people, Alexander Graham Bell

Extra help for weaker students

Teacher's Resource File: All Clear Basics, pages 6–10

Material for fast finishers

Workbook: Grammar Extension, page 19
Teacher's Resource File: Vocabulary Extension, page 7
Teacher's Resource File: Grammar Extension, page 8
Teacher's Resource File: Language Excellence, pages 3–4

2 Connected

Objectives

Vocabulary	IT activities; jobs
Grammar	Past simple; past continuous
Speaking	Making requests and offers (1)
Writing	A thank you letter

Vocabulary

IT activities

1 1.15 **Listen and repeat the words. Match them with pictures 1–14.**

charge a mobile phone • download / upload a video clip • go online • make a phone call • play a video game • plug in a memory stick • post a comment • print a document • read an e-book • scan a document • send an email • store data • take a photo • write a blog

Exercise 1
1 plug in a memory stick
2 scan a document
3 read an ebook
4 charge a mobile phone
5 store data
6 make a phone call
7 take a photo
8 post a comment
9 go online
10 download/upload a video clip
11 send an email
12 play a video game
13 write a blog
14 print a document

1

2
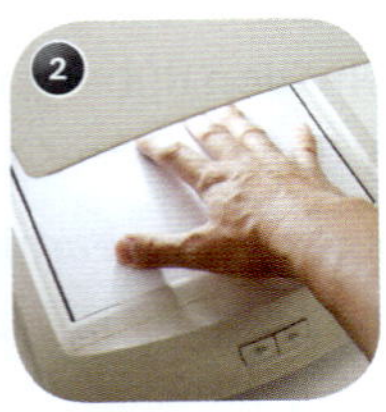
3

4

5

6

7

8

9

10

11
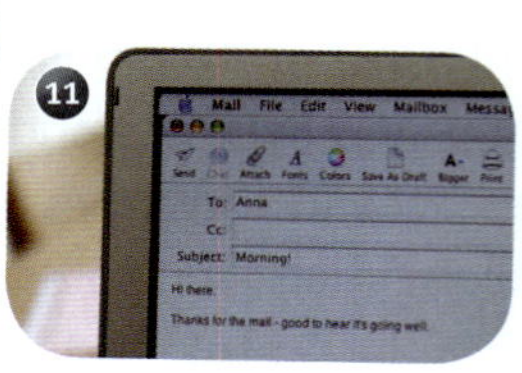
12

13

14

2 **Write the correct words in your notebook.**

1 I need to **store** / **charge** my mobile phone because the battery's dead.
2 He **stores** / **scans** data on a memory stick.
3 Do you know how to **upload** / **download** a video onto the internet?
4 This blog is really funny. I'm going to **post** / **download** a comment.
5 I use the internet to help me with my homework. I **go online** / **store data** to search for information.

Exercise 2
1 charge
2 stores
3 upload
4 post
5 go online

3 1.16 **Listen to Sophie and Chen. How many hours does Chen watch TV every week?**

Exercise 3
About four or five

4 **In pairs, ask and answer questions about IT activities.**

How many hours do you use a computer every day?

About two hours. What about you?

Vocabulary Reference

Lesson Aims:

Students learn and practise the names of technology items and IT-related activities.
Students listen to two young people talking about IT activities and ask and answer questions about their own IT activities.

Vocabulary

IT activities

Warmer

Books closed. Brainstorm with the class what type of things they use a smartphone or computer for and write the words on the board. Help with vocabulary when needed.

1 1.15

- Play the audio. Students listen and repeat the words.
- Check understanding.
- Practise the pronunciation, paying particular attention to word stress.
- Students match the words with the pictures.
- Check answers with the class.

2
- Students complete the sentences with the correct words.
- Check answers with the class.
- Check the pronunciation.

Extra activity

Revise adverbs of frequency, expressions of frequency (eg *every day*, *once a week*, etc) and the question *How often do you … ?* with the class.
Ask students questions using the activities in the box, eg *How often do you go on line?*
Students ask each other questions in pairs.

3 1.16

- Students read the question.
- Play the audio. Students listen for the number of hours Chen watches TV every week.
- Check the answer with the class.

4

- Read the example question and answer with the class.
- Students ask and answer questions about IT activities in pairs.

Mixed-ability solutions

Students who need extra help: Exercise 3. Give students two options: *four or five* / *ten*.

Fast finishers: Exercise 3. Students write down the other activities that Sophie and Chen talk about.

Self-study and extra practice

Workbook
- Vocabulary, page 14
- Vocabulary Reference, page 85

Teacher's Resource File
- All Clear Basics, page 6
- Vocabulary Consolidation, page 5
- Vocabulary Extension, page 7

Lesson Aims:

Students read and listen to a news report about a man who went from being homeless to designing his own app.

Reading

A news report

Warmer

Ask students if they know who the following people are and why they're famous. (Answers in brackets.)
Bill Gates (co-founder of Microsoft)
Steve Jobs (co-founder of Apple)
Mark Zuckerberg (co-founder of Facebook)
Larry Page and Sergey Brin (founders of Google)

1 • In pairs, students look at the pictures and discuss the answers to the questions.

Word Check

Check students understand the new words: *homeless, skill, car rides*. Explain any they don't know.

2 1.17
- Play the audio. Students read and listen to the text and check their answers to exercise 1.
- Check answers with the class.

3 • Read through the sentences with the class and make sure that they understand them.
- Students read the text again and correct the sentences.
- Check answers with the class.

4 • Students read the text again and answer the questions.
- Check answers with the class.

All Clear Facts

Read the fact with the class. Ask students if they've ever heard of Summly and if they know what it does. (See *Cultural note*.)

Cultural note

Summly is an application that aims to improve the way news articles are presented on smartphones. It condenses news into only a few sentences so that you can understand the gist of a story without reading hundreds of words. The initial version was downloaded by over 200,000 users.

Web info

Type these words in your search engine for more information about the homeless man who designed an app: 'Leo homeless coder'
For information on how Summly condenses news on smartphones go to google images and then type 'Summly app'

Mixed-ability solutions

Students who need extra help: Exercise 3. Correct the first sentence with the class as an example. Ask them where the information is located in the text, why the statement is incorrect and how it needs to be changed to make it correct.

Fast finishers: Exercise 3. Students work in pairs and try to think of a good new smartphone application. Once they have finished, ask them to share their ideas with the rest of the class.

Self-study and extra practice

Teacher's Resource File
- Key Competences: Reading, page 3

Reading

A news report

Word Check
homeless skill car rides

November 1st News **24**

THE POWER OF TECHNOLOGY

Patrick and Leo are both from New York. Patrick is a computer programmer. He started designing websites when he was just 12 years old. Leo doesn't have a job. He was working for an insurance company when he lost his job. As a result, he also lost his apartment and became **homeless**.

Patrick was walking to work when he first saw Leo. After that, he walked past him every day for five months. Then one day he decided to help him. He offered Leo two options: $100 in cash or free lessons in writing computer code. Leo chose the lessons.

Patrick taught Leo every day for two months. He bought him a second-hand laptop and three books on Java – the language of computers. Leo used computers at school but he didn't know much about them. At first, he couldn't send Patrick emails because he didn't have an email address. However, he found programming interesting and learnt very quickly.

When they started the lessons, Patrick wrote a blog about the project. Many people posted positive comments, but there were also negative comments. They said that Leo needed food and a home, not computer lessons. But computer programming is a very useful **skill**. You need it to build apps, websites or video games, for example.

Trees for Cars

And only a few months after he started his lessons, Leo built and launched his own app to encourage people to share **car rides** and reduce pollution. It's called Trees for Cars. Why don't you download it?

All Clear Facts

Nick D'Aloisio is a teenager who builds apps. In 2013, when he was just 17, he sold his app, Summly, to Yahoo for more than 20 million euros!

Exercise 1
1 A computer programmer (Patrick) and someone he is teaching to write computer code (Leo)
2 The man on the right (Patrick) is a computer programmer. The man on the left (Leo) doesn't have a job.

1 Look at the pictures and answer the questions.

1 Who are the two people in the photo?
2 What are their jobs?

2 1.17 Read and listen. Check your answers to exercise 1.

3 Read the text again. Correct these sentences in your notebook.

1 Leo lost his job because he became homeless.
2 Patrick decided to help Leo the first day he saw him.
3 Patrick offered Leo money, a laptop and computer lessons.
4 Patrick bought Leo a new computer.
5 Leo found programming boring and he learnt slowly.

Exercise 3
Possible answers:
1 Leo became homeless because he lost his job.
2 Patrick decided to help Leo five months after he saw him.
3 Patrick offered Leo money or free lessons in writing computer code.
4 Patrick bought Leo a second-hand computer.
5 Leo found programming interesting and he learnt quickly.

4 Answer the questions in your notebook.

1 Where did Leo work before he became homeless?
2 How often did Patrick agree to teach Leo?
3 Why did some people make negative comments?
4 What can you use computer code for?
5 How did Leo first use his new skill?

Exercise 4
1 He worked for an insurance company.
2 Every day for two months
3 Because they thought that Leo needed food and a home, not computer lessons
4 To build apps, websites and video games
5 To build and launch his own app (Trees for Cars)

Grammar

Past simple

was / were	
Affirmative	She **was**
Negative	We **weren't**
Interrogative	**Were** you …?

Language Reference p26

1 Complete the questions with *was* or *were*.

Were your friends online yesterday?

1 What … your favourite birthday present last year?
2 Where … you on Saturday afternoon?
3 … your friends at school yesterday?
4 … your mobile phone a gift from your parents?
5 … you tired last night?
6 … Jim at the concert last night?

Exercise 1
1 was
2 were
3 Were
4 Was
5 Were
6 Was

2 Match answers a–f with questions 1–6 in exercise 1.

a) No, they weren't. It was Sunday.
b) No, it wasn't.
c) Yes, I was.
d) I was at the shopping centre.
e) It was my mp3 player.
f) Yes, he was.

Exercise 2
1 e
2 d
3 a
4 b
5 c
6 f

Regular verbs	
Affirmative	She **played**
Negative	We **didn't play**
Interrogative	**Did** you **play** …?

Language Reference p26

All Clear Rules

Remember to check if verbs are regular or irregular in the past. There are no spelling rules for irregular verbs, so look at the Irregular verbs list on p110 if you aren't sure.

3 Copy and complete the table with the past simple form of the verbs in the box.

buy charge decide realize see take think want

Regular	Irregular
want – wanted	take – took

Exercise 3
Regular: charge – charged, decide – decided, realize – realized, want – wanted (example), **Irregular:** buy – bought, see – saw, take – took (example), think – thought

4 Sam made a list of things to do yesterday. Look at the list and write sentences about what he did / didn't do in your notebook.

He didn't send three emails.

✗ send three emails
✓ upload some photos
✓ buy a memory stick
✗ play a new computer game
✓ upload a video to my blog
✗ post comments on my blog

Exercise 4
He didn't send three emails. (example)
He uploaded some photos.
He bought a memory stick.
He didn't play a new computer game.
He uploaded a video to his blog.
He didn't post comments on his blog.

5 Write six questions about last weekend in your notebook. Use the ideas in the box or your own ideas.

buy something go to the park / cinema listen to music meet your friends play football / basketball read watch TV

Did you watch TV last weekend?

Exercise 5
Students' own answers

6 In pairs, ask and answer your questions in exercise 5.

7 Complete the text with the past simple form of the verbs in brackets.

www.historyoftheweb.com

The World Wide Web

Twenty years ago, there (1)… (not be) a World Wide Web and there (2)… (not be) any social networking sites. By 1994, there (3)… (be) about a hundred big websites, but today there are millions! The web (4)… (develop) when search engines such as Google (5)… (become) available and more people (6)… (get) high-speed broadband in their homes. Then, the development of wi-fi and the increase in the use of smartphones (7)… (make) the internet accessible almost anywhere. Today, it's hard to imagine life without the web.

Exercise 7
1 wasn't
2 weren't
3 were
4 developed
5 became
6 got
7 made

Lesson Aims:

Students revise and practise the past simple (affirmative, negative, interrogative and short answers) with the verb *be* and regular and irregular verbs.

Grammar

Past simple

Warmer

Students re-read the first paragraph of the text on page 19 and identify all the verbs in the past simple (*started*, *was*, *lost*, *became*). Ask them if any of the verbs are regular (only *started*).

1 • Elicit the past simple forms of *be* from the class.
• Read through the first grammar table and the example with the class.
• Students complete the questions with *was* or *were*.
• Check answers with the class.

2 • Students match the answers with the questions in exercise 1.
• Check answers with the class.

All Clear Rules

Read through the second grammar table with the class. Remind students that in the past simple regular verbs end in *-ed* but that there are many verbs that are irregular in the past.

3 • Students copy the table and write the verbs and their past simple form in the correct columns.
• Ask them to say the verbs in each column aloud. Remind them of the rules for pronouncing the endings of regular past simple affirmative verbs:
We pronounce the *-ed* ending:
/t/ after /p/, /k/, /s/, /f/, /ʃ/ and /tʃ/ sounds: *stopped*, *washed*, etc.
/ɪd/ after /d/ and /t/ sounds: *ended*, *wanted*, etc.
/d/ after all other sounds: *arrived*, *opened*, etc.

4 • Elicit the negative form of the past simple verbs in the table in exercise 3.
• Read through the example with the class.
• Students write the sentences.
• Check answers with the class.

5 • Ask students some questions about last weekend using the activities in the box. Encourage short answers.
• Students look at the ideas in the box. They write six questions with *Did you … ?* and the ideas in the box or their own ideas.

6
• Students ask and answer their questions from exercise 5 in pairs. Monitor and help as necessary.
• Ask some students to report back on their partner, using the affirmative and negative.

Extra activity

Students write about their partner's weekend.

7 • Students complete the text with the correct past simple form of the verbs in brackets.
• Check answers with the class.

Mixed-ability solutions

Students who need extra help: Exercise 3.
Tell students that only *want* (the example), *charge*, *decide* and *realize* are regular. Instruct them to consult the list of irregular verbs on page 110 to find the past simple form of the other verbs.

Fast finishers: Exercise 3. Students find nine irregular past simple verbs in the text on page 19 (excluding *was* and *were*).

Lesson Aims:

Students learn and practise using the past continuous and contrast it with the past simple.

Grammar

Past continuous

Warmer

Write on the board *What were you doing at six o'clock last night?* Elicit the translation. Make sure that students translate it with the equivalent of the past continuous, and not the past simple, in their own language.
Ask questions using this structure with different times, eg *last Saturday, five minutes ago*, etc.

All Clear Rules

Read the grammar table with the class.
Read the rule with the class.
Elicit the difference in use between the past continuous and the past simple.

8
- Explain that all the sentences describe what other people were doing when Sara arrived and therefore they need to use the past continuous.
- Students complete the sentences with the past continuous form of the verbs in brackets.
- Check answers with the class.

Extra activity

Practise extracts from the answers, eg *her brother Miguel wasn't writing an email, he was watching TV.*, to make students aware of which words are stressed.

9
- Read the example with the class.
- Students write questions with the past continuous.
- Check answers with the class, making sure students spell the *-ing* form of the verb correctly.

10
- Ask a student the example question from exercise 9 and elicit the answer from the sentences in exercise 8 (*No, he wasn't. He was watching TV.*).
- Students ask and answer the questions in exercise 9 in pairs.
- Check answers by asking some pairs to ask and answer the questions again in open class.

11
- Read the first sentence of the text with the class.
- Students complete the text with the past continuous form of the verbs in brackets.
- Check answers with the class.

All Clear Grammar

12
- Tell students that this is a cumulative check of the grammar in Units 1 and 2.
- Before students do the exercise, you may like to go back to exercise 8. Ask students to look at the first sentence and ask which tenses are used and why (*arrived* – past simple because it is a single action completed in the past; *wasn't writing* and *was watching* – past continuous because they are actions in progress in the past).
- As this exercise is quite challenging, you may want students to do it in pairs.
- Students choose the correct words to complete the text.

13 1.18
- Play the audio. Students listen and check their answers.
- Check answers with the class. This is a good moment to check they have understood the new grammar and to review the grammar from the previous units.

Mixed-ability solutions

Students who need extra help: Exercise 10. Students write their answers to the questions first.

Fast finishers: Exercise 8. Students write three sentences about what other members in their family were doing when they arrived home yesterday.

Self-study and extra practice

Workbook
- Grammar, pages 16–7
- Grammar Reference and Practice, pages 68–9

Teacher's Resource File
- All Clear Basics, pages 8–9
- Grammar Consolidation, page 6
- Grammar Extension, page 8
- Language Excellence, pages 3–4

Digital Activities
- Student's Digital Material

Exercise 9

1 Were her parents preparing a meal when she arrived?
2 Was Elisa chatting online when Sara arrived?
3 Was Elisa listening to music when she arrived?
4 Was Nahuel using the computer when Sara arrived?
5 Were Jimmy and Johnny sleeping when she arrived?

Past continuous

Affirmative	She **was** reading
Negative	We **weren't** reading
Interrogative	**Were** you reading ...?

Language Reference p26

All Clear Rules

We use the past continuous to talk about an action in progress in the past.

Exercise 8

1 wasn't writing; was watching
2 were looking; weren't preparing
3 wasn't listening; was chatting
4 was waiting; wasn't using
5 were sleeping; weren't eating

8 **Complete the sentences with the past continuous form of the verbs in brackets.**

When Sara arrived home ...

1 her brother Miguel ... (not write) an email, he ... (watch) TV.
2 her parents ... (look) at a holiday website, they ... (not prepare) a meal.
3 her sister Elisa ... (not listen) to music on her mp3 player, she ... (chat) online.
4 her friend Nahuel ... (wait) for her, he ... (not use) the computer.
5 the cats Jimmy and Johnny ... (sleep), they ... (not eating).

9 **Write complete questions in your notebook about what was happening when Sara arrived.**

Miguel / write an email / when Sara arrived?
Was Miguel writing an email when Sara arrived?

1 her parents / prepare a meal / when she arrived?
2 Elisa / chat online / when Sara arrived?
3 Elisa / listen to music / when she arrived?
4 Nahuel / use the computer / when Sara arrived?
5 Jimmy and Johnny / sleep / when she arrived?

10 **In pairs, ask and answer the questions in exercise 9.**

Exercise 10

1 No, they weren't. They were looking at a holiday website.
2 Yes, she was.
3 No, she wasn't. She was chatting online.
4 No, he wasn't. He was waiting for her.
5 Yes, they were.

11 **Complete the text with the past continuous form of the verbs in brackets.**

A robber took Dave's laptop when he *was sleeping* (sleep). Two days later, when Dave (1)... (search) for a new laptop on the internet, he saw a laptop similar to his old one. Dave went to the seller's house to buy it. As he (2)... (look) at the laptop, he realized it was his! When the seller (3)... (not look), Dave sent a message to the police. When the police arrived, Dave (4)... (talk) to the seller. The police found more of Dave's things when they (5)... (search) the house.

Exercise 11

1 was searching
2 was looking
3 wasn't looking
4 was talking
5 were searching

All Clear Grammar

1 2 3 4 5 6 7 8 9

Exercise 12

1 were
2 couldn't
3 installed
4 stopped
5 was travelling
6 connected
7 started
8 use

12 **Write the correct words in your notebook.**

Before mobile phones, there (1)**was / were** two-way radios in taxis, police cars and ambulances, but users (2)**can't / couldn't** connect to the phone network. In 1910, Lars Ericsson (3)**installed / was installing** a phone in his car. He (4)**stopped / was stopping** at different places while he (5)**travelled / was travelling** across the country. Then he (6)**connected / was connecting** his phone to the national telephone network with long wires. The first real mobile phone system (7)**started / was starting** in 1956, in Sweden. Today, people (8)**use / are using** mobile phones every day.

13 1.18 **Listen and check your answers.**

Grammar Reference

Vocabulary

Jobs

1 1.19 **Listen and repeat the words. How do you say them in your language?**

actor • artist • builder • doctor • electrician • firefighter • journalist • lab technician • lawyer • police officer • politician • postal worker • researcher • scientist

Exercise 1
Students' own answers

2 **Match pictures 1–14 with the jobs in exercise 1.**

Exercise 2
1 doctor
2 firefighter
3 electrician
4 journalist
5 politician
6 artist
7 actor
8 lawyer
9 builder
10 police officer
11 lab technician
12 researcher
13 scientist
14 postal worker

3 **Complete the sentences with jobs from exercise 1.**

1 A … is someone who treats people who are ill.
2 A … uses special equipment or machines in a laboratory.
3 A … collects and delivers letters and parcels.
4 Picasso was an … . He painted many pictures.
5 A … collects information and analyses it.
6 A … studies law and advises people on legal matters.

Exercise 3
1 doctor
2 lab technician
3 postal worker
4 artist
5 researcher / scientist
6 lawyer

4 **What work-related verbs and nouns can you find in the jobs above?**

builder → build (verb)   *artist → art (noun)*

Exercise 4
actor → act (noun / verb)
artist → art (noun) (example)
builder → build (verb) (example), building (noun)
electrician → electricity (noun)
fighter → fight (noun / verb), fighting (noun)
journalist → journal (noun)
technician → technology (noun)
lawyer → law (noun)
politician → politics (noun)
postal → post (verb / noun)
worker → work (verb / noun)
researcher → research (verb / noun)
scientist → science (noun)

Listening

5 1.20 **Listen to the news story. How did Martin Jones become blind?**

Exercise 5
He had an accident at work.

6 **Listen again and answer the questions in your notebook.**

1 What was Martin's job?
2 How long was he blind for?
3 What part of Martin's body did doctors implant in his eye?
4 Who was the first person Martin saw?
5 Do scientists think they can use this technology for other blind people?

Exercise 6
1 a builder
2 12 years
3 a tooth
4 his wife, Gill
5 Yes, they do.

Vocabulary Reference

Lesson Aims:

Students revise some words for jobs and professions and learn and practise some new words.
Students identify specific information in an audio report about someone whose blindness was cured using new technology.

Vocabulary

Jobs

Warmer

Books closed. Write the heading *Jobs* on the board and tell students they have a minute to write down as many jobs in English as they can. Then see who has the longest list and ask them to read it out. Write the words on the board. Other students add any different words they have to the list on the board.

1 1.19

- Play the audio. Students listen and repeat the words.
- Elicit the translations.
- Practise each word carefully, pointing out the pronunciation features, such as the silent *u* in *builder* and the vowel sound /ɔː/ in *lawyer*.

2
- Students look at the pictures and match them with the words in exercise 1.
- Check answers with the class.

3
- Students complete the sentences with jobs from exercise 1.
- Check answers with the class.

4
- Explain to students that many words come from the same root and look at the examples in the Student's Book with them.
- Elicit some more examples from the class based on the words in exercise 1.
- In pairs, students write down any words they can think of with the same root as those in exercise 1.
- Check answers with the class, writing the words on the board.

Extra activity

Dictate some of the jobs that are more difficult to spell, eg *electrician, lawyer*. Check by asking individuals to write them on the board. Elicit corrections as needed.

Language note

Many women are now doing jobs which were traditionally done by men and vice versa. As a result, gender-neutral job titles such *police officer*, *firefighter*, *bartender* and *flight attendant* are now in common use.

Listening

Warmer

Brainstorm with the class ways in which advances in medical science have made our lives better. This may require some prompting. Possible ideas include hearing aids, glasses, operations to correct eyesight, prosthetics, cancer screening and cures for many diseases that were fatal in the past.

5 1.20

- Read the question with the class.
- Play the audio. Students listen and answer the question. You may want to stop the audio after the words *he couldn't see at all*.
- Check the answer with the class.

6
- Read the questions with the class.
- Play the audio again. Students listen and answer the questions.
- Check answers with the class.

Web info

Type 'Martin Jones eye operation' in your search engine for more information about Martin Jones

Mixed-ability solutions

Students who need extra help: Exercise 6.
Write the following options on the board.

1 *teacher / builder*
2 *12 years / 20 years*
3 *mouth / tooth*
4 *his wife / his girlfriend*
5 *yes / probably not*

Fast finishers: Exercise 3. Students choose the five jobs from exercise 1 they think would be the most interesting.

Self-study and extra practice

Workbook
- Vocabulary, page 15
- Vocabulary Reference, page 85

Teacher's Resource File
- All Clear Basics, page 7
- Vocabulary Consolidation, page 5
- Vocabulary Extension, page 7
- Key Competences: Listening, page 4

Digital Activities
- Student's Digital Material

Lesson Aims:

Students learn and practise functional language to make requests and offers.

Speaking

Making requests and offers (1) / Shopping for electronic gadgets

Warmer

Books closed. Ask students if they have bought a smartphone recently. What did they buy? What questions did they ask the shop assistant? Did they find it easy to choose?

Model Dialogue

1 1.21

- Read the question with the class.
- Play the audio. Students listen to and read the dialogue.
- Elicit the answer to the question.

Extra activity

Revise how we say prices in English, eg £25.50 = *Twenty-five pounds fifty* or, less commonly, *Twenty-five pounds (and) fifty pence.*

2
- Play the audio again. Students listen again and this time repeat the dialogue.
- Focus on the use of *Can I … ?* to both make an offer and make a request: *Can I help you?* and *Can I see that one over there?*. Also highlight *I'm looking for … ; What features has it got?; How much is it?* and *I'll take the other one* (not ~~I take~~). Get the class to pay attention to stress and intonation.

Speaking Task

1 Talk to a shop assistant

Students look at the pictures and read the information. If necessary, clarify the meaning of *screen*, *front and back cameras* and *touch screen*. They choose one of the gadgets.

2 Prepare a dialogue

Students look at the Model Dialogue and change the words in blue to make their own dialogue.

3 Speak

Students practise their dialogues in pairs.

Cultural note

Although the UK is a full member of the EU, it has never joined the euro and has kept its own currency, known as the pound sterling.

Mixed-ability solutions

Students who need extra help: Speaking Task. Students write out their dialogue before they do step 3.

Fast finishers: Speaking Task. Students act out another dialogue about buying something, not necessarily an electronic gadget. Encourage them to use their imagination! If possible, they do this without looking at the Model Dialogue.

Self-study and extra practice

Workbook
- Speaking, page 121

Teacher's Resource File
- Key Competences: Speaking, pages 21–2

Digital Activities
- Student's Digital Material

Speaking

Making requests and offers (1) / Shopping for electronic gadgets

Exercise 1
Because it's too expensive.

1 1.21 **Listen to the dialogue. Why doesn't Carla buy the second phone?**

Model Dialogue

Shop assistant: Can I help you?

Carla: Yes, I'm looking for a new smartphone.

Shop assistant: This one's on special offer. It's £75.

Carla: What features has it got?

Shop assistant: It's got an HD video camera, a music player and 4G mobile internet.

Carla: Right. What about that one over there? Can I see it?

Shop assistant: Sure. This is a really good one.

Carla: How much is it?

Shop assistant: It's £200.

Carla: Oh! That's too expensive for me. OK, I'll take the other one.

Shop assistant: That's £75 then, please.

Carla: Here you are. Thanks. Bye.

2 **Listen again and repeat the dialogue.**

Speaking Task

1 Talk to a shop assistant

Read the information and choose a gadget.

Gadgets 128

smartphone
a 3D screen, an HD camera, 4G mobile internet
~~£450~~ £350

tablet
a music player, front and back cameras, an HD video camera
£120

smartwatch
a music player control, bluetooth, a touch screen
£95

camera
wi-fi, digital zoom, face detection
£75

2 Prepare a dialogue

Look at the Model Dialogue and change the words in blue.

3 Speak

In pairs, practise your dialogue.

Can I help you?

Yes, I'm looking for a new smartphone.

Useful Language Making requests and offers (1)

Can I help you?
This one's on special offer.
How much is it?
Can I see that one over there?
Yes, I'm looking for a new smartphone.
What features has it got?
That's £75 then, please.
I'll take this / that / the other one.

Writing

A thank you letter

Exercise 1
1 Because she is very busy at school.
2 A smartwatch.
3 She can read texts and emails, take photos and make phone calls.
4 With her friends at home. They had pizza and a birthday cake. Then they went to the cinema.

1 1.22 **Read the Model Text and listen. Answer the questions in your notebook.**

1 Why didn't Luciana write before?
2 What was her birthday present from her aunt and uncle?
3 What can Luciana do with her present?
4 How did she celebrate her birthday?

Model Text

Dear Aunty Laura and Uncle Harry,

How are you? I hope you're well. I'm very busy at school, so that's why I didn't write before!

Thanks very much for the smartwatch. It was exactly what I wanted! I use it all the time. I can read texts and emails, take photos and make phone calls. I really like it.

I had a great birthday. When I arrived home from school, my friends were waiting with pizza and a birthday cake. I wasn't expecting it, so it was a lovely surprise! Then we all went to the cinema.

Hope to see you soon.

Lots of love,

Luciana

Exercise 2
Beginning a letter:
I'm writing to thank you for …
How are you? I hope you're well.
Saying thank you:
It was exactly what I wanted!
Thanks a lot / very much for my present.
I really like it / them.
Ending a letter:
Lots of love,
All the best,
Hope to see you soon.

2 **Look at the All Clear Tips. Copy the phrases into your notebook under the following headings.**

Beginning a letter   Ending a letter
Saying thank you

All Clear Tips

Thank you letters

I'm writing to thank you for …
It was exactly what I wanted!
Lots of love,
Thanks a lot / very much for my present.
How are you? I hope you're well.
All the best,
I really like it / them.
Hope to see you soon.

Exercise 3
1 e
2 d
3 b
4 c
5 a

3 **Match 1–5 with a–e to make expressions for a thank you letter.**

1 I'm writing
2 Thanks a lot for
3 A camera is
4 Hope to
5 Lots of love,

a) Oscar
b) exactly what I wanted.
c) see you soon.
d) my new headphones.
e) to thank you for my smartphone.

Writing Task

1 Plan

Make notes for a thank you letter and include:

Beginning: *who you are writing to, why you didn't write before*
Say thank you: *describe the present you received and explain why you like it*
Ending: *describe what you did on your birthday*

2 Write

Use the Model Text, your notes and this structure:

Paragraph 1: Beginning
Paragraph 2: Say thank you
Paragraph 3: Ending

3 Check

☑ past simple, past continuous
☑ IT activities
☑ expressions for thank you letters

Lesson Aims:

Students learn to use appropriate expressions for opening and closing a letter and expressing thanks.
Students write a thank you letter.

Writing

A thank you letter

Warmer

Ask students if they have ever written a letter or email to relatives or friends thanking them for a present. If so, elicit who they wrote to and what the present was.

1 1.22

- Students look at the picture and read the questions.
- Play the audio. Students read and listen to the letter and find the answers.
- Check answers with the class.
- Highlight the structure of the letter. Point out that there are three paragraphs, each with a specific topic. The first is an introduction; the second is about the present and the third is about how she celebrated her birthday.

All Clear Tips

2
- Tell students that there are some useful expressions that they can use for writing emails and letters of thanks.
- Look at the expressions in the All Clear Tips box and elicit translations.
- Ask them to identify which expressions Luciana uses in her letter.
- Students write the phrases under the correct headings.
- Check answers with the class.

3
- Students match the words and phrases to make expressions for a thank you letter.
- Check answers with the class.

Extra activity

Students re-read the third paragraph and identify all the examples of the past simple and the past continuous and say why the tense is used in each case.

Writing Task

1 Plan

Read the notes with the class. Students make notes for their own thank you letter.

2 Write

Look at the structure with the class. Students use their notes to write a thank you letter. Emphasize that they should use some of the expressions from the All Clear Tips.

3 Check

Encourage students to check their work, paying particular attention to the points mentioned.

Web info

Type these words in your search engine to read some thank you letters written by famous people: 'mental floss + amazing thank you note'

Mixed-ability solutions

Students who need extra help: Writing Task. Students just write the notes in step 1.

Fast finishers: Writing Task. Students exchange their text with a partner. They read each other's letter and write a short reply.

Self-study and extra practice

Workbook
- Writing Guide, pages 104–5

Teacher's Resource File
- Key Competences: Writing, page 4

Lesson Aims:

Students learn about Alexander Graham Bell, the inventor of the telephone.
Students practise word stress.

Culture Reading

Famous inventions and inventors

Warmer

Write the following on the board:
The name of the inventor of the telephone was ....
He was from ....
His first call was to ....
His first words on the phone were ....
Students write possible endings to the sentences. Encourage them to be imaginative.

1.23

- Play the audio. Students read and listen to the text. They check their predictions from the warmer.
- Read the questions with the class.
- Students read the text again and find the answers.
- Check answers with the class.

Pronunciation

Word stress

a
- Write some words on the board with one, two, three and four syllables, eg *mouse*, *modem*, *computer*, *explanation*, and ask students how many syllables they have.
- Students copy the table and in pairs complete it with the words in the box.
- Check answers with the class.

b 1.24
- Repeat one of the words from exercise a and ask the class where the stress falls.
- Play the audio. Students listen and mark the stress in the other words.
- Check answers with the class.
- Practise all the words, making sure students pronounce them correctly.

c 1.25
- Play the audio. Students listen to the words and add them to their table.
- Play the audio again. Students listen and mark the stress in the words.
- Practise all the words, checking pronunciation.

Web info

Type these words in your search engine
- for more information about Alexander Graham Bell: 'soft schools + Alexander Graham Bell timeline'
- to see a silent film re-enactment of the first phone call: 'youtube + Alexander Graham Bell invents telephone'

Mixed-ability solutions

Students who need extra help: Reading text. To help students understand the text, you may want to pre-teach the words *deaf*, *as early as*, *develop*, *voice* and *landline phone subscriptions*.

Fast-finishers: Reading text. Students write four sentences based on the text, two true and two false. They pass their sentences to their partner who has to decide if they are true or false.

Self-study and extra practice

Workbook
- Culture: Reading and Listening, page 94

Culture Reading

EXTRA

Famous inventions and inventors

Alexander Graham Bell

Alexander Graham Bell (1842–1922) was a scientist, inventor and engineer. He was born in Scotland, but he moved to Canada and then the USA when he was a young man. Bell produced his first invention when he was just 12 and continued to invent things all his life.

Interest in sound

Bell's mother became deaf when he was a child and this started his interest in sound. He worked with deaf students for many years and started designing machines to transmit sound as early as 1863.

The first telephone

Bell started to develop a machine to transmit the human voice while he was teaching in Boston in the 1870s. The result? The telephone. The first phone call was to his assistant, Thomas Watson, on 10th March 1876. The first words? 'Watson. Come here. I want to see you.' The Bell Telephone Company began in 1877 and by 1886 over 150,000 people in America had telephones.

Today

There are approximately 1.14 billion landline phone subscriptions in the world and nearly 7 billion mobile phone subscriptions – 95.5% of the world's population! In the UK, 93% of people have a mobile phone, and in the USA it's 90%.

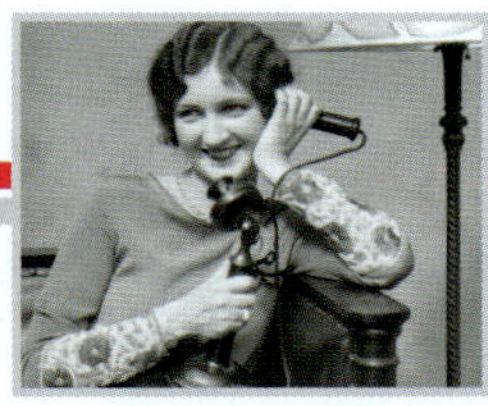

1.23 Read and listen. Then answer the questions in your notebook.

1 Where was Bell born?
2 When did he produce his first invention?
3 Why did he become interested in sound?
4 Where did he develop the first telephone?
5 How many people in America had telephones by 1886?

Reading text exercise

1 Scotland
2 when he was 12
3 because his mother became deaf
4 Boston
5 Over 150,000

Pronunciation

Word stress

a Copy and complete the table with the words in the box.

engineer inventor landline mobile phone population scientist sound

1 syllable	2 syllables	3 syllables	4 syllables
		engineer	

b 1.24 Listen and mark the stress.

c 1.25 Listen to the words and add them to the table. Then mark the stressed syllable.

blog data digital electrician invention online scan technology

Pronunciation exercises a and b

1 syllable	2 syllables	3 syllables	4 syllables
phone	landline	engineer	population
sound	mobile	inventor	
		scientist	

Pronunciation exercise c

1 syllable	2 syllables	3 syllables	4 syllables
blog	data	digital	electrician
scan	online	invention	technology

Unit 2 Language Reference

Vocabulary IT activities

charge a mobile phone • download / upload a video clip • go online • make a phone call • play a video game • plug in a memory stick • post a comment • print a document • read an e-book • scan a document • send an email • store data • take a photo • write a blog

Jobs

actor • artist • builder • doctor • electrician • firefighter • journalist • lab technician • lawyer • police officer • politician • postal worker • researcher • scientist

Grammar *was / were*

Affirmative	Negative	Interrogative	Short answers
I **was** an actor.	I **was not** an actor.	**Was** I an actor?	Yes, I **was**.
You **were** an actor.	You **were not** an actor.	**Were** you an actor?	No, you **were not**.
He / She / It **was** an actor.	He / She / It **was not** an actor.	**Was** he / she / it an actor?	Yes, he **was**.
We / You / They **were** actors.	We / You / They **were not** actors.	**Were** we / you / they actors?	No, we **were not**.

Past simple: regular verbs

Affirmative	Negative	Interrogative	Short answers
I / You **uploaded** a video.	I / You **did not upload** a video.	**Did** I / you **upload** a video?	Yes, I / you **did**.
He / She / It **uploaded** a video.	He / She / It **did not upload** a video.	**Did** he / she / it **upload** a video?	No, he / she / it **did not**.
We / You / They **uploaded** a video.	We / You / They **did not upload** a video.	**Did** we / you / they **upload** a video?	Yes, we / you / they **did**.

Past continuous

Affirmative	Negative	Interrogative	Short answers
I **was making** a phone call.	I **was not making** a phone call.	**Was** I **making** a phone call?	Yes, I **was**.
You **were making** a phone call.	You **were not making** a phone call.	**Were** you **making** a phone call?	No, you **were not**.
He / She / It **was making** a phone call.	He / She / It **was not making** a phone call.	**Was** he / she / it **making** a phone call?	Yes, he **was**.
We / You / They **were making** a phone call.	We / You / They **were not making** a phone call.	**Were** we / you / they **making** a phone call?	No, we **were not**.

Speaking Making requests and offers (1)

Can I help you?
This one's on special offer.
How much is it?
Can I see that one over there?

Yes, I'm looking for a new smartphone.
What features has it got?
That's £75 then, please.
I'll take this / that / the other one.

Unit 2 Progress Check

Vocabulary IT activities

1 Complete the phrases with vowels.

1 pl_y _ v_d_ _ g_m_
2 s_nd _n _m_ _l
3 ch_rg_ _ m_b_l_ ph_n_
4 g_ _nl_n_
5 p_st _ c_mm_nt

Exercise 1
1 play a video game
2 send an email
3 charge a mobile phone
4 go online
5 post a comment

Jobs

2 Complete the sentences with the correct jobs.

1 Kathy is investigating new technology at the moment. She is a … .
2 Joe works in construction. He's a … .
3 Sarah works in the local hospital. She is a … .
4 Ben works for a newspaper. He is a … .
5 My favourite film star is Robert Pattinson. Who is your favourite … ?

Exercise 2
1 researcher
2 builder
3 doctor
4 journalist
5 actor

Grammar Past simple

3 Complete the sentences with the correct form of *be*.

1 At 11 pm last night Mark … in bed.
2 Where … you at 7 pm yesterday?
3 They … (not) at school yesterday because it … Sunday.
4 My family and I … (not) at home last night because we … at my grandma's house.
5 … Kevin at the party last Saturday?

Exercise 3
1 was
2 were
3 weren't; was
4 weren't; were
5 Was

4 Complete the sentences with the correct past simple form of the verbs in brackets.

1 Eva … (send) an email to Chen last night.
2 We … (not go) dancing last Saturday.
3 Carla and her sister … (play) games on their tablets last weekend.
4 … (you / write) on your blog yesterday?
5 Nick … (post) a comment last night.

Exercise 4
1 sent
2 didn't go
3 played
4 Did you write
5 posted

Past continuous

5 Write complete questions in your notebook using the past continuous. Then answer the questions so they are true for you.

1 What / you / do / at 10 pm last night?
2 What / your parents / do / at 3 pm on Sunday?
3 you and your friend / watch a DVD / at 9 pm yesterday?
4 your friend / sleep / at 10 am this morning?
5 What / your friends / do / five minutes ago?

Exercise 5
1 What were you doing at 10 pm last night?
2 What were your parents doing at 3 pm on Sunday?
3 Were you and your friend watching a DVD at 9 pm yesterday?
4 Was your friend sleeping at 10 am this morning?
5 What were your friends doing five minutes ago?
Students' own answers

All Clear Self-Check

Check your answers

Write your scores for exercises 1–5 in your notebook. What did you get for:

- IT activities?
- jobs?
- past simple?
- past continuous?

Extra Practice

If you need extra practice, go to:

Unit 2 Grammar Reference
Unit 2 Vocabulary Reference
Unit 2 Grammar Exercises
Unit 2 Vocabulary Exercises

Correct the activities with the class. Students who need extra revision and practice can go to:

Workbook
- Unit 2 Revision, page 18
- Grammar Reference and Practice, pages 68–9
- Vocabulary Reference, page 85

Student's Digital Material
www.allclear.macmillan.es

3 Incredible stories

Overview

Unit objectives and key competences

- Understand, memorize and correctly use *-ed* / *-ing* adjectives and prepositions of movement after certain verbs CLC
- Read two shorts text in which people take the initiative and overcome difficulties SIE
- Identify the gist and main ideas of two short texts about unusual incidents CLC
- Understand, contrast and correctly use the past simple and past continuous with *when* and *while*; differentiate between and correctly use present and past tenses CLC, L2L
- Listen and identify the main events in a news report CLC
- Use appropriate functional language to tell an anecdote CLC, SCC
- Write a description of an accident using appropriate tenses and time expressions CLC, SIE, CAE
- Find specific information in a text about a famous English writer and his work CLC
- Learn about a famous English writer and his work CAE
- Assimilate the All Clear Tips and Rules and study the Language Reference from the unit CLC, L2L, SIE
- Identify areas of language which need improvement and use ICT for extra practice DC, CLC, L2L

More information on Key Competences, page v

Linguistic content

Grammar

- Past simple and past continuous with *when* and *while*
- Contrast past and present tenses

Recycled grammar

- Present simple (Unit 1)
- Present continuous (Unit 1)
- Past simple (Unit 2)
- Past continuous (Unit 2)

Main vocabulary

- Prepositions of movement after certain verbs: *across*, *along*, etc
- *-ed* / *-ing* adjectives: *annoyed* / *annoying*, etc

Functional language

- Telling anecdotes / Talking with friends

Pronunciation

- Sentence stress

Skills: learning outcomes

- **Reading** Understand specific information in two clearly structured descriptions of incidents. The student can re-read the more difficult parts, page 29
- **Listening** Identify the gist and main ideas of a report about an event. Delivered slowly and with clarity, page 32
- **Speaking** Communicate effectively in an everyday situation, telling an anecdote, page 33
- **Writing** Write a description of an accident with the events in a logical order, page 34
- **Reading** Understand specific information in a clearly structured text about a famous English writer and his work. The student can re-read the more difficult parts, page 35

Lifelong learning skills and content-based learning

Life skills

- **Social development** Interest in news stories from different countries, pages 29, 31 and 32
- **Social responsibility** The importance of honesty, page 29
- **Self knowledge** The ability to overcome difficult situations or experiences through determination, pages 29 and 32
- **Communication** Telling an anecdote, page 33
- **Socio-cultural awareness** Learn about a famous British writer, page 35

Learning strategies

- Classify words together with their opposite to facilitate understanding and retention, page 28
- Finding examples of rules in a text, page 34

Cross-curricular content

- Natural science: behaviour of sharks and dolphins, page 31
- Literature: a famous writer and his work, page 35

Further materials and evaluation

Digital material

- Student's and Teacher's Resource Centres
- Teacher's Presentation Kit
- Student's Digital Material: interactive vocabulary and grammar activities
- Video *Sport* (Revision Units 1–3, page 40)

Student's website www.macmillansecondary.es

Workbook

- Vocabulary, pages 20–1
- Vocabulary Reference, page 86
- Grammar, pages 22–3
- Grammar Reference and Practice, pages 70–1
- Revision, page 24
- Culture: Reading and Listening, page 95
- Writing Guide, pages 106–7
- Speaking, page 122

Teacher's Resource File

Multi-level Materials Bank

- All Clear Basics, pages 11–5
- Vocabulary and Grammar Consolidation and Extension, pages 9–12
- Language Excellence, pages 5–6
- Translation and Dictation, pages 3 and 12

Lifelong Learning

- Digital Competence, pages 5–6
- Culture Video Material, pages 1–2
- Study Skills, pages 1–12

Evaluation and Key Competences

- Evaluation Rubrics, pages 1–7
- Key Competences, pages 5–6 and 23–4

Content-based Learning

- CLIL, pages 1–10
- Macmillan Readers, pages 1–7

Evaluation material

- Unit 3 end-of-unit test: Basic, Standard and Extra
- End-of-term test, Units 1–3: Basic, Standard and Extra
- CEFR Skills Exam Generator

Web info

Tips to find extra information on: the activities that can be done in the Mont Blanc area, someone who survived a skydiving accident, funny and allegedly true descriptions of accidents made on insurance claims, *Robinson Crusoe*

Extra help for weaker students

Teacher's Resource File: All Clear Basics, pages 11–5

Material for fast finishers

Workbook: Grammar Extension, page 25
Teacher's Resource File: Vocabulary Extension, page 11
Teacher's Resource File: Grammar Extension, page 12
Teacher's Resource File: Language Excellence, pages 5–6

3 Incredible stories

Objectives

Vocabulary	Prepositions; *-ed* / *-ing* adjectives
Grammar	Past tenses: past simple and past continuous; *when* and *while*; present and past tenses
Speaking	Telling anecdotes
Writing	A description of an accident

Vocabulary

Prepositions

1 1.26 **Listen and repeat the words. Match them with pictures 1–12.**

across • along • away from • down • into • out of • over • round • through • towards • under • up

Exercise 1
1 under
2 towards
3 out of
4 away from
5 through
6 down
7 up
8 across
9 round
10 along
11 into
12 over

2 Which prepositions are opposites? In pairs, write them in your notebook.

Exercise 2
away from – towards
down – up
into – out of
over – under

3 Write the correct words in your notebook.

James Bond is always very active in his films. He often jumps (1)**out of / towards** aeroplanes and parachutes (2)**over / down** to the ground, and then he runs (3)**up / under** to the top of mountains, dives (4)**into / out of** rivers and then swims (5)**under / over** the water to the other side. He jumps (6)**into / over** obstacles and moves (7)**towards / over** his objective. After that, he drives (8)**into / away from** his enemies in his car!

Exercise 3
1 out of
2 down
3 up
4 into
5 under
6 over
7 towards
8 away from

4 1.27 **Listen to William, Fatima and Charlotte. What are their superstitions?**

Exercise 4
Charlotte never walks under ladders.
Fatima jumps over lines in the road.
William walks away from black cats.

5 **In pairs, ask and answer the question.**

Have you got any superstitions?

I never walk under ladders!

Vocabulary Reference

Lesson Aims:

Students learn and practise prepositions of movement and how to combine them with verbs of movement.
Students listen to three people talking about their superstitions and identify them and talk about their own superstitions.

Vocabulary

Prepositions

Warmer

Do some simple line drawings on the board and elicit the prepositions of movement, eg *He's walking across the road.*; *They're walking along the street.*; etc. Alternatively, you can do the same by bringing a poster to class which shows lots of different types of movement.

1 1.26

- Play the audio. Students listen and repeat the words.
- Highlight the vowel sounds, especially /əʊ/ in *over*, /aʊ/ in *round*, /ɔː/ in *towards*, /uː/ in *through*.
- Students work in pairs and match the prepositions with the pictures.
- Check answers with the class.
- Elicit the *meaning* of the words. (This will help students more than a direct translation because in many cases a direct word-for-word translation may not exist in the students' own language.)
- Make sure students understand that we can use different action verbs, such as *fly*, *jump*, *run*, *swim*, *walk*, with the prepositions.

2
- In pairs, students write the prepositions with their opposites when they have one.
- Check answers with the class.

3
- Check students understand the words *parachutes*, *ground* and *dives*.
- Students read the text about James Bond and choose the correct prepositions to complete it.
- Check answers with the class.

Extra activity

Read the text and pause at key places. Elicit from the class what comes next. For example: *James Bond is always very active in his films. He often jumps … aeroplanes and parachutes … to the ground*, etc.

4 1.27

- Elicit some popular superstitions from the students. If they don't know any, tell them some well-known ones, eg breaking a mirror brings seven years' bad luck, knocking on wood brings good luck, etc.
- Play the audio. Students listen for the superstitions mentioned.
- Let students listen again before checking answers with the class.

5

- Give students time to think about the answer to the question and provide possible ideas, eg what they do before exams, special clothes they wear for good luck, etc.
- Students talk about their superstitions in pairs.
- Ask some pairs to give feedback to the class. They decide who has the strangest superstitions.

Cultural note

In the United States and most European countries, a black cat passing in front of you means that you will have bad luck. In the United Kingdom and Japan however, a black cat crossing your path means that good fortune is on its way.

Mixed-ability solutions

Students who need extra help: Exercise 1.
Give students two options for each picture, eg:
1 *round / under*
2 *along / towards*, etc
3 *out of / through*

Fast finishers: Exercise 3. Students add a sentence to the text including a preposition of movement.

Self-study and extra practice

Workbook
- Vocabulary, page 20
- Vocabulary Reference, page 86

Teacher's Resource File
- All Clear Basics, page 11
- Vocabulary Consolidation, page 9
- Vocabulary Extension, page 11

Reading

True stories

Warmer

Students look at the pictures accompanying the texts and the titles of the texts. They make predictions about what the texts might be about.

1 • Students skim the texts quickly and decide which text the words relate to.
• Emphasize that they should not attempt to read every word or to worry about completely understanding both texts.

Word Check

Check students understand the new words: *stick out*, *precious*, *emeralds*, *rubies*, *owner*. Explain any they don't know. You may want to explain *stick out* (*of the snow*) using a simple illustration on the board.

2 1.28
• Play the audio. Student read and listen to the text to check their answers to exercise 1.
• Check answers with the class.

3 • Students read text A again and decide if the statements are true or false.
• Check answers with the class, eliciting the words from the text that helped them decide.

Extended answers
Exercise 3

1 false – He was walking across a glacier near the top of the mountain when he saw a metal box …
2 false – It probably came from one of two Air India planes …
3 false – The climber carried the box down the mountain and took it to the police.
4 true – The Indian authorities are trying to find the owner of the box or their family.
5 true – Now the authorities are worried about inexperienced climbers going up to look for 'treasure' buried under the snow.

4 • Students read the sentences. Clear up any vocabulary problems.
• Students read text B again and order the events.
• Check the answer with the class.

All Clear Facts

Read the fact with the class. Ask students if they know what the highest mountain in Spain is (*Mount Teide*), where it is (*Tenerife*) and how high it is (*3,718 metres*).

Extra activity

Ask the class which story they prefer and why.

Cultural note

Mont Blanc ('White Mountain' in French) is located on the border between France and Italy. The first recorded ascent was in 1786, while the first woman reached the summit in 1808. Now it is climbed by around 20,000 people every year.

Web info

Type these words in your search engine for more information about

- the activities that can be done in the Mont Blanc area and a live webcam: 'Mont Blanc Chamonix + tourist office'
- Joan Murray: 'beating odds + Joan Murray skydiving'

Mixed-ability solutions

Students who need extra help: Exercise 3.
Read out the relevant part of the text where the answer to each question is to be found.

1 *He was walking across a glacier near the top of the mountain when he saw a metal box …*
2 *It probably came from one of two Air India planes …*
3 *The climber carried the box down the mountain and took it to the police.*
4 *The Indian authorities are trying to find the owner of the box or their family.*
5 *Now the authorities are worried about inexperienced climbers going up to look for 'treasure' buried under the snow.*

Fast finishers: Exercise 3. Students find all the verbs + prepositions of movement in text A.

Self-study and extra practice

Teacher's Resource File

- Key Competences: Reading, page 5

Reading

True stories

Word Check
stick out precious emeralds rubies owner

Ⓐ

A surprising discovery

In 2013, a French mountaineer made a surprising discovery while he was climbing Mont Blanc in Switzerland. He was walking across a glacier near the top of the mountain when he saw a metal box **sticking out** of the snow and ice. The box contained about 100 **precious** stones including **emeralds** and **rubies**. It probably came from one of two Air India planes that crashed into the mountain in 1950 and 1966.

The climber carried the box down the mountain and took it to the police. 'The climber was very honest,' said the police. Later, experts valued the stones at about €200,000. The Indian authorities are trying to find the **owner** of the box or their family.

Mont Blanc is a beautiful mountain, but it is also very dangerous. Now the authorities are worried about inexperienced climbers going up to look for 'treasure' buried under the snow.

Ⓑ

A lucky escape

Joan Murray loves adventure and she often goes skydiving. She doesn't normally have any problems, but one day she had a bad experience. She was falling towards the ground at about 200km per hour, when her main parachute didn't open.

At the last moment, her emergency parachute opened just 210 metres from the ground. Joan crashed into a field and her heart stopped. Luckily, she fell onto a mound of fire ants. The ants climbed up her clothes and bit her.

Doctors believe the bites from the ants started her heart again. Joan was in hospital for two weeks, but then she recovered completely. The accident didn't stop Joan – she started skydiving again a year later.

Exercise 1
Text A: treasure
Text B: ant, skydive
Both: accident, crash

1 **Look at the words below. Do they relate to text A or B, or both?**

accident ant crash skydive treasure

All Clear Facts
Mont Blanc is the highest mountain in Europe. It is 4,810m high.

2 1.28 **Read and listen. Check your answers to exercise 1.**

3 **Read text A again. Write true or false in your notebook. Copy the text that shows your answers.**

Exercise 3
See Extended answers on T29.

1 The climber found the box at the bottom of the mountain.
2 The police know which plane it came from.
3 The climber gave the box to the owner.
4 The Indian authorities didn't know who owned the box.
5 The authorities are worried about people getting into problems on Mont Blanc.

4 **Order the events from text B and write them in your notebook.**

Exercise 4
The correct order is b (example), e, g, a, d, c, f.

a) Joan's heart stopped.
b) Joan went skydiving. *1*
c) Joan went to hospital and recovered.
d) The fire ants bit Joan.
e) Joan's parachute didn't open.
f) Joan started skydiving again.
g) Joan fell onto a mound of ants.

Grammar

Past tenses

Past simple and past continuous
Joan **was parachuting** down when her parachute didn't open.
Joan **crashed** into the ground and her heart **stopped**.

All Clear Rules

We use the past continuous to describe actions in progress in the past, sometimes interrupted by other actions. We use the past simple to describe completed actions in the past.

1 **Write the correct words in your notebook.**

Last week, Ben Hawkins (1)**went / was going** to Scout Camp. One day, he (2)**did / was doing** a survival activity in the woods when he (3)**got / was getting** lost. Ben (4)**survived / was surviving** for four days alone in the woods! When rescuers finally (5)**found / were finding** Ben, he (6)**hid / was hiding** in the trees because he (7)**didn't recognize / wasn't recognizing** them!

Exercise 1
1 went
2 was doing
3 got
4 survived
5 found
6 was hiding
7 didn't recognize

2 **Answer the questions about the text in exercise 1. Write answers in your notebook.**

1 Where did Ben go last summer?
2 What happened when he was doing a survival activity?
3 How many days did he survive alone?
4 What was Ben doing when rescuers found him?
5 Why was Ben hiding?

Exercise 2
1 He went to Scout Camp.
2 He got lost.
3 He survived alone for four days.
4 He was hiding in the trees.
5 Because he didn't recognize the rescuers.

when and *while*

Past simple and past continuous, *when* and *while*
He was running away **when** the bear attacked.
When the bear attacked, he was running away.
The bear attacked **while** he was running away.
While he was running away, the bear attacked.

3 **Look at the sentences in the table and answer the questions in your notebook.**

1 Which action was in progress?
2 Which action interrupted the action in progress?
3 Which tense usually comes after *while*?
4 Which tense usually comes after *when*?

Exercise 3
1 he was running away
2 the bear attacked
3 past continuous
4 past simple

4 **Complete the sentences with the correct form of the verbs in brackets.**

He *was walking* (walk) in the forest when the dog *appeared* (appear).
1 While the children … (play), they … (see) a snake.
2 While they … (sail) along the coast, there … (be) a storm.
3 The plane … (fly) over the area when the pilot … (see) the explorers.
4 When we … (arrive), the rescuers … (look) for the lost girl.
5 I … (have) an accident while I … (cycle) home.
6 I … (walk) through the park when you … (phone) me.

Exercise 4
1 were playing; saw
2 were sailing; was
3 was flying; saw
4 arrived; were looking
5 had; was cycling
6 was walking; phoned

5 **Write complete questions in your notebook using the past simple or past continuous form of the verbs.**

What time / you / go to bed / last night?
What time did you go to bed last night?
1 What / you / do / at 5 pm yesterday?
2 What / you and your friends / do / when / the English teacher / arrive / today?
3 you / use / a dictionary / while / you / do / your English homework / last night?
4 What / you / watch / on TV / last night?

Exercise 5
1 What were you doing at 5 pm yesterday?
2 What were you and your friends doing when the English teacher arrived today?
3 Did you use a dictionary while you were doing your English homework last night?
4 What did you watch on TV last night?

6 **In pairs, ask and answer the questions in exercise 5.**

What time did you go to bed last night?
I went to bed at 11 pm last night.

Lesson Aims:

Students contrast the past simple and past continuous with *when* and *while* and practise using them.

Grammar

Past tenses

Warmer

Students look back at the first paragraph of text A on page 29 and find examples of the past simple and the past continuous.

All Clear Rules

Read out the sentences in the grammar table and ask students to identify which verb is in the past simple and which is in the past continuous. Elicit why the past simple or the past continuous is used in each case.
Read the All Clear Rules with the class.
Emphasize that we use the past simple for completed actions and not the past continuous, even if the action lasted a long time, eg *I waited two hours for the bus.* (not ~~*I was waiting*~~); *I lived in Barcelona for five years.* (not ~~*I was living*~~).

1 • Explain that in each case students have to decide if the verb should be in the past simple or the past continuous. Check that students understand potentially difficult vocabulary in the text, eg *survival*, *rescuers*, *hide* and *recognize*.
- With weaker classes, you may want to do the first question with the class, eliciting why *went* and not *was going* is the correct answer.
- Students choose the correct words to complete the text.
- Check answers with the class.

2 • Students answer the questions about the text in exercise 1.
- Check answers with the class.

Extra activity

Students ask and answer the questions in exercise 2 in pairs, with one student playing the role of Ben. So, for example, question 1 would be *Where did you go last summer?*.

3 • Ask different students to read out the sentences in the grammar table. After each sentence, elicit the translation.
- Students answer the questions.
- Check answers with the class.

4 • Look at the example with the class and elicit why each tense is used.
- Elicit from or remind students which tense we usually use after *when* and which after *while*.
- Students complete the sentences with the correct form of the verbs in brackets.
- Check answers with the class.

Extra activity

Teams of four. Give the teams two verbs each. They have to invent one sentence using both verbs – one in the past continuous and one in the past simple. They write the sentence on the board. If the sentence is correct, they get a point.

5 • Look at the example with the class. Ask why we use the past simple and not the past continuous.
- Students write the questions. Emphasize that sometimes they will need to use the past simple and sometimes the past continuous.
- Check answers with the class.

6
- Practise the questions in exercise 5, focusing on stress and intonation.
- Read the example question and answer with the class.
- Ask a few students the other questions.
- Students ask and answer the questions in exercise 5 in pairs.

Mixed-ability solutions

Students who need extra help: Exercise 6. Students write their answers before asking and answering the questions in pairs.

Fast finishers: Exercise 5. Students write three more questions about what their partner was doing at a particular time in the past. Then they ask their partner the questions.

Lesson Aims:

Students revise and contrast the use of present and past tenses and practise their use.

Grammar

Present and past tenses

Warmer

Books closed. Read out the sentences in the grammar table. After you read out each one, ask the class to identify the tense of the verb in blue.

7
- Students look at the sentences in the grammar table and match the sentences with the uses.
- Check answers with the class.

8
- Students choose the correct words to complete the questions. You may want to do the first one with the class, eliciting the answer and why it is correct.
- Check answers with the class, clarifying any confusions about tense usage.

9
- Practise the questions from exercise 8 with the class. Remind students of stress and weak forms.
- Students ask and answer the questions in pairs.
- Ask a few pairs to ask and answer the questions for the class.

10
- Read the first sentence of the story with the class. Look at the example and elicit the answer for the first gap (*heard*).
- Students complete the text with the correct form of the verbs in brackets. Tell them they need to read the story carefully to decide on the correct verb forms. As this is a challenging exercise, you may want students to do it in pairs so that they can help each other.
- Check answers with the class.

All Clear Grammar

11
- Tell students that this is a cumulative check of the grammar in Units 1 to 3 and explain any vocabulary they may not know, eg *shark*, *hit*, *release*, *recover*.
- As this exercise is quite challenging, you may want students to do it in pairs.
- Students choose the correct words to complete the text.

12 1.29
- Play the audio. Students listen and check their answers.
- Check answers with the class. This is a good moment to check they have understood the new grammar and to review the grammar from previous units.

Mixed-ability solutions

Students who need extra help: Exercise 10. Write two options on the board for each gap, eg

1 *heard / was hearing*
2 *goes / went*
3 *saw / was seeing*, etc

Fast finishers: Exercise 10. In pairs students make a list of all the animals they have seen in real life.

Self-study and extra practice

Workbook
- Grammar, pages 20–1
- Grammar Reference and Practice, pages 70–1

Teacher's Resource File
- All Clear Basics, pages 13–4
- Grammar Consolidation, page 10
- Grammar Extension, page 12
- Language Excellence, pages 5–6

Digital Activities
- Student's Digital Material

Present and past tenses

Present and past tenses	
1	Every year we **go** to the mountains.
2	We**'re playing** tennis in Salou at the moment.
3	He **was climbing** up the mountain when he saw a box in the snow.
4	He **carried** the box down the mountain.

Exercise 7
a 1
b 2
c 4
d 3

7 **Look at sentences 1–4 above and match the verbs in bold with uses a–d. Write them in your notebook.**

a) present simple for habits
b) present continuous for an action happening now
c) past simple for a completed action in the past
d) past continuous for an action in progress in the past

Exercise 8
1 do you usually do
2 do you go
3 did you do
4 were you doing
5 are you thinking

8 **Write the correct words in your notebook.**

1 What **do you usually do / are you usually doing** on your birthday?
2 How often **are you going / do you go** swimming?
3 What **do you do / did you do** yesterday?
4 What **are you doing / were you doing** when the teacher arrived in class?
5 What **are you thinking / do you think** about now?

9 **In pairs, ask and answer the questions in exercise 8.**

10 **Complete the text with the correct form of the verbs in brackets.**

Vanessa Horrocks *was watching* (watch) TV in her apartment when she [1]… (hear) a strange noise in the bathroom. She [2]… (go) to the bathroom and she [3]… (see) a two-metre python in the toilet. The snake [4]… (try) to get out of the toilet, so she [5]… (run) out of the bathroom. Then she [6]… (call) Fred, the building manager, and he [7]… (catch) the snake. Now, Vanessa often [8]… (feel) nervous when she [9]… (use) her bathroom.
Building manager Fred Murray said: 'Pet pythons sometimes [10]… (escape) from their owners. We [11]… (look) for this python's owner now. At the moment, it [12]… (live) in a cage in my flat.'

Exercise 10
1 heard
2 went
3 saw
4 was trying
5 ran
6 called
7 caught
8 feels
9 uses
10 escape
11 are looking for
12 is living

All Clear Grammar
1 2 3 4 5 6 7 8 9

11 **Write the correct words in your notebook.**

Todd Endris often [1]**goes / is going** surfing in his free time. One day last summer an enormous white shark [2]**attacked / was attacking** him while he [3]**is surfing / was surfing** at Marina Beach. Todd [4]**hit / was hitting** the shark on the nose, but it [5]**didn't release / wasn't releasing** him. He [6]**got / was getting** desperate when suddenly six dolphins attacked the shark and Todd escaped. Two surfers helped Todd to the beach and [7]**call / called** an ambulance. Todd [8]**was / were** in hospital for a long time, but he recovered. After a shark attack most people are frightened and [9]**don't / didn't** want to go surfing again, but not Todd. What [10]**does he do / is he doing** at the moment? Surfing, of course!

Exercise 11
1 goes
2 attacked
3 was surfing
4 hit
5 didn't release
6 was getting
7 called
8 was
9 don't
10 is he doing

12 1.29 **Listen and check your answers.**

Vocabulary

-ed / *-ing* adjectives

Exercise 1
Students' own answers

1 1.30 **Listen and repeat the words. How do you say them in your language?**

annoyed / annoying • bored / boring • excited / exciting • frightened / frightening • interested / interesting • surprised / surprising • tired / tiring • worried / worrying

Exercise 2
a *-ed*
b *-ing*

2 **Look at the example and complete the rules with *-ed* or *-ing*.**

The couple are frightened because the forest is frightening.
a) We use … adjectives to describe how we feel.
b) We use … adjectives to describe the thing or person that causes the feeling.

Exercise 3
1 bored; boring
2 surprising; worried
3 annoyed; annoying
4 tired; interesting

3 **Write the correct word in your notebook.**

1 John is **bored / boring** because the film is **bored / boring**.
2 The results of the experiments are very **surprised / surprising**. The scientists are **worried / worrying**.
3 I'm **annoyed / annoying** because my friend is late – again! It's very **annoyed / annoying** when people are always late.
4 We're **tired / tiring** because it's very late, but the documentary is really **interested / interesting**.

Listening

4 1.31 **Look at the pictures and answer the questions in your notebook. Then listen and check your answers.**

1 What do you think the people were doing?
2 What do you think happened?

Exercise 4
1 The people in the pictures were looking for a Christmas tree.
2 Their car got trapped in the snow.

5 **Listen again and answer the questions. Write short answers in your notebook.**

1 Why do Keith and Jennifer Lee go to the mountains every year?
2 What happened on the way home?
3 Why didn't they use their phones?
4 How many nights did they spend in their car?
5 Who did they phone on the way home?
6 Are they planning to go again next year?

Exercise 5
1 to get a Christmas tree
2 their car got trapped in the snow
3 because their phones weren't working (because they were so high up)
4 two
5 the police and their friend Sophie
6 Keith is planning to go, but Jennifer doesn't want to

Vocabulary Reference

Speaking

Telling anecdotes / Talking with friends

Exercise 1
running, cycling and cooking in the dark

1 1.32 **Listen to the dialogue. What three things is the head torch useful for?**

Model Dialogue

Sarah: What's that on your head? A new fashion accessory?

Connor: No, it's a head torch. It's really useful.

Sarah: Really? What for?

Connor: For one thing, it's good for running or cycling in the dark. In fact, it's great for lots of things, as I discovered last year when I was camping.

Sarah: Why? What happened?

Connor: I was cooking in the dark when two spiders fell into the spaghetti. As you can imagine, it was quite annoying. But thanks to my head torch I didn't eat them!

Sarah: That was lucky!

2 **Listen again and repeat the dialogue.**

Speaking Task

1 Tell a friend a similar anecdote

First, choose one of the situations below.

last week / go home / walk along road / my keys / fall down a drain / annoying / not lose them

last summer / go camping / try to put up tent / drop my hammer / frustrating / put up tent

2 Prepare a dialogue

Look at the Model Dialogue and change the words in blue.

3 Speak

In pairs, practise your dialogue.

What's that? A new fashion accessory?

No, it's a head torch. It's really useful.

Useful Language

Telling anecdotes

For one thing, it's good for running or cycling in the dark.

In fact, it's great for lots of things, as I discovered last year when I was camping.

As you can imagine, it was quite annoying.

But thanks to my head torch …

Writing

A description of an accident

Exercise 1
The correct order is c, b, a.

1 1.33 **Read the Model Text and listen. Order the events in your notebook.**

a) the reporter arrived **b)** the car crashed **c)** it started raining

Model Text

Last Saturday evening, I was walking home from the sports centre with my friend Zoe. It was raining hard and very windy. We were a bit frightened.

Suddenly, a big branch fell from a tree onto the road! We were trying to move it when a car appeared. The driver didn't see the branch and crashed into it. I ran towards the car. Meanwhile, Zoe called an ambulance. The driver wasn't conscious although he was breathing.

The ambulance took the man to hospital. Then, a reporter arrived as we were leaving. We told her about the accident and the next day our story appeared in the newspaper – it was really exciting!

Exercise 2
Students' own answers
Suddenly, a big branch fell from a tree onto the road!
Meanwhile, Zoe called an ambulance.
Then, a reporter arrived as we were leaving.

2 **Look at the All Clear Tips and translate the words in bold. Then find examples in the Model Text.**

All Clear Tips

Time expressions

We were walking along the road. ***Suddenly****, we heard a loud noise.*
The police moved people and evacuated the area. ***Meanwhile****, the firefighters tried to put out the fire.*
We called an ambulance. ***Then****, we helped the accident victims.*

Exercise 3
1 Then
2 Suddenly
3 Meanwhile
4 Suddenly
5 Meanwhile

3 **Complete the sentences with *suddenly*, *meanwhile* or *then*.**

1 The rescuers carried the boy down the mountain. …, they took him to hospital.
2 We were walking across the ice. …, we heard a loud crack!
3 I started building a fire. …, my friends looked for food.
4 I was surfing in the sea. …, I saw an enormous shark!
5 Jake was trying to find the camp. …, his friends were looking for him.

Writing Task

1 Plan

Make notes about an imaginary or real accident and include:

Background: *time, place, people, weather, your feelings*
Description: *what happened, how and why*
Consequences: *what happened in the end, your feelings*

2 Write

Use the Model Text, your notes and this structure:

Paragraph 1: Background
Paragraph 2: Description
Paragraph 3: Consequences

3 Check

☑ past simple and past continuous, *when* and *while*
☑ prepositions of movement, *-ed* / *-ing* adjectives
☑ time expressions: *suddenly*, *meanwhile* and *then*

Lesson Aims:

Students practise using time expressions.
Students write a description of an accident.

Writing

A description of an accident

Warmer

In pairs, students look at the picture but cover the text. They describe what they can see and speculate about what is happening.

1 1.33

- Students read the events.
- Play the audio. Students read and listen to the description and order the events.
- Check the answer with the class.
- Elicit or explain the meaning of *raining hard*, *a bit*, *branch* and *breathing*.

Extra activity

To further check comprehension of the Model Text, ask the class the following questions.
Why were they a bit frightened?
Why did the driver crash into the branch?
What appeared in the newspaper?

All Clear Tips

2
- Read the All Clear Tips with the class. Students translate the words in bold.
- Emphasize that these words make it easier to follow the sequence of events in a description.
- Make sure students understand the difference between *meanwhile* and *while*, eg we cannot say ~~*Meanwhile*~~ *we were watching TV, the phone rang.*
- Point out the use of the comma in all three cases.
- Students find examples in the Model Text.

3
- With weaker classes, you may want to do question 1 with the class as an example.
- Students choose the correct words to complete the sentences.
- Check answers with the class.

Writing Task

1 Plan

Read the notes with the class. Students make notes about an imaginary or real accident.

2 Write

Look at the structure with the class. Students use their notes to write a description of an accident. Emphasize that they should use some of the time expressions they have just practised (*meanwhile*, *suddenly* and *then*) to sequence events in their description.

3 Check

Encourage students to check their work, paying particular attention to the points mentioned.

Web info

Type these words in your search engine to read some funny and allegedly true descriptions of accidents made on insurance claims: 'things people said + car accident reports'

Mixed-ability solutions

Students who need extra help: Writing task. Students just write the notes in step 1.

Fast finishers: Writing task. Students read their partner's description of an accident and try to decide whether it is true or made up.

Self-study and extra practice

Workbook
- Writing Guide, pages 106–7

Teacher's Resource File
- Key Competences: Writing, page 6

Lesson Aims:

Students learn about the writer Daniel Defoe and some facts about his famous novel *Robinson Crusoe*.
Students practise sentence stress.

Culture Reading

Famous writers and books

Warmer

Write *Robinson Crusoe* on the board and ask students what they know about it. Elicit the fact that it is a novel about a man stranded on a desert island. Ask if they have read the book or seen any films of *Robinson Crusoe* or about anyone stranded on a desert island.

1.34

- Students read the questions.
- Play the audio. Students read and listen to the text to find the answers to the questions.
- Check answers with the class.

Extra activity

Students work in groups to brainstorm ideas for a good story or novel, including the title. Then each group presents their ideas.

Cultural note

There are many film versions of *Robinson Crusoe*. The first was a silent film made in 1902. Other well-known versions are *The Adventures of Robinson Crusoe* directed by the Spanish film director Luis Buñuel (1954), *Robinson Crusoe on Mars* (1964) and the 1997 version with Pierce Brosnan playing the part of Robinson Crusoe.

Pronunciation

Sentence stress

a 1.35

- Students read the sentences silently.
- Play the audio. Students listen and repeat the sentences.
- Play the audio again. Students listen again and decide which words they think are stressed.
- Check answers with the class.
- Ask the class if they can see a pattern to which words are stressed (Answer: *the important words in the sentence*).

b 1.36

- Play the audio. Students listen and repeat the sentences. Make sure that they stress the correct words.

Web info

Type these words in your search engine for a simple description of the plot of *Robinson Crusoe*: 'Robinson Crusoe + kidsgen'

Mixed-ability solutions

Students who need extra help: Reading text. Write the following prompts on the board:

1 *first*
2 *writer; Robinson*
3 *sailor*
4 *trade; scientific*

Fast-finishers: Reading text. Students try to work out the meaning from the context of the following words and expressions: *sinks* (paragraph 1), *rescue* (paragraph 3), *accurate* (paragraph 4), *increase trade* (paragraph 4).

Self-study and extra practice

Workbook

- Culture: Reading and Listening, page 95

Culture Reading

EXTRA

America Asia Africa Australasia Europe

History *then and* now

Famous writers and books

The first English novel?

Robinson Crusoe is a novel by Daniel Defoe, published in 1719. It is a fictional story about a man who spends 28 years on a remote tropical island after his ship sinks. Many people think that *Robinson Crusoe* is the first novel in English. There are many film versions of the book.

Daniel Defoe (c1659–1731)

Defoe was an English writer and journalist. He wrote hundreds of books on different topics, including politics, crime and psychology. He is famous for *Robinson Crusoe* and for making novels popular in Britain.

Defoe's inspiration

Alexander Selkirk was a Scottish sailor who lived on an island near Chile for four years. After his rescue, his story was in British newspapers. Defoe probably got the idea for his story after reading about Selkirk.

Exploration and discovery

In the 18th century, Europeans travelled all over the world exploring its oceans and continents. They began to produce much more accurate maps and this helped to increase trade. Their expeditions helped to expand scientific knowledge in areas such as geography, astronomy, anthropology and mathematics.

1.34 **Read and listen. Then answer the questions in your notebook.**

1 Why is *Robinson Crusoe* an important book?
2 Who was Daniel Defoe and why is he famous?
3 Who was Alexander Selkirk?
4 What did the Europeans' expeditions help to develop?

Reading text exercise

1 *Robinson Crusoe* is important because many people think that it is the first novel in English.
2 Daniel Defoe was an English writer and journalist. He's famous for *Robinson Crusoe* and for making novels popular in Britain.
3 Alexander Selkirk was a Scottish sailor who lived on an island near Chile for four years.
4 The expeditions helped to increase trade and expand scientific knowledge.

Pronunciation

Sentence stress

a 1.35 **Listen and repeat the sentences. Which words are stressed?**

1 Defoe was an English writer.
2 They were travelling to America.
3 He wasn't an explorer.
4 Was he a writer?

b 1.36 **Listen and repeat the sentences.**

Pronunciation exercise a

1 Defoe was an English writer.
2 They were travelling to America.
3 He wasn't an explorer.
4 Was he a writer?

Unit 3 Language Reference

Vocabulary Prepositions

across • along • away from • down • into • out of • over • round • through • towards • under • up

-ed / *-ing* adjectives

annoyed / annoying • bored / boring • excited / exciting • frightened / frightening • interested / interesting • surprised / surprising • tired / tiring • worried / worrying

Grammar Past simple and past continuous

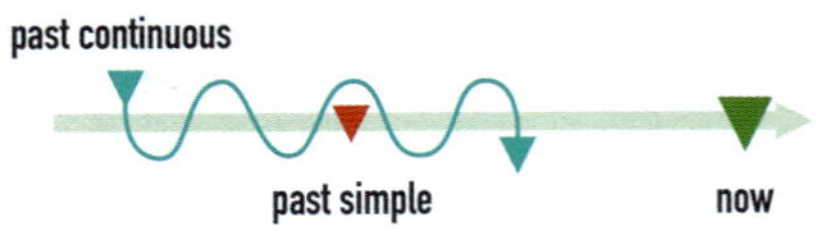

She **was falling** towards the ground when her main parachute **didn't open**.

Joan **crashed** into the ground and her heart **stopped**.

when and *while*

He was running away **when** the bear attacked.
While he was running away, the bear attacked.

Present and past tenses

See page 16 for present simple and present continuous grammar tables.

See page 26 for past simple and past continuous grammar tables.

Present simple	Every year we **go** to the mountains.
Present continuous	We**'re playing** tennis in Salou at the moment.
Past simple	He **carried** the box down the mountain.
Past continuous	He **was climbing** up the mountain when he saw a box in the snow.

Speaking Telling anecdotes

For one thing, it's good for running or cycling in the dark.
In fact, it's great for lots of things, as I discovered last year when I was camping.
As you can imagine, it was quite annoying.
But thanks to my head torch …

Unit 3 Progress Check

Vocabulary Prepositions

1 Complete the sentences with the words in the box.

out of under up into across

1 When John woke up, he climbed … his tent and ate breakfast.
2 Then he walked to the river and dived … the water.
3 While he was swimming … the river to the other side, it started to rain.
4 When he reached the other side, he sheltered … a tree.
5 When the rain stopped, he ran … a big hill.

Exercise 1
1 out of
2 into
3 across
4 under
5 up

-ed / *-ing* adjectives

2 Complete the sentences with the correct form of the words in brackets.

1 They are very late. I am … (worry).
2 The film was really … (bore).
3 Were you … (surprise) when you saw me?
4 I'm reading a really … (interest) book.
5 Jackie was very … (annoy) when Ruth arrived late again.

Exercise 2
1 worried
2 boring
3 surprised
4 interesting
5 annoyed

Grammar Past tenses

3 Complete the sentences with the correct form of the verbs in brackets. Use the past simple or the past continuous.

1 John … (not get up) early yesterday.
2 At six o'clock yesterday I … (do) my homework.
3 They … (not go) to the cinema last week.
4 Kate … (meet) Kevin while she … (walk) to school.
5 They … (get lost) when they … (look) for the lost boy!

Exercise 3
1 didn't get up
2 was doing
3 weren't doing; saw
4 met; was walking
5 got lost; were looking

4 Complete the questions using the past simple or the past continuous form of the verbs in brackets.

1 … (you / go) to a party last Saturday?
2 What … (you / do) at 3 am this morning?
3 What … (you / do) last night?
4 What … (your mother / do) when you … (wake up) this morning?
5 What … (the other students / do) when your teacher … (arrive) today?

Exercise 4
1 Did you go
2 were you doing
3 did you do
4 was your mother doing; woke up
5 were the other students doing; arrived

Present and past tenses

5 Write complete sentences in your notebook using the present simple, present continuous, past simple or past continuous.

1 Nicky / watch a DVD / when / her friend / arrive.
2 I / look for my friends / now.
3 Maggie / go swimming / twice a week.
4 They / not usually eat / meat.
5 While / they / swim / they / see a shark.

Exercise 5
1 Nicky was watching a DVD when her friend arrived.
2 I'm looking for my friends now.
3 Maggie goes swimming twice a week.
4 They don't usually eat meat.
5 While they were swimming, they saw a shark.

All Clear Self-C…

Check your answers

Write your scores for exercises 1–5 in your notebook. What did you get for:

- prepositions?
- *-ed* / *-ing* adjectives?
- past tenses?
- present and past tenses?

Extra Practice

If you need extra practice, go to:

Unit 3 Grammar Reference
Unit 3 Vocabulary Reference
Unit 3 Grammar Exercises
Unit 3 Vocabulary Exercises

Correct the activities with the class. Students who need extra revision and practice can go to:

Workbook
- Unit 3 Revision, page 24
- Grammar Reference and Practice, pages 70–1
- Vocabulary Reference, page 86

Student's Digital Material
www.allclear.macmillan.es

Revision Units 1–3

Vocabulary

- Free-time activities
- Character adjectives
- IT activities
- Jobs
- Prepositions
- *-ed* / *-ing* adjectives

Work with a partner to complete the sentences in your notebooks. Who finishes first?

START

Do you like m… models?

I'm reading a book about the Arctic. It's really i… .

Can I use your phone? I need to s… a text message.

On Saturdays, I play t… with my friend Lisa.

When I see something interesting, I like to take a p… of it.

We sailed r… the island yesterday. It was great!

The river is very wide. We can't swim a… it.

It's my brother's birthday tomorrow. He's really e… .

Manu likes exploring the mountains. He's really a… .

My mum works for the emergency services. She's a firef… .

FINISH

Revision Units 1–3 Vocabulary

making
interesting
send
tennis
photo
round
across
excited
adventurous
firefighter

Lesson Aims:

Students revise and practise vocabulary from Units 1 to 3.

Revision Units 1–3

Vocabulary

Warmer

Students look through Units 1 to 3 and tell you what vocabulary areas they have seen. Alternatively, you could get the class to do this from memory and then to check by looking in the Student's Book.

- Do the board game as a competition. Explain these rules to the class before you start.
- Students work in pairs. They complete the words in the sentences.
- When they have finished, they shout *Stop!* All the other teams must stop writing.
- Check answers with the class and write them on the board.
- Teams get two points for each correct answer and minus one point for each wrong answer. For a blank, they get zero points.
- Ask how many points the teams have, starting at 20 (the maximum) and working down.

Extra activity

In pairs, students take turns to mime one of the words in the board game. Their partner says the word in English.

Lesson Aims:

Students revise and practise the grammar from Units 1 to 3.

Revision Units 1–3

Grammar

Present simple and present continuous

Warmer

Say and write on the board *I often play video games, but I'm not playing one now.* Students identify the tenses and say why they are used.

1
- Students choose the correct words to complete the sentences.
- Check answers with the class.
- If you detect any major problems, you might want to read through the grammar section of the Language Reference on page 16 with the class.

Past simple

Warmer

Ask students how we form the past simple of regular verbs. Then, write on the board *I arrived* and elicit the negative and interrogative forms.
Write on the board *I go*, *I meet* and *I see* and ask students to put the verbs in the past simple. Then, ask the class for the negative and interrogative forms.

2
- Students complete the sentences with the correct form of the verbs in the box.
- Check answers with the class.
- If you detect any major problems, you might want to read through the grammar section of the Language Reference on page 26 with the class.

Past simple and past continuous

Warmer

Ask a couple of good students these questions.
What were you doing at seven o'clock last night?
What time did you go to bed last night?
Make sure that they answer in the correct tense and write the answers on the board. Elicit what tense is used in each answer and why.

3
- Students choose the correct words to complete the sentences.
- Check answers with the class.
- If you detect any major problems, you might want to read through the grammar section of the Language Reference on page 36 with the class.

when and *while*

Warmer

Write on the board:
Tom rang me while I was having dinner.
I got up when I heard someone at the door.
Ask students to translate each sentence and elicit which tense we usually use after *when* and which tense we usually use after *while*.

4
- Students complete the sentences with the correct form of the verbs in brackets.
- Check answers with the class.
- If you detect any major problems, you might want to read through the grammar section of the Language Reference on page 36 with the class.

Grammar check

5
- Tell students that this exercise revises all the grammar they have seen in Units 1 to 3 and it will give them a good idea of how well they have learnt it.
- Explain any potentially difficult vocabulary in the text, eg *Web browser* and *prize*.
- Students choose the correct words to complete the text.
- Check answers with the class.

Grammar

- Present simple
- Adverbs of frequency
- Present continuous
- Time expressions
- Gerunds
- Past simple
- Past continuous
- *when* and *while*

Present simple and present continuous

1 **Write the correct words in your notebook.**

1 He hardly ever chats / is hardly ever chatting online.
2 We are never using / never use computers in the classroom.
3 Are you doing / Do you do a sport now?
4 I don't learn / 'm not learning Chinese at the moment.
5 I play / 'm playing tennis twice a week.

Exercise 1
1 hardly ever chats
2 never use
3 Are you doing
4 I'm not learning
5 play

Past simple

2 **Complete the sentences with the correct form of the verbs in the box.**

download	go	meet	not see	not visit

1 I … the new Lorde song onto my tablet yesterday.
2 … you … to the beach last weekend?
3 We … the Alhambra when we were in Granada.
4 She … her friends in the shopping centre.
5 I … the last *X-Men* film at the cinema.

Exercise 2
1 downloaded
2 Did (you) go
3 visited
4 met
5 didn't see

Past simple and past continuous

3 **Write the correct words in your notebook.**

1 I was going / went to the USA for the first time in 2014.
2 I'm sorry, I didn't recognize / wasn't recognizing you.
3 What were you doing / did you do at 8 pm last night?
4 We watched / were watching that film on DVD last year.
5 Did you buy / Were you buying any souvenirs on holiday?

Exercise 3
1 went
2 didn't recognize
3 were you doing
4 watched
5 Did you buy

when and *while*

4 **Complete the sentences with the correct form of the verbs in brackets.**

1 She … (have) dinner when I … (arrive).
2 … you … (watch) TV when I … (call) you last night?
3 While I … (chat) online, my computer … (crash).
4 I … (surf) in the ocean when I … (see) a jellyfish.
5 While Jenna … (travel) in Italy, she … (not speak) Italian.

Exercise 4
1 was having; arrived
2 Were (you) watching; called
3 was chatting; crashed
4 was surfing; saw
5 was travelling; didn't speak

Grammar check

5 **Write the correct words in your notebook.**

Tim Berners-Lee (1) is / are a scientist and inventor. But (2) are you knowing / do you know what he invented?
Tim (3) was / is born in London in 1955. When he was a boy, he liked (4) play / playing with model trains and he became interested in (5) learn / learning about the electronics of the trains. He (6) was studying / studied physics at Oxford University from 1973–1976.
While Tim (7) worked / was working in a scientific laboratory in Switzerland, he (8) was inventing / invented the World Wide Web. He (9) built / were building the first Web browser in 1990. Then, in 1991, he (10) created / create the first website.
Tim (11) has / is having many prizes for his work. In 2012, he (12) was appearing / appeared at the opening ceremony of the London Olympic Games.

Exercise 5
1 is
2 do you know
3 was
4 playing
5 learning
6 studied
7 was working
8 invented
9 built
10 created
11 has
12 appeared

Cultural Awareness: Sport

Multimedia

1 How much do you know about sport in Britain? Do the quiz.

1 What is the most popular sport in Britain?
a tennis b cricket c football

2 Which football club did David Beckham become famous at?
a Arsenal b Manchester United c Liverpool

3 Which sport did not originate in Britain?
a cricket b football c basketball

4 When is the cricket season?
a April to September b September to April c September to December

5 What year were the summer Olympics held in London?
a 2004 b 2008 c 2012

6 How many runners usually take part in the London Marathon?
a around 20,000 b around 40,000 c around 60,000

Exercise 1
1 c
2 b
3 c
4 a
5 c
6 b

WATCH

2 Watch the documentary about sport and answer the questions.

1 In what year did England last win the football World Cup?
2 What happened in the 1978 Oxford and Cambridge university boat race?
3 Why do people run in sponsored runs in the UK?

Exercise 2
1 1966
2 The Cambridge boat sank
3 To raise money for charity and to have fun

Lesson Aims:

Students do a quiz to see how much they know about sport in Britain.
Students watch a video about sport in Britain.

Cultural Awareness:

Sport

Warmer

Ask students if they can think of any famous British sportsmen. You may want to prompt them giving the names of various sports, eg football, cycling, tennis, athletics.

1
- Tell students they are going to do a quiz about sport in Britain. Read through the questions with the class.
- Students do the quiz individually.
- Students compare answers in pairs.
- Check answers with the class.

Extra activity

Books closed. Read out the questions in the quiz without the options. Students try to answer from memory.

2
- Tell students that they are going to watch a documentary about sport in Britain.
- Read through the questions with the class, clearing up any vocabulary or cultural problems, eg *the Oxford and Cambridge boat race*, *a sponsored run*.
- Play the video. Students watch and listen.
- Students answer the questions.
- Check answers with the class. Replay the video if necessary.

Web info

Type these words in your search engine for more information about the Oxford and Cambridge boat race: 'youtube + Oxford prepares for the boat race'

Culture Video: *Sport*

This Culture video and accompanying worksheet, teaching notes, videoscript and answer key are in the Teacher's Resource Centre.
The worksheet, teaching notes, videoscript and answer key can also be found in the Teacher's Resource File.

Lesson Aims:

Students look at a digital wall about tennis and then make one themselves.

Digital Competence:

A digital wall

Warmer

Ask the class if they have ever posted pictures, videos or ideas online. If so, ask them what they were about and where they posted them.
Ask students to look at the digital wall. Ask them what the wall shows in general (*different types of information about tennis*).
Look at the words in the box with the class. Students look at the wall and find examples. Check answers with the class.

Task

Explain to students that they are going to make a digital wall about a different sport.

Step 1 Divide the class into groups of five or six.

Students discuss in their groups which sport they want to do their wall about.

Step 2 Students look for information, videos and photos about the sport of their choice. It can be their own material, eg a drawing, a few lines describing what they think of the sport, etc, or something they find on the web, eg a video, a striking picture, a profile of a famous player, etc.

Step 3 Students pool their information and decide how to present it.

To help them make a digital wall, write the URL of a digital wall generator (see *Web info*) on the board. Alternatively, they can create a poster. If appropriate, make it clear to the class that this is a project which they will need to organize in their free time and that they will need to take responsibility for it.

Step 4 Each group sends a link to their wall to the other groups and asks them to add more information. Alternatively, each group can display their poster in class.

Step 5 Students show their wall to the rest of the class, either projected onto a screen or as a physical poster. Encourage positive feedback and *constructive* criticism and suggestions.

Web info

Type these words in to your search engine for more information about digital walls: 'online collaborative wall for schools'

Term Project

For a different type of collaborative project, see the Life Skills Collaborative Project in the Workbook, pages 130–1.

Digital Competence: A digital wall

Multimedia

Look at the digital wall and find an example of:

the history of the game | a description of the rules | a video clip | a photo

LOG IN | HOME | SPORTS | FAQS | SEARCH

Tennis

The French Open is named after a person – Roland Garros! He was a famous pilot and a great tennis player.
Juan, 3 days ago

Tennis is a game for two or four players. When two people play, it's called 'singles' and when four people play, it is called 'doubles'.
Silvia, 7 days ago

The final of the men's singles at Wimbledon in 2013 was very exciting! British player, Andy Murray, played Novak Djokovic. See the highlights here!
Juan, 2 days ago

Venus and Serena Williams became the first sisters to win Olympic gold medals in tennis.
Silvia, 6 days ago

Wimbledon is the oldest tennis tournament in the world. It started in 1877. Other famous tennis tournaments are the French Open, the US Open and the Australian Open.
Silvia, 4 days ago

You must hit the ball with your racket inside the white lines. If you hit it outside the white lines, it is 'Out' and you lose a point.
Juan, yesterday

TASK **Create a digital wall. Follow the steps below.**

Step 1 Choose a sport that you like and are familiar with.

Step 2 Find information, videos and photos about

Step 3 Decide how you are going to arrange your information. Put the information

Step 4 Send the link to your digital wall to your classmates. Ask

Step 5 Read your classmates' walls. Add your comments.

Exercise 1

Possible answers:

The history of the game: Venus and Serena Williams became the first sisters to win Olympic gold medals in tennis.
Wimbledon is the oldest tennis tournament in the world. It started in 1877. Other famous tournaments are the French Open, the US Open and the Australian Open.
The French Open is named after a person – Roland Garros! He was a famous pilot and a great tennis player.
The final of the men's singles at Wimbledon in 2013 was very exciting! Scottish player, Andy Murray, played Novak Djokovic. See the highlights here!

A description of the rules: Tennis is a game for two or four players. When two people play, it's called 'singles' and when four people play, it is called 'doubles'.
You must hit the ball with your racket inside the white lines. If you hit it outside the white lines, it is 'Out' and you lose the point.

A video clip: The final of the men's singles at Wimbledon in 2013 was very exciting! Scottish player, Andy Murray, played Novak Djokovic. See the highlights here!

A photo: There is a photo of the Wimbledon courts.

4 A wonderful world

Overview

Unit objectives and key competences

- Understand, memorize and correctly use vocabulary related to places to visit and adverbs CLC, DC
- Identify the gist and main ideas from a text about different places in the world CLC
- Learn about different World Heritage sites CAE
- Understand, contrast and correctly use grammar structures related to comparatives and superlatives, (*not*) *as … as* and *too*, *enough* and *not enough* CLC, L2L
- Identify general and specific information through a listening activity about a trip to New York CLC
- Learn about different places in New York CAE
- Use appropriate functional language to ask about and describe a day out CLC, SCC
- Identify the general content of an entry in a travel guide about Central Park CLC
- Write an entry for a travel guide CLC, SIE, CAE
- Learn about Buckingham Palace CAE
- Assimilate the All Clear Tips and Rules and study the Language Reference from the unit CLC, L2L, SIE
- Identify areas of language which need improvement and use ICT for extra practice DC, CLC, L2L

More information on Key Competences, page v

Linguistic content

Grammar

- Comparatives and superlatives
- (*not*) *as … as*
- *too*, *enough* and *not enough*

Recycled grammar

- Present simple (Unit 1)
- Present continuous (Unit 1)
- Past simple (Unit 2)

Main vocabulary

- Places to visit: *castle*, *cathedral*, etc
- Adverbs: *angrily*, *badly*, etc

Functional language

- Describing your weekend / A day out

Pronunciation

- The sounds /ɑː/ /eɪ/ /uː/

Skills: learning outcomes

- **Reading** Understand specific information from a clearly structured website about World Heritage sites. The student can re-read the more difficult parts, page 43
- **Listening** Understand specific information from a conversation which is delivered in a slow, clear way. Clearly recorded and without any interference, page 46
- **Speaking** Participate effectively in a face-to-face informal dialogue, describing a day out, page 47
- **Writing** Write a short travel guide entry with simple and relevant information and facts to describe places in a city, page 48
- **Reading** Understand specific information from a clearly structured text about Buckingham Palace. The student can re-read the more difficult parts, page 49

Lifelong learning skills and content-based learning

Life skills

- **Socio-cultural awareness** World Heritage sites, page 43
- **Learning how to learn** Use factual information in a table to complete sentences, page 44
- **Socio-cultural awareness** Respect for the natural environment, page 45
- **Recognizing diversity** Famous buildings and sites in the UK, New York and other places around the world, pages 45, 46, 48 and 49

Learning strategies

- Use factual information in a table to complete sentences, page 44

Cross-curricular content

- History and Geography: historical and natural sites and their location, pages 45, 46, 48 and 49
- Maths: comparing data, numbers, page 44
- Language: ways of describing things with qualifiers, page 48

Further materials and evaluation

Digital material

- Student's and Teacher's Resource Centres
- Teacher's Presentation Kit
- Student's Digital Material: interactive vocabulary and grammar activities
- Video *Literature* (Revision Units 4–6, page 74)

Student's website www.macmillansecondary.es

Workbook

- Vocabulary, pages 26–7
- Vocabulary Reference, page 87
- Grammar, pages 28–9
- Grammar Reference and Practice, pages 72–3
- Revision, page 30
- Culture: Reading and Listening, page 96
- Writing Guide, pages 108–9
- Speaking, page 123

Teacher's Resource File

Multi-level Materials Bank

- All Clear Basics, pages 16–20
- Vocabulary and Grammar Consolidation and Extension, pages 13–6
- Language Excellence, pages 7–8
- Translation and Dictation, pages 4 and 13

Lifelong Learning

- Digital Competence, pages 7–8
- Culture Video Material, pages 3–4
- Study Skills, pages 1–12

Evaluation and Key Competences

- Evaluation Rubrics, pages 1–7
- Key Competences, pages 7–8 and 25–6

Content-based Learning

- CLIL, pages 1–10
- Macmillan Readers, pages 1–7

Evaluation material

- Unit 4 end-of-unit test: Basic, Standard and Extra
- CEFR Skills Exam Generator

Web info

Tips to find extra information on: World Heritage sites in the UK and Spain, tourist attractions in New York, Central Park, Buckingham Palace

Extra help for weaker students

Teacher's Resource File: All Clear Basics, pages 16–20

Material for fast finishers

Workbook: Grammar Extension, page 31
Teacher's Resource File: Vocabulary Extension, page 15
Teacher's Resource File: Grammar Extension, page 16
Teacher's Resource File: Language Excellence, pages 7–8

4 A wonderful world

Objectives

Vocabulary	Places to visit; adverbs
Grammar	Comparatives and superlatives; (*not*) *as … as*; *too, enough* and *not enough*
Speaking	Describing your weekend
Writing	A travel guide entry

Vocabulary

Places to visit

1 1.37 **Listen and repeat the words. Match them with pictures 1–12.**

castle • cathedral • cave • coastline • lighthouse • opera house • pyramid • rainforest • reef • ruin • temple • tomb

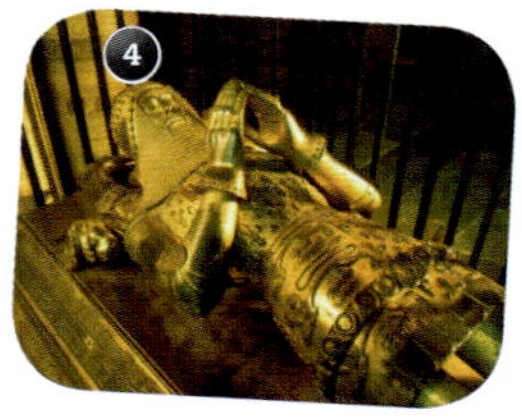

Exercise 1
1 cave
2 reef
3 ruin
4 tomb
5 cathedral
6 coastline
7 lighthouse
8 rainforest
9 opera house
10 castle
11 pyramid
12 temple

2 **Write the correct words in your notebook. Test your knowledge!**

1 The city of Pompeii is full of Roman **ruins** / **pyramids**.
2 La Scala in Milan is the world's most famous **tomb** / **opera house**.
3 The Tower of Hercules in A Coruña is a very old **castle** / **lighthouse**.
4 The most famous **reef** / **cave** in the world is in the Pacific Ocean near the coast of Australia.
5 The Tower of London is a famous **lighthouse** / **castle**.
6 Burgos has a famous **temple** / **cathedral**.

Exercise 2
1 ruins
2 opera house
3 lighthouse
4 reef
5 castle
6 cathedral

3 1.38 **Listen to Emma and Ryan. What is Mérida famous for?**

Exercise 3
Its Roman ruins.

4 **In pairs, ask and answer questions about famous places.**

What's Sydney famous for?

Its opera house.

Vocabulary Reference

Lesson Aims:

Students learn and practise words for places to visit.
Students listen to two young people talking about a famous place and then talk about other famous places.

Vocabulary

Places to visit

Warmer

Brainstorm with the class places where you can go at the weekend or when on holiday, eg the beach, a park, a sports centre, the cinema, etc.

1 1.37

- Play the audio. Students listen and repeat the words.
- Highlight the pronunciation features, such as the stress on *cathedral* and *pyramid* and the silent letters in *tom(b)* and *cas(t)le*.
- Ask students which of the words they know and which they can guess the meaning of.
- Students match the words with the pictures, guessing if necessary.
- Check answers with the class.

2
- Tell students they are going to test their knowledge of famous places.
- Students read the sentences and choose the correct words to complete them.
- Check answers with the class.

3 1.38

- Ask students about Mérida. Ask them where it is and whether they've been there.
- Students read the question. Pre-teach the expression *Give me a clue*.
- Play the audio. Students listen for the answer to the question.
- Check the answer with the class.

Extra activity

Ask students what other Roman ruins they can name in Spain or in Britain.

4

- Read out the question and answer.
- Ask similar questions, eg about Paris or San Francisco, etc.
- Give students time to think about some famous places. Help with the names in English, if necessary.
- Students ask and answer the questions in pairs.
- Ask some pairs to repeat their questions and answers for the class.

Extra activity

Play a guessing game. Tell students you are thinking of a famous place. They must ask you questions to guess the place, eg *Is it in Europe?*; *Is it in France?*; *Is it a building?*, etc. You can only answer *yes* or *no*. This provides revision of countries as well as words for places to visit. When a student guesses correctly, he or she thinks of a place for the class to guess. You could also play the game in teams.

Cultural note

The pictures show:

1 A cave, Davenport, California, USA
2 The Great Barrier Reef, Australia
3 Colosseum, Rome, Italy
4 The tomb of Edward the Black Prince, Canterbury Cathedral, England
5 Burgos Cathedral, Spain
6 Coastline, Cornwall, England
7 The Tower of Hercules Lighthouse, A Coruña, Spain
8 Rainforest, Borneo, Malaysia
9 The Palais Garnier opera house, Paris, France
10 Bodiam Castle, Sussex, England
11 Pyramid of Kukulkan, Chichen Itza, Yucatan, Mexico
12 Temple of Ulun Danu, Bali, Indonesia

Mixed-ability solutions

Students who need extra help: Exercise 1. Translate the words before students match them with the pictures.

Fast finishers: Exercise 1. Students write down the names of all the places they recognize in the pictures. (See *Cultural note*.)

Self-study and extra practice

Workbook
- Vocabulary, page 26
- Vocabulary Reference, page 87

Teacher's Resource File
- All Clear Basics, page 16
- Vocabulary Consolidation, page 13
- Vocabulary Extension, page 15

Lesson Aims:

Students read a website about World Heritage sites for gist and specific information.

Reading

A website

Warmer

Write *Word Heritage Sites* on the board. Elicit or provide the translation. Ask students if they can name any World Heritage sites in their own country or elsewhere.

1 • Students looks at the pictures and brainstorm the questions in pairs.

Word Check

Check students understand the new words: *endangered, limestone, narrow*. Explain any they don't know.

2 1.39

- Play the audio. Students read and listen to the text and check their answers to exercise 1.

3 • Students read the questions and the multiple-choice options.
- They read the text again and choose the correct options.
- Check answers with the class. Ask students to read out the relevant part in the text in each case.

4 • Check that students know how to say these numbers. Remind them that a comma in numbers has a different meaning in English.
- Students locate the numbers in the text and say what they refer to.
- Check answers with the class.

All Clear Facts

Read the fact with the class.
Ask students why they think it is important to preserve cultural and natural sites. Look at the list of Spanish sites online if you have access to the internet (see *Web info*) and ask students if there are any other sites they think should be included on the list and why.

Extra activity

Students think about the World Heritage sites in the text and give each one a mark out of 5 depending on how much they would like to visit it. They think of a reason for each of the marks they give.
Read out the name of each site and ask students to raise their hand if they have given it the highest mark.
Ask some students to justify their choice.

Cultural note

The UK has over 25 World Heritage sites. The most famous are the Tower of London, Stonehenge, the city of Edinburgh and Westminster Abbey. Part of the south-west coast in Cornwall is also a World Heritage site.

Web info

Type these words in your search engine for a map and list of World Heritage sites
- in the UK: 'World Heritage sites UK'
- in Spain: 'World Heritage sites Spain'

Mixed-ability solutions

Students who need extra help: Exercise 4.
Write on the board:
a *different species of fish that live in the Great Barrier Reef*
b *limestone blocks to build the Great Pyramid*
c *types of coral that live in the Great Barrier Reef*
d *species of bird and endangered marine animals that live in the Great Barrier Reef*
e *UNESCO World Heritage sites*
f *miles to transport the limestone blocks to the site of the Great Pyramid*
Students match the numbers with the items a–f.

Fast finishers: Exercise 4. Students write down all the different types of man-made construction mentioned in the text.

Self-study and extra practice

Teacher's Resource File
- Key Competences: Reading, page 7

Reading

A website

Word Check
endangered limestone narrow

Exercise 1
The places in the pictures are the Great Barrier Reef, the Great Pyramid of Giza and the Great Mosque in Córdoba.
They are all World Heritage sites.

1 Where are the places in the pictures? What do they have in common?

2 1.39 Read and listen. Check your answers to exercise 1.

WORLD HERITAGE SITES

The Alhambra, Burgos Cathedral, and the Roman ruins of Mérida. Yes, they are all tourist sites in Spain, but they are also UNESCO World Heritage sites. Click here to find out more.

Home
News
Visits
Contact

There are 890 UNESCO World Heritage sites. Not all of them are buildings or cultural sites like temples or castles. Some are natural places like rainforests and caves. Let's visit some famous sites from around the world, one natural and two cultural.

The Great Barrier Reef is on the north-east coast of Australia. It is larger than any other coral reef ecosystem in the world. It contains 400 types of coral, 1,500 different species of fish, 240 species of bird and many **endangered** marine animals like the dugong ('sea cow').

The Egyptian Pharaoh Khufu ordered his slaves to build the Great Pyramid as his tomb. They needed over two million **limestone** blocks, and they had to transport them over 500 miles to the site. They used boats to bring the blocks down the River Nile because they were too heavy to move by land.

The Historic Centre of Córdoba isn't as old as the Great Pyramid, but it has a rich, multicultural history. There is a magnificent Roman Bridge over the River Guadalquivir. The **narrow** streets and the patios with flowers and fountains are a sign of the city's Arabic influence. One of the greatest buildings in the world is Córdoba's Great Mosque which has a Christian Cathedral at its centre. It is a symbol of religious and cultural tolerance.

Are there are any World Heritage sites near you?

All Clear Facts
One of UNESCO's missions is to preserve sites of cultural and natural importance for humanity.

3 Read the text again and write the correct answers in your notebook.

1 The Great Pyramid and the Historic Centre of Córdoba are both …
a) buildings.
b) cultural sites.
c) natural sites.

2 The dugong …
a) is a type of coral.
b) is in danger of extinction.
c) is a species of fish.

3 How did the builders move the limestone to build the Great Pyramid?
a) by elephant
b) by chariot
c) by boat

4 Which is older?
a) the Great Pyramid
b) the Historic Centre of Córdoba
c) they are the same age

Exercise 3
1 b
2 b
3 c
4 a

4 What do these numbers refer to in the text? Write short answers in your notebook.

1 890 2 two million 3 240 4 500 5 400 6 1,500

Exercise 4
1 UNESCO World Heritage sites
2 limestone blocks to build the Great Pyramid
3 species of bird and endangered marine animals that live in the Great Barrier Reef
4 miles to transport the limestone blocks to the site of the Great Pyramid
5 types of coral that live in the Great Barrier Reef
6 different species of fish that live in the Great Barrier Reef

Grammar

Comparatives and superlatives

	Adjective	Comparative	Superlative
One-syllable adjectives	old	old**er than**	**the** old**est**
Two syllables ending in -y	early	earl**ier than**	**the** earl**iest**
Two or more syllables	famous	**more** famous **than**	**the most** famous
Irregular	good bad	**better** than **worse** than	**the best** **the worst**

Exercise 1
1 bigger
2 larger
3 than
4 the most
5 best

1 **Write the correct words in your notebook.**

1 Paris is **more big / bigger** than Málaga.
2 The Tower of London is **larger / more large** than the Sydney Opera House.
3 The caves at Lascaux are older **than / that** the Alhambra.
4 The Amazon Basin has **the most / the more** important rainforest in the world.
5 I think New York is the **goodest / best** city in the world.

Exercise 2
1 bigger
2 the most beautiful
3 smaller
4 more expensive
5 better

2 **Complete the sentences with the comparative or superlative form of the adjectives in brackets.**

1 My flat is … (big) than yours.
2 What's … (beautiful) place in Spain?
3 Spain is not … (small) than the UK.
4 I think Oslo is … (expensive) than Paris.
5 The pyramid is … (good) than the castle.

3 **Compare two buildings in your town.**

The football stadium is bigger than the library.

(not) as … as

New York is **as** famous **as** London.
The historic centre of Córdoba is **not as** old **as** the Great Pyramid.

All Clear Rules

As … as is used to show that two things are the same.
Not as … as is used to show that two things are different.

4 **Complete the sentences using the information in the table and the words in brackets.**

	The Empire State Building	The Eiffel Tower
year completed	1931	1889
height	381 metres	324 metres
entry cost	$27 dollars (about €20)	15€
opening time	8 am	9 am
number of visitors a year	3.5 million	6 million
famous	***	***

The Empire State Building *isn't as old as* the Eiffel Tower. (be / old)
1 The Eiffel Tower … the Empire State Building. (be / tall)
2 The Eiffel Tower … the Empire State Building. (be / expensive)
3 The Eiffel Tower's opening time … as the Empire State Building's. (be / early)
4 The Empire State Building … the Eiffel Tower. (be / popular)
5 The Empire State Building … the Eiffel Tower. (be / famous)

Exercise 4
1 isn't as tall as
2 isn't as expensive as
3 isn't as early as
4 isn't as popular as
5 is as famous as

Lesson Aims:

Students revise and practise comparative and superlative forms of adjectives.

Grammar

Comparatives and superlatives

Warmer

Write on the board *motorbike / fast / bicycle*. Ask students for a sentence comparing the two. Once they've done this, write *faster than* on the board. Now write *maths / difficult / English* and elicit another sentence. Once they've done this, write *more difficult than* on the board. Elicit why the different forms are used. Then add *plane* to the first group and *physics* to the second and elicit a superlative sentence and write the superlative form in each case.

1
- Tell students to cover the last two columns of the grammar table and elicit the comparative and superlative forms.
- Elicit why the final consonant of *big* is doubled when the comparative *bigger* is formed. (*Because it is a stressed combination of consonant + vowel + consonant.*)
- Students choose the correct words to complete the sentences in exercise 1.
- Check answers with the class.

2
- Tell students they need to decide first whether a comparative or superlative form is needed, and then to write the adjective in the correct form.
- You may want students to do this exercise in pairs as it is quite challenging.
- Check answers with the class.

3
- Read out the speech bubble. Ask students to work in pairs and say three or four sentences comparing two buildings in their town. You might want to put these prompts on the board.
  buildings: our school, the town hall, my house, the park, the sports centre
  adjectives: big, small, beautiful, ugly, interesting

(not) as … as

All Clear Rules

Read out the sentences in the box and ask students to translate them.
Point out that with *as … as* the form of the adjectives does not change – we don't say ~~*as older as*~~.
Read the All Clear Rules with the class.
Elicit more sentences from the students by writing some prompts on the board, eg *Ronaldo / Messi / good* (*Ronaldo is as good as Messi.*; *Ronaldo isn't as good as Messi.*).

4
- Ask students to look at the pictures and say which building they think is more impressive. Ask the class which cities the buildings are located in.
- Students look at the information in the table. Make sure they understand what each term means.
- Read the example with the class and refer to the table.
- In pairs, students complete the sentences using (*not*) *as … as*.
- Check answers with the class.

Extra activity

Students work in pairs. They take turns to compare buildings or places in their town, saying both true and false sentences. Their partner has to say if each sentence is true or false.

Mixed-ability solutions

Students who need extra help: Exercise 3. Students write their sentences before talking about the two buildings.

Fast finishers: Exercise 4. Students rewrite the sentences using the comparative.

Lesson Aims:

Students learn and practise using *too*, *enough* and *not enough*.

Grammar

too, enough and *not enough*

Warmer

Say *The wall was too high. I couldn't climb it.* and do a simple drawing on the board to illustrate this.
Then write the sentence on the board and elicit the meaning of *too*.
Repeat the same process with *His house is big enough for 20 people.*, eliciting the meaning of *enough*.

5 • Students look at the sentences in the table and translate them into their language.
- Point out that *too* comes before the adjective and *enough* comes after.
- Also make sure students understand that *too* is not the same as *very* as they are often confused.

6 • Look at the example with the class.
- Students order the words to make sentences.
- Check answers with the class.

All Clear Rules

Read the All Clear Rules with the class.
Ask them to look at the word order with *enough* + noun and elicit the fact that it comes before the noun, not after. If you think it is helpful, compare with the students' own language. You might also want to point out that we cannot use *too* with nouns.

7 • Look at the example with the class.
- Students complete the sentences with *too* or *enough* and the adjectives in brackets.
- Check answers with the class.

Extra activity

Students write some more sentences using *too*, *enough* and *not enough*. Help with vocabulary if necessary. Ask some students to read out their sentences.

8 • If you have a map of the UK, show students roughly where Hadrian's Wall is (in the north of England roughly between Carlisle and Newcastle upon Tyne).
- Students read the text about Hadrian's Wall and choose the correct words to complete it.
- Check answers with the class.

Cultural note

Hadrian's Wall is a World Heritage site. The Romans started building the wall in AD 122 during the rule of the emperor Hadrian. It contains several forts including Housesteads, the best preserved Roman fort in Britain. It runs across the north of England through Newcastle in the east and Carlisle in the west.

All Clear Grammar

9 • Tell students that this is a cumulative check of the grammar in Units 1 to 4.
- As this exercise is quite challenging, you may want students to do it in pairs.
- Students choose the correct words to complete the text.

10 1.40
- Play the audio. Students listen and check their answers.
- Check answers with the class. This is a good moment to check they have understood the new grammar and to review the grammar from the previous units.

Mixed-ability solutions

Students who need extra help: Exercise 7. Write two options on the board for each gap, eg *too warm / warm enough*, etc.

Fast finishers: Exercise 7. Write the following prompts on the board and ask students to write sentences about themselves.
I / not old enough
my bedroom / too small
I / not enough money

Self-study and extra practice

Workbook
- Grammar, pages 28–9
- Grammar Reference and Practice, pages 72–3

Teacher's Resource File
- All Clear Basics, pages 18–9
- Grammar Consolidation, page 14
- Grammar Extension, page 16
- Language Excellence, pages 7–8

Digital Activities
- Student's Digital Material

too, *enough* and *not enough*

We were **too** late. The museum was closed.
My burger was big **enough** for two people.
The tour of the Eiffel Tower was OK but it wasn't exciting **enough** for me.

Exercise 5
Students' own answers

5 **Look at the sentences in the table. How do you say them in your language?**

6 **Order the words to make sentences.**

to visit / the caves / We / late / were / too / .
We were too late to visit the caves.

1 The / wasn't / cheap / restaurant / enough / .
2 cathedral / The / is / enough / for 2,000 people / big / .
3 hot / It / too / to go sightseeing / was / .
4 The / enough / hotel / wasn't / good / so we left / .
5 When / I'm / enough / old / I'm / with my friends / going to go on holiday / .

Exercise 6
1 The restaurant wasn't cheap enough.
2 The cathedral is big enough for 2,000 people.
3 It was too hot to go to sightseeing.
4 The hotel wasn't good enough so we left.
5 When I'm old enough I'm going to go on holiday with my friends.

All Clear Rules

We also use *to have enough* with nouns.
I don't have ***enough*** *money.*
We have ***enough*** *time.*

7 **Complete the sentences with *too* or *enough* and the words in brackets.**

We didn't have enough money to go to the opera. It was *too expensive* (expensive).

1 It was too cold to visit the caves. It wasn't … (warm).
2 We had enough time to visit the castle, but it was … (crowded).
3 Six people wanted to go to the museum. Luckily, Carla's car was … (big).
4 I wanted to go to the opera, but I didn't have … (money).
5 The reef is not safe for children. It's … (dangerous).

Exercise 7
1 warm enough
2 too crowded
3 big enough
4 enough money
5 too dangerous

8 **Write the correct words in your notebook.**

Hadrian's Wall is a Roman wall in the north of England. For centuries it was [(1)]**big enough / enough big** to protect Roman Britain from invasion.
Now it is the most popular tourist attraction in the area. You cannot walk on the entire wall because it [(2)]**is strong enough / isn't strong enough** and it's [(3)]**too old / not old enough**. If you have [(4)]**too time / enough time**, you can walk next to the wall for 135km, but go in the summer because in the winter it's [(5)]**too wet / wet enough**!

Exercise 8
1 big enough
2 isn't strong enough
3 too old
4 enough time
5 too wet

All Clear Grammar

1 2 3 4 5 6 7 8 9

9 **Write the correct words in your notebook.**

I [(1)]**love / am loving** travelling. I think the [(2)]**more / most** interesting place in the world is China. The Forbidden City in Beijing is amazing. It [(3)]**isn't / wasn't** as old as the Alhambra, but it's [(4)]**biggest / bigger**. The Great Wall of China is also incredible. It's [(5)]**longer / more long** than the coastline of Spain! The only problem with China is that it's [(6)]**too big / big enough**. I never have [(7)]**too / enough** time to go everywhere. Perhaps I'll go and live there when I'm [(8)]**enough old / old enough**.

Exercise 9
1 love
2 most
3 isn't
4 bigger
5 longer
6 too big
7 enough
8 old enough

10 1.40 **Listen and check your answers.**

Vocabulary

Adverbs

Exercise 1
Students' own answers

1 1.41 **Listen and repeat the words. How do you say them in your language?**

angrily • badly • carefully • easily • fast • happily • hard • noisily • quickly • quietly • well

Exercise 2
a) adverb
b) adjective

2 **Read the sentences below. Which has an adverb and which has an adjective?**

Exercise 3

	Adjective	Adverb
add *-ly*	*quick*	*quickly*
	bad	badly
	careful	carefully
	quiet	quietly
remove *-y*, add *-ily*	*happy*	*happily*
	angry	angrily
	easy	easily
	noisy	noisily
irregular	*good*	*well*
	fast	fast
	hard	hard

a) He drove home carefully.
b) He's a careful driver.

3 **Copy and complete the table with the adverbs from exercise 1 and their adjective form.**

	Adjective	Adverb
add *-ly*	quick	quickly
remove *-y*, add *-ily*	happy	happily
irregular	good	well

4 **Order the words to make sentences.**

1 works / My / sister / hard / very / .
2 in / England / very / speak / People / quickly / .
3 I / homework / carefully / did / my / .
4 badly / I / the / play / guitar / .
5 drive / very / fast / People / Italy / in / .
6 My / speak / can / dad / well / French / .

Exercise 4
1 My sister works very hard.
2 People in England speak very quickly.
3 I did my homework carefully.
4 I play the guitar badly
5 People in Italy drive very fast.
6 My dad can speak French well.

Listening

Exercise 5
The Metropolitan Museum of Art
It was too late. / They didn't have enough time.

5 1.42 **Listen to Ben and Michela's conversation. Which place in the pictures didn't Ben visit? Why not?**

Exercise 6
1 No, he didn't.
2 Yes, he did.
3 It was too small.

6 **Listen again and answer the questions.**

1 Did Ben buy some trainers in New York?
2 Did he buy a baseball cap for Michela?
3 Why did Michela not keep her present?

Brooklyn Bridge

The Metropolitan Museum of Art

The Statue of Liberty

Vocabulary Reference

Lesson Aims:

Students learn and practise how to form adverbs.
Students listen to a conversation about a trip to New York and identify general and specific information.

Vocabulary

Adverbs

Warmer

Mime eating slowly and eating quickly. Ask students *How am I eating?* Elicit *slowly* and *quickly* and write them on the board. Ask students if the words are adjectives, and elicit the difference between adjectives and adverbs in formation and use.

1 1.41

- Play the audio. Students listen and repeat the words.
- Elicit the translation of each one.
- Ask students why *fast* and *hard* are exceptions (*because they have the same form as the adjective*). You might also want to point out that we use *hard* with verbs such as *rain*, *try* and *work*.

2
- Read the two sentences and ask students to identify the adverb and the adjective.

3
- Students look at the different ways to form adverbs shown in the table.
- They copy and complete the table in their notebooks by adding the adverbs from exercise 1, together with their adjective form.
- Check the spelling of the adjectives and adverbs with the class.

4
- Students order the words to make sentences. You may want to do the first sentence together with the class so they can see that adverbs usually go after the verb.
- Check answers with the class.

Listening

Warmer

Books closed. Ask students if they can think of any famous places in New York.

5 1.42

- Read the questions with the class.
- Play the audio. Students listen and find which place Ben didn't visit and why.
- Check answers with the class.

6
- Students read the questions.
- Play the audio again. Students listen again and answer the questions.
- Check answers with the class.

Extra activity

Ask the class which city in the world they would like to visit and what they would like to see and do there.

Web info

Type these words in your search engine for more information about tourist attractions in New York: 'things to see in New York'

Mixed-ability solutions

Students who need extra help: Exercise 3. Elicit the first three adverb / adjective combinations (*angrily / angry*; *badly / bad*; *carefully / careful*) and where they should go in the table.

Fast finishers: Exercise 3. Students add the following adjectives and the corresponding adverbs to the table: *beautiful*, *bright*, *heavy*, *sad*, *slow*.

Self-study and extra practice

Workbook
- Vocabulary, page 27
- Vocabulary Reference, page 87

Teacher's Resource File
- All Clear Basics, page 17
- Vocabulary Consolidation, page 13
- Vocabulary Extension, page 15
- Key Competences: Listening, page 8

Digital Activities
- Student's Digital Material

Lesson Aims:

Students learn and practise functional language to ask about and describe what they did at the weekend.

Speaking

Describing your weekend / A day out

Warmer

Ask students when was the last time they went away at the weekend and where they went.

Model Dialogue

1 1.43

- Read the question with the class.
- Play the audio. Students listen to and read the dialogue and find what you can do in Cambridge.
- Elicit the answer to the question.
- If you have a map in the class, show students where Cambridge is.

2
- Play the audio again. Students listen again and this time repeat the dialogue.
- Point out that the question *Did you have a good time?* does not refer to the weather. Get the class to pay attention to intonation, both of questions and answers.

Speaking Task

1 Talk about a day out

Students look at the information in the Student's Book. Students choose one of the towns or use their own ideas.

2 Prepare a dialogue

Students look at the Model Dialogue and change the words in blue to make their own dialogue.

3 Speak

Students practise their dialogues in pairs.

Mixed-ability solutions

Students who need extra help: Speaking Task. Students write out their dialogue before they do step 3.

Fast finishers: Speaking Task. Students act out another dialogue using a different town and ideas. Encourage them to use their imagination! If possible, they do this without looking at the Model Dialogue.

Self-study and extra practice

Workbook
- Speaking, page 123

Teacher's Resource File
- Key Competences: Speaking, pages 25–6

Digital Activities
- Student's Digital Material

Speaking

Describing your weekend / A day out

Exercise 1
You can go to museums and visit the university.

1 1.43 Listen to the dialogue. What can you do in Cambridge?

Model Dialogue

Alex: Hi, Maisie. What did you do at the weekend?

Maisie: I went to Cambridge with Leah.

Alex: That sounds more interesting than my weekend. Why did you go there?

Maisie: We went to visit my cousin who lives there.

Alex: So, what is there to do there?

Maisie: Well, you can go to museums and visit the university.

Alex: Was the weather good?

Maisie: Yeah. It was very sunny.

Alex: Did you have a good time?

Maisie: Yes, it was a lot of fun. We went on a boat trip.

2 Listen again and repeat the dialogue.

Speaking Task

1 Talk about a day out

First, choose a town to visit. Use the ideas below or your own ideas.

What? Bristol with my family
Why? see my granny
To do go shopping, visit the university
Weather good? no / cold and wet
Good time? terrible / a horrible meal

What? Brighton with my friend
Why? stay with my sister
To do go to the cinema / beach
Weather good? yes / hot and sunny
Good time? fantastic / to a great concert

2 Prepare a dialogue

Look at the Model Dialogue and change the words in blue.

3 Speak

In pairs, practise your dialogue.

What did you do at the weekend?
I went to Bristol with my family.

Useful Language Describing your weekend

What did you do at the weekend?	**I went to** Cambridge with Leah.
Why did you go there?	**We went to** visit my cousin.
What is there to do there?	**You can go to** museums and visit the university.
Was the weather good?	Yeah. **It was** very sunny.
Did you have a good time?	Yes, **it was** a lot of fun.

Writing

A travel guide entry

Exercise 1
The correct order is b, c, a, d.

1 1.44 **Read the Model Text and listen. Order the information in your notebook.**

a) food **b)** places to visit **c)** things to do **d)** recommendations

Model Text

New York's garden

Central Park is one of the most famous parks in the world. It's a really good place to hang out, especially when the weather is sunny.

The park has beautiful gardens, lakes and caves. In the summer, there are free music concerts. There is also a castle and a zoo with a rainforest! It's a very good place for rollerblading, but that's too energetic for me! I prefer walking quietly through the trees. I also like going on the lake in a boat. It's not very expensive and it's very relaxing. There are restaurants in the park but they are quite expensive. I usually take a sandwich from home because it's cheaper.

When you need to escape from New York, just visit Central Park!

Exercise 2
Students' own answers
It's a **really** good place to hang out, …
It's a **very** good place for rollerblading, …
It's **not very** expensive and it's **very** relaxing.
There are restaurants in the park but they are **quite** expensive.

2 **Look at the All Clear Tips and translate the words in bold. Then find examples in the Model Text.**

All Clear Tips

Qualifiers

\+ *It's **really** interesting.*
*It's **very** interesting.*
*It's **quite** interesting.*
\- *It's **not very** interesting.*

Exercise 3
1 Seville is a really beautiful city.
2 The museum is quite expensive.
3 The castle is not very interesting.
4 It is a really good place for shopping.
5 The cathedral is not very old.
6 The tickets are very cheap.

3 **Order the words to make sentences.**

1 city / Seville / a / beautiful / is / really / .
2 The / museum / expensive / is / quite / .
3 is / interesting / The / very / castle / not / .
4 really / good / It / place / shopping / for / is / a / .
5 cathedral / not / The / old / very / is / .
6 tickets / very / The / cheap / are / .

Writing Task

1 Plan

Make notes about a place and include:

Introduction: *location, why it is special*
Description: *landscape, activities, food and entertainment, why you like it*
Conclusion: *a recommendation*

2 Write

Use the Model Text, your notes and this structure:

Paragraph 1: Introduction
Paragraph 2: Description
Paragraph 3: Conclusion / Recommendation

3 Check

☑ comparatives and superlatives, *too, enough, not enough*
☑ places to visit, adverbs
☑ qualifiers: *really, very, quite* and *not very*

Lesson Aims:

Students practise using qualifiers.
Students write an entry for a travel guide.

Writing

A travel guide entry

Warmer

Ask students if they can remember the places in New York that were mentioned in the listening activity (*the Statue of Liberty, Central Park, the Empire State Building, the Metropolitan Museum of Art*).

1 1.44

- Read the options with the class.
- Play the audio. Students read and listen to the text and put the information in the correct order.
- Check the answer with the class.

Extra activity

Students read the text again and make a list of everything you can do in Central Park. In pairs they then compare their lists and talk about which activity they would most like to do.

All Clear Tips

2
- Students read the sentences in the All Clear Tips and translate the qualifiers (*really*, *very*, *quite*, *not very*). Make it clear that the meaning of *really* and *very* is similar, but *really* is a little more emphatic.
- Explain that we can use qualifiers with adjectives to make our descriptions more precise.
- Students look for examples of the qualifiers in the Model Text.
- Check answers with the class.

3
- Students order the words to make sentences.
- Check answers with the class.

Writing Task

1 Plan

Read the notes with the class. Students choose a place and make notes about it.

2 Write

Look at the structure with the class. Students use their notes to write their travel guide entry. Emphasize that they should try to use qualifiers to make their descriptions more precise.

3 Check

Encourage students to check their work, paying particular attention to the points mentioned.

Web info

Type these words in your search engine for more information about Central Park: 'go travel go + 10 facts Central Park'

Mixed-ability solutions

Students who need extra help: Writing Task. Students just complete the notes in step 1.

Fast finishers: Writing Task. Students read their partner's entry and give them their opinion of the place.

Self-study and extra practice

Workbook
- Writing Guide, pages 108–9

Teacher's Resource File
- Key Competences: Writing, page 8

Lesson Aims:

Students read about Buckingham Palace.
Students practise the /ɑː/ /eɪ/ and /uː/ sounds.

Culture Reading

Famous places

Warmer

Books closed. Ask students to tell you everything they know about Buckingham Palace: where it is, who lives there, whether they have visited it, etc.
Books open. Students look at the pictures and describe what they can see.

1.45

- Students read the questions.
- Teach the word *flag*.
- Play the audio. Students read and listen to the text to find the answers.
- Check answers with the class.

Extra activity

Say the following places. Students tell you who lives there. (Answers in brackets.)
10 Downing Street (The Prime Minister of Great Britain)
The Zarzuela Palace (The King of Spain)
The White House (The President of the USA)
The Moncloa Palace (The Prime Minister of Spain)
The Kremlin (The President of the Russian Federation)
The Élysée Palace (The President of the French Republic)
The Quirinal Palace (The President of the Italian Republic)

Pronunciation

/ɑː/ /eɪ/ /uː/

a 1.46

- Play the audio. Students listen and repeat the words.

b 1.47

- Play the audio. Students listen and repeat the sentences.

Cultural note

Queen Elizabeth II is Queen of the United Kingdom of Great Britain and Northern Ireland.
Apart from Buckingham Palace in London, the Queen has official or state residences at Windsor Castle in Windsor, the Palace of Holyroodhouse in Edinburgh and Hillsborough Castle in County Down, Northern Ireland. These residences belong to the state and are not part of the Queen's personal possessions. The Queen owns Sandringham House in Norfolk and Balmoral Castle in Scotland.

Web info

Type these words in your search engine

- for a simple description of Buckingham Palace: 'Woodlands Junior + Buckingham Palace'
- to take a virtual tour of Buckingham Palace (video): 'royal gov + virtual tour Buckingham Palace'

Mixed-ability solutions

Students who need extra help: Reading text.
Write the following prompts on the board:

1 *royal*
2 *flag*
3 *not 775*
4 *parties*

Fast-finishers: Reading text. Students read the text again and write down the numbers in the text and what they refer to.

Self-study and extra practice

Workbook

- Culture: Reading and Listening, page 96

Culture Reading

EXTRA

Famous places

Buckingham Palace

Buckingham Palace is the London home of the British royal family. It is in Westminster, in the city centre.

A royal home

The palace was built in 1703, but it didn't become the home of the royal family until 1837. People know when the queen is there because they can see her flag on top of the palace. When she's away, the flag isn't there.

The palace today

Queen Elizabeth II does a lot of her work in the palace and over 400 people work there too. The palace has 775 rooms, including 52 royal and guest bedrooms and 188 bedrooms for people who work in the palace. The most impressive room is probably the White Drawing Room. The palace has got a huge garden. In fact, it is the largest private garden in London.

Visiting the palace

Thousands of people visit the palace every year. Many tourists watch the Changing of the Guard, a famous ceremony which happens every day outside the palace. In the summer, tourists can visit some of the rooms inside the palace. Also in the summer, the queen invites about 50,000 people to her garden parties.

1.45 **Read and listen. Then answer the questions in your notebook.**

1 Who lives in Buckingham Palace?
2 How do you know if the queen is at home?
3 How many bedrooms are there?
4 What does the queen do every summer?

Reading text exercise

1 the British royal family
2 because you can see her flag on top of the palace
3 240
4 She invites about 50,000 people to her garden parties.

Pronunciation

/ɑː/ /eɪ/ /uː/

a 1.46 **Listen and repeat the words.**

/ɑː/ garden, large, party
/eɪ/ away, famous, day
/uː/ room, true, beautiful

b 1.47 **Listen and repeat the sentences.**

Unit 4 Language Reference

Vocabulary Places to visit

castle • cathedral • cave • coastline • lighthouse • opera house • pyramid • rainforest • reef • ruin • temple • tomb

Adverbs

angrily • badly • carefully • easily • fast • happily • hard • noisily • quickly • quietly • well

Grammar Comparatives and superlatives

Comparatives
The Great Pyramid is **older** than the Taj Mahal.
Central Park is **larger** than the Retiro Park.
London is **bigger** than Madrid.
I think pizza is **tastier** than spaghetti.
The Taj Mahal is **more beautiful** than the Great Pyramid.
Do you think cycling is **better** than rollerblading?

Superlatives
This is **the oldest** building in the city.
The Pacific is **the largest** ocean in the world.
It is **the biggest** pyramid in the world.
In my opinion, cheese is **the tastiest** food.
The Taj Mahal is **the most beautiful** monument in India.
What is **the best** monument in your town?

too, *enough* and *not enough*

We were **too** late. It was closed. We were**n't too** late.
My tent was big **enough** for two people. My tent was**n't** big **enough** for eight people.

(*not*) *have enough*

We have **enough** chocolate for ten people.
I do**n't** have **enough** money to buy a car.

(*not*) *as … as*

We use *as … as* to show that two things are the same.

*New York is **as** famous **as** London.*

We use *not as … as* to show that two things are different.

*The Taj Mahal is **not as** old **as** the Great Pyramid.*

Speaking Describing your weekend

What did you do at the weekend?	**I went to** Cambridge with Leah.
Why did you go there?	**We went to** visit my cousin.
What is there to do there?	**You can go to** museums and visit the university.
Was the weather good?	Yeah. **It was** very sunny.
Did you have a good time?	Yes, **it was** a lot of fun.

Unit 4 Progress Check

Vocabulary Places to visit

1 Complete the sentences with the words in the box.

coastline lighthouse reefs ruins tomb

1 Rome has some important historical … .
2 When the sailors saw the …, they knew they were safe.
3 Egyptian pharaohs were often buried in a … inside a pyramid.
4 The USA has an Atlantic and a Pacific … .
5 Pollution is killing coral … in many seas.

Exercise 1
1 ruins
2 lighthouse
3 tomb
4 coastline
5 reefs

Adverbs

2 Write the correct words in your notebook.

1 My uncle always drives very slow / slowly.
2 I always do my homework careful / carefully.
3 The Golden Temple is a beautiful / beautifully building.
4 The Great Pyramid was built very well / good.
5 The museum was very interesting / interestingly.

Exercise 2
1 slowly
2 carefully
3 beautiful
4 well
5 interesting

Grammar Comparatives and superlatives

3 Complete the sentences with comparative or superlative forms of the adjectives in brackets.

1 Russia is … country in the world. (big)
2 China's population is … than Russia's. (large)
3 The weather in Spain is … than in the UK. (good)
4 Paris is … city in the world. (beautiful)
5 Mont Blanc is … mountain in Europe. (high)

Exercise 3
1 the biggest
2 larger
3 better
4 the most beautiful
5 the highest

4 Complete the sentences with *(not) as … as* and the verbs and adjectives in brackets.

1 Moscow … St Petersburg. (not be / beautiful)
2 Prague … Paris now. (be / popular)
3 The cave … the reef. (be / interesting)
4 The Pyrenees … the Alps. (not be / high)
5 Spain … Italy. (be / hot)

Exercise 4
1 is not as beautiful as
2 is as popular as
3 is not as interesting as
4 are not as high as
5 is as hot as

too, enough and *not enough*

5 Complete the sentences with *too, enough* or *not enough*.

1 The restaurant was … expensive.
2 We did … have … money to go to Bali.
3 Are you old … to travel alone?
4 There's … time to visit the cave. I'm sorry.
5 The caves are … small. We can't go in.

Exercise 5
1 too
2 not (have) enough
3 enough
4 not enough
5 too

Check your answers

Write your scores for exercises1–5 in your notebook. What did you get for:

- places to visit?
- adverbs?
- comparatives and superlatives?
- *too, enough* and *not enough*?

Extra Practice

If you need extra practice, go to:

Unit 4 Grammar Reference
Unit 4 Vocabulary Reference
Unit 4 Grammar Exercises
Unit 4 Vocabulary Exercises

Correct the activities with the class. Students who need extra revision and practice can go to:

Workbook
- Unit 4 Revision, page 30
- Grammar Reference and Practice, pages 72–3
- Vocabulary Reference, page 87

Student's Digital Material
www.allclear.macmillan.es

5 Real-life heroes

Overview

Unit objectives and key competences

- Understand, memorize and correctly use vocabulary related to fundraising ideas and expressions with *make* and *do* CLC, DC
- Identify the gist and main ideas in an article about two people involved in education projects CLC
- Learn about two charities providing education for deprived children SCC, SIE
- Understand, contrast and correctly use grammar structures related to the present perfect CLC, L2L
- Identify general and specific information through a listening activity about a celebrity charity worker CLC

More information on Key Competences, page v

- Learn about a celebrity Goodwill Ambassador SCC, CAE
- Use appropriate functional language to make requests and offers CLC, SCC
- Write a magazine article CLC, SIE, CAE
- Identify the general content of a text about Elizabeth Fry CLC
- Learn about Elizabeth Fry SCC, CAE
- Assimilate the All Clear Tips and Rules and study the Language Reference from the unit CLC, L2L, SIE
- Identify areas of language which need improvement and use ICT for extra practice DC, CLC, L2L

Linguistic content

Grammar

- Present perfect
- *ever* and *never*
- *How long … ?* with *for* and *since*

Recycled grammar

- Present simple (Unit 1)
- Present continuous (Unit 1)
- Use of gerund after *love* (Unit 1)
- Past simple (Unit 2)
- Comparatives and superlatives (Unit 4)

Main vocabulary

- Fundraising activities: *collect money, do a sponsored swim*, etc
- Expressions with *make* and *do*: *make a decision, do your best*, etc

Functional language

- Making requests and offers (2) / A fundraising event

Pronunciation

- Contractions

Skills: learning outcomes

- **Reading** Understand the gist and specific information in a clearly structured article about two young women involved in education projects for deprived children. The student can re-read the more difficult parts, page 53
- **Listening** Identify the gist and main ideas from a report about a celebrity UNICEF Goodwill Ambassador, page 56
- **Speaking** Communicate effectively in an everyday situation. Follow norms of basic courtesy while talking about a fundraising event, page 57
- **Writing** Write a short magazine article about a fundraising event with simple and relevant information, set out in a logical order, page 58
- **Reading** Understand the gist and specific information in a clearly structured biography of Elizabeth Fry. The student can re-read the more difficult parts, page 59

Lifelong learning skills and content-based learning

Life skills

- **Socio-cultural awareness** Education projects for deprived children, page 52, A UNICEF Goodwill Ambassador, page 56, Elizabeth Fry, page 59
- **Social development** Awareness of people less fortunate than ourselves and how we can help them, pages 52, 56 and 59; organizing fundraising activities, pages 52 and 57

Learning strategies

- Become aware of, and use, simple collocations, pages 52 and 56
- Deduce rules by analysing examples, page 54

Cross-curricular content

- History: Elizabeth Fry, page 59

Further materials and evaluation

Digital material

- Student's and Teacher's Resource Centres
- Teacher's Presentation Kit
- Student's Digital Material: interactive vocabulary and grammar activities
- Video *Literature* (Revision Units 4–6, page 74)

Student's website www.macmillansecondary.es

Workbook

- Vocabulary, pages 32–3
- Vocabulary Reference, page 88
- Grammar, pages 34–5
- Grammar Reference and Practice, pages 74–5
- Revision, page 36
- Culture: Reading and Listening, page 97
- Writing Guide, pages 110–1
- Speaking, page 124

Teacher's Resource File

Multi-level Materials Bank

- All Clear Basics, pages 21–5
- Vocabulary and Grammar Consolidation and Extension, pages 17–20
- Language Excellence, pages 9–10
- Translation and Dictation, pages 5 and 14

Lifelong Learning

- Digital Competence, pages 9–10
- Culture Video Material, pages 3–4
- Study Skills, pages 1–12

Evaluation and Key Competences

- Evaluation Rubrics, pages 1–7
- Key Competences, pages 9–10 and 27–8

Content-based Learning

- CLIL, pages 1–10
- Macmillan Readers, pages 1–7

Evaluation material

- Unit 5 end-of-unit test: Basic, Standard and Extra
- CEFR Skills Exam Generator

Web info

Tips to find extra information on: the Street Academy project in Ghana, the Akosia educational project around the world, UNICEF, ideas for fundraising activities, Elizabeth Fry

Extra help for weaker students

Teacher's Resource File: All Clear Basics, pages 21–5

Material for fast finishers

Workbook: Grammar Extension, page 37
Teacher's Resource File: Vocabulary Extension, page 19
Teacher's Resource File: Grammar Extension, page 20
Teacher's Resource File: Language Excellence, pages 9–10

5 Real-life heroes

Objectives

Vocabulary	Fundraising ideas; *make* and *do*
Grammar	Present perfect; *ever* and *never*; *How long ... ?* with *for* and *since*
Speaking	Making requests and offers (2)
Writing	A magazine article

Vocabulary

Fundraising ideas

Exercise 1
1 make a charity CD
2 sell cakes
3 have a bring and buy sale / organize a jumble sale
4 have a barbecue
5 collect money
6 sell raffle tickets
7 sell badges
8 have a bring and buy sale / organize a jumble sale
9 do a sponsored swim
10 wash cars

1 2.01 **Listen and repeat the words. Match them with pictures 1–10.**

collect money • do a sponsored swim • have a barbecue • have a bring and buy sale • make a charity CD • organize a jumble sale • sell badges • sell cakes • sell raffle tickets • wash cars

1 
2 
3 
4 
6 
8 
9 
5 

7 
10 

Exercise 2
1 cakes
2 sponsored
3 cars
4 a jumble sale
5 barbecue
6 charity

2 **Complete the text with words from exercise 1.**

After Typhoon Haiyan struck the Philippines, lots of people from around the world wanted to help. People collected money in the street and sold (1)... for people to eat. Schoolchildren did (2)... walks and swims and washed (3)... to raise money. In the UK, one charity shop organized (4)... with second-hand clothes from Victoria and David Beckham. They raised a lot of money! In Canada, people had a (5)... and bought burgers for $5. In many countries, pop stars worked together to make (6)... CDs. Everyone wanted to help.

Exercise 3
a bring and buy sale

3 2.02 **Listen to Alex and Lucy. What fundraising idea do they choose for their class?**

4 **In pairs, think of three fundraising ideas to raise money for a school trip.**

I think having a barbecue is a good idea because everyone likes burgers.

Lesson Aims:

Students learn and practise vocabulary related to fundraising ideas.
Students listen to two young people talking about fundraising ideas and identify the one they choose.

Vocabulary

Fundraising ideas

Warmer

Books closed. Write the following on the board: *Oxfam, Caritas, UNICEF*. Ask what they are and what they do. Students suggest ways they can raise money. Teach the word *fundraising*. Explain that *a fund* is an amount of money and *raise* means collect.

1 2.01

- Play the audio. Students listen and repeat the words.
- Look at the phrases one by one to make sure students understand them. Expressions such as *bring and buy sale* and *jumble sale* (see *Cultural note*) and *raffle tickets* (a type of lottery ticket to win a physical prize or money) will need to be explained. Also explain that sponsored activities such as runs, swims and walks are very common in the UK.
- Check pronunciation, paying particular attention to the stress in each expression.
- Students say what they can see in the pictures. They match the expressions with the pictures.

Extra activity

Books closed. Dictate some of the expressions or play the audio. Students write down the expressions and underline the stress.

2
- Students complete the text with words from exercise 1.
- Check answers with the class.

3 2.02

- Read the question with the class.
- Students listen to the conversation and answer the question.
- Check the answer with the class.

4

- Read the example sentence with the class. Highlight the use of *I think* followed by the gerund.
- Students suggest ideas in pairs.

Cultural note

In Britain and the United States, many young people are involved in fundraising through their schools and communities. For example, they organize carnivals for charity, they sell raffle tickets and they offer to do odd jobs such as mowing the lawn.
A bring and buy sale is an informal sale, often to raise money for charity, in which people bring items to sell and buy items that other people have brought.
A jumble sale is a sale of articles which are usually cheap and second-hand, often to raise money for charity.

Mixed-ability solutions

Students who need extra help: Exercise 2. Write the following options on the board.

1 *charity / cakes*
2 *sponsored / raffle*
3 *money / cars*
4 *a jumble sale / badges*
5 *sponsored swim / barbecue*
6 *expensive / charity*

Fast finishers: Exercise 4. Students do the exercise again but this time they disagree with their partner's ideas and to try to convince them that their ideas are better.

Self-study and extra practice

Workbook
- Vocabulary, page 32
- Vocabulary Reference, page 88

Teacher's Resource File
- All Clear Basics, page 21
- Vocabulary Consolidation, page 17
- Vocabulary Extension, page 19

Lesson Aims:

Students read and listen to a text about two people involved in charity projects for children.

Reading

An article

Warmer

Ask students if they know anyone personally who is involved in charity activities, either as a volunteer or full-time. If so, what do they do?

1
- Students read the titles.
- Students read the text quickly to decide which is the best title.
- Check the answer with the class, asking students to justify their choice.

Word Check

Check students understand the new words: *wooden hut, deprived, teamwork, set up*. Explain any they don't know.

2 2.03
- Students read the statements.
- Play the audio. Students read and listen to the text to decide if the statements are true or false.
- They copy the sentences with the information that helped them decide.
- Check answers with the class.

3
- Read the questions with class and make sure that they understand them.
- Students read the text again and answer the questions.
- Check answers with the class.

4
- You might want to make this a timed exercise to train students to look quickly for information. If so, give them two minutes to write down all the fundraising ideas.
- Check answers with the class.

All Clear Facts

Read the fact with the class. Ask the class if they think Red Nose Day is a good or a bad idea, and why.

Extra activity

Books closed. Read out the following incorrect statements. Elicit corrections (given in brackets).

Felicity Marks spent four months teaching adults at the Street Academy school. (She taught children.)

The building is a small metal hut and it has got only two classrooms. (The hut is made of wood and there is only one classroom.)

Felicity's charity has organized quiz nights and it has sold badges. (It hasn't sold badges; it has organized quiz nights, sold cakes and done sponsored walks and skydives.)

Cultural note

Ghana is a relatively small coastal country in the west of Africa. (It is less than half the size of Spain.) It was the first African country to declare independence from European colonization, in 1957. Economically, Ghana is one of the fastest-growing countries in Africa and it is rich in natural resources (in particular, petroleum, natural gas, gold and diamonds). It is also one of the largest cocoa producers in the world. Most children in Ghana have access to primary and secondary education. All teaching is done in English.

Web info

Type these words in your search engine for more information about

- the Street Academy: 'the Street Academy Ghana'
- Akosia: 'Akosia'

Mixed-ability solutions

Students who need extra help: Exercise 3. Write the following options on the board.

1 *four months / four years*
2 *free education, books and meals / free education and specialist sports training*
3 *better teachers / more classrooms and better facilities*
4 *how to cook / cooperation and teamwork*
5 *Ghana, Mexico and Mongolia / many countries in Africa*

Fast finishers: Exercise 4. Students write their opinion relating to which of the two projects is more interesting and why.

Self-study and extra practice

Teacher's Resource File

- Key Competences: Reading, page 9

Reading

An article

Word Check
wooden hut   deprived   teamwork   set up

Exercise 1
c) Two inspiring fundraisers

1 **Read the text quickly and choose the best title.**

a) How to build your own school   b) Ideas for fundraising projects   c) Two inspiring fundraisers

Have you ever noticed whenever there's a natural disaster people respond by donating time and money? But some people dedicate their lives to helping others. Here are two examples.

Felicity Marks

Felicity Marks spent four months teaching children at The Street Academy school in Accra, Ghana. She wanted to do more to help the city's children so she started a charity called the Street Academy Annexe Project.

The Street Academy offers free education to children aged 8–18, as well as books and meals. But the building is a small **wooden hut** and it has only got one classroom. The aim of the project is to build a school with four rooms and better facilities.

Her charity has organized quiz nights and it has sold cakes and done sponsored walks and skydives. So far, the school has bought the land for the new building. When it has raised enough money, it can start construction.

Maria Schonfeld

Maria Schonfeld is the co-founder of a charity called Akosia. The aim of Akosia is to develop the creativity and confidence of **deprived** children around the world. They also learn about cooperation and **teamwork**.

Akosia has organized a film-making project for children in Ghana every year since 2009. It has **set up** similar projects in Mexico and Mongolia. The charity has organized fundraising dinners, music festivals and sports tournaments. It has also used platforms like Kickstarter to collect money online.

Maria is passionate about helping children and believes that the sky is the limit for Akosia!

All Clear Facts
In the UK, Red Nose Day is an annual fundraising day. People wear red noses and do something funny to raise money for charity.

2 2.03 **Read and listen. Write true or false in your notebook. Copy the text that shows your answers.**

1 Felicity started her charity to help to pay for a new building.
2 The school has started the construction of the new building.
3 Maria started Akosia on her own.
4 Maria is optimistic about the future of Akosia.

3 **Read the text again. Answer the questions in your notebook.**

1 How long was Felicity at the Street Academy school?
2 What do children receive at the Street Academy school?
3 What does the Street Academy school need?
4 What do children learn on Akosia projects?
5 Where has Akosia organized projects?

Exercise 3
1 four months
2 free education, books and meals
3 more classrooms and better facilities
4 They learn about cooperation and teamwork.
5 Ghana, Mexico and Mongolia

4 **Make a list of all the fundraising ideas that the text mentions in your notebook.**

Exercise 2
1 true – … she started a charity called the Street Academy Annexe Project. … The aim of the project is to build a school …
2 false – So far, the school has bought the land for the new building. When it has raised enough money, it can start construction.
3 false – Maria Schonfeld is the co-founder of a charity called Akosia.
4 true – Maria … believes that the sky is the limit for Akosia!

Exercise 4
organize quiz nights, sell cakes, do sponsored walks and skydives, organize fundraising dinners, music festivals and sports tournaments, collect money online using fundraising platforms

Grammar

Present perfect

Affirmative	She **has** collected
Negative	We **haven't** collected
Interrogative	**Have** you collected …?

Language Reference p60

Exercise 1
1 's had
2 haven't organized
3 's sold
4 's made
5 haven't sold

1 Complete the sentences with the present perfect form of the verbs in brackets.

I*'ve done* (do) lots of sponsored swims.
1 My dad … (have) a barbecue for charity in our garden.
2 We … (not organize) a jumble sale.
3 She … (sell) raffle tickets.
4 He … (make) a charity CD.
5 I … (not sell) cakes for charity.

Exercise 2
1 I've done a sponsored swim.
2 We haven't organized a jumble sale.
3 He hasn't bought a raffle ticket.
4 My brother hasn't collected second-hand books for a bring and buy sale.
5 My mum has raised £2,000 for charity.

2 Write complete sentences with the affirmative or negative form of the present perfect in your notebook.

My friends / have / lots of barbecues. ✓
My friends have had lots of barbecues.
1 I / do / a sponsored swim. ✓
2 We / organize / a jumble sale. ✗
3 He / buy / a raffle ticket. ✗
4 My brother / collect / second-hand books for a bring and buy sale. ✗
5 My mum / raise / £2,000 for charity. ✓

Exercise 3
1 has organized
2 has bought
3 have made
4 (have) sold
5 haven't (even) bought
6 haven't collected

3 Complete the text with the present perfect form of the verbs in brackets.

Have you ever raised money for charity? I *haven't done* (not do) anything before, but I really want to be a volunteer. My brother (1)… (organize) a raffle to raise money for cancer research and he (2)… (buy) lots of charity badges. My sisters (3)… (make) cakes and (4)… (sell) them outside school to raise money for the Red Cross. I (5)… even … (not buy) a charity CD!

I want to do a sponsored swim because I think it is a good way to raise money. My brother and sisters (6)… (not collect) money for an animal charity, so I want to raise money for the RSPCA.

ever and *never*

Present perfect with *ever* and *never*
Have you **ever** done charity work?
Has she **ever** organized a sponsored swim?
I've **never** bought a charity CD.
She's **never** had a bring and buy sale.

All Clear Rules

We can use ***ever*** in questions and ***never*** in negative sentences to talk about experiences.
*I've **never** done a sponsored swim.*

4 Write questions in your notebook. Use the present perfect and *ever*.

sell raffle tickets for charity
Have you ever sold raffle tickets for charity?
1 collect money for charity
2 learn to play a musical instrument
3 do a sponsored sports event
4 buy a charity badge
5 meet a famous person
6 wash cars for charity

Exercise 4
1 Have you ever collected money for charity?
2 Have you ever learned / learnt to play a musical instrument?
3 Have you ever done a sponsored sports event?
4 Have you ever bought a charity badge?
5 Have you ever met a famous person?
6 Have you ever washed cars for charity?

5 In pairs, ask and answer the questions in exercise 4.

6 Write the correct words in your notebook.

Anna My life is boring. I've (1)**ever / never** done anything interesting.
Rob I don't believe you. Everyone (2)**has / have** done something interesting.
Anna I (3)**hasn't / haven't**.
Rob OK, have you ever (4)**eat / eaten** Thai food?
Anna No, I've (5)**never / ever** eaten it.
Rob Have you ever (6)**ride / ridden** a horse?
Anna No, (7)**I / I've** never done that.
Rob Have you ever (8)**be / been** in a film?
Anna You mean as an actor? No, of course I (9)**have / haven't**!
Rob Errr, well have you (10)**never / ever** met a famous person?
Anna Yes! I met Pablo Alborán last year!

Exercise 6
1 never
2 has
3 haven't
4 eaten
5 never
6 ridden
7 I've
8 been
9 haven't
10 ever

Lesson Aims:

Students revise and practise making affirmative and negative sentences using the present perfect tense.
Students practise using *ever* and *never* with the present perfect tense to ask and answer questions about experiences.

Grammar

Present perfect

Warmer

Write on the board *I've travelled by plane.* Ask students to identify the tense. Then ask the class if we use the present perfect to talk about a past action if we're interested in *when* it was done or if we're *not* interested in when it was done.

1
- Ask students how the present perfect is formed (*have* / *has* + past participle).
- Look at the grammar table with the class. Point out that *collect* is a regular verb but that many verbs have an irregular past participle. Write the following prompts with irregular verbs on the board.
  I / ride bike
  She / spend / a lot of money
  They / not come / home
- Elicit the complete sentences. Tell students to consult the list of irregular verbs on page 110 if they're not sure of the past participles of these verbs.
- Look at the example sentence in exercise 1 with the class.
- Students complete the sentences with the present perfect form of the verbs in brackets. Remind them to consult the list of irregular verbs on page 110 if they're not sure of the past participle of any of these verbs.
- Check answers with the class.

2
- Go over the example with the students. Note that the tick mark is for an affirmative sentence and the cross is for a negative sentence.
- Students write present perfect sentences with the prompts given.
- Check answers with the class.

3
- Check that students remember the meaning of the words *raise money*, *raffle* and *charity badges*.
- Read the first two sentences of the text with the class, looking at the example.
- Students complete the rest of the text with the present perfect form of the verbs in brackets.
- Check answers with the class.

ever and *never*

All Clear Rules

Read the sentences in the grammar table with the class and ask students to translate them.
Read the All Clear Rules with the class.

4
- Look at the example with the class.
- Students write questions with the present perfect and *ever*.
- Check answers with the class.

5
- Practice the pronunciation of the questions in exercise 4, paying attention to stress and intonation.
- Point out that the short answers to questions in the present perfect are *Yes, I/you/they/we have.*; *Yes, he/she/it has.* and *No, I/you/they/we haven't.*; *No, he/she/it hasn't.* We do not repeat the main verb.
- Encourage students to ask a follow-up question if their partner's answer is *yes*, eg *When did you sell raffle tickets for charity? I sold raffle tickets at a fundraising dinner last year.*
- Students ask and answer the questions in exercise 4 in pairs.
- Ask some students to report back their partner's answers using the third person.

6
- Students choose the correct words to complete the conversations.
- Check answers with the class.

Mixed-ability solutions

Students who need extra help: Exercise 1. Write the correct form of *have* on the board for each question. Students just add the past participle.

Fast finishers: Exercise 3. Students write three things that they have done today, two true and one false. They then show their sentences to their partner who has to guess the false sentence.

Lesson Aims:

Students learn and practise asking questions with *How long … ?* and the present perfect and answering with the present perfect and *for* or *since*.

Grammar

How long … ? with *for* and *since*

Warmer

Write on the board:

1 *She has been a teacher for 20 years. She likes her job a lot.*

2 *She was a teacher for 20 years. Now she works for a charity.*

Ask which tenses the underlined verbs are.

Ask if she is still a teacher in sentence 1 and then in sentence 2.

Explain that we can use the present perfect to talk about situations that started in the past and continue now. Ask students to translate statement 1. Elicit whether the verb tenses are the same in English and their own language.

7
- Read through the grammar table with the class. Ask students to translate the sentences. Make sure that students understand that the question and answers refer to a situation that is still continuing.
- Check that students understand the difference between *a period of time* and *a point in time*.
- Students choose the correct words to complete the rules.
- Check answers with the class.

8
- Look at the examples in the table with the class. Ask why we say *for three weeks* but *since 2010*.
- Students copy and complete the table with the time expressions in the box.
- Check answers with the class.

9
- Look at the example with the class. Elicit why the answer is *since* and not *for*.
- Students complete the sentences with *for* or *since*.
- Check answers with the class.

10
- Look at the example with the class. Explain that they must begin the question with *How long* and put the verb in the present perfect interrogative.
- Ask the class to translate the question and make sure that they understand that it refers to the time up to now.
- Students write questions with *How long* … .
- Check answers with the class.

11
- Read the example with the class. Elicit how to say the same thing as *for two years* with *since*.
- Practise the pronunciation of the questions in exercise 10, emphasizing the stressed syllables and weak form /həv/.
- Students ask and answer the questions in pairs.
- Ask some pairs to report their partner's answers using the third person.

12
- Students complete the text with *for* or *since*.
- Check answers with the class.

All Clear Grammar

13
- Tell students that this is a cumulative check of the grammar in Units 1 to 5.
- As this exercise is quite challenging, you may want students to do it in pairs.
- Students choose the correct words to complete the text.
- Check answers with the class.

14 2.04
- Play the audio. Students listen and check their answers.
- Check answers with the class. This is a good moment to check they have understood the new grammar and to review the grammar from the previous units.

Mixed-ability solutions

Students who need extra help: Exercise 11. Students write their answer to each question first.

Fast finishers: Exercise 12. Students write three sentences about someone they admire a lot.

Self-study and extra practice

Workbook
- Grammar, pages 34–5
- Grammar Reference and Practice, pages 74–5

Teacher's Resource File
- All Clear Basics, pages 23–4
- Grammar Consolidation, page 18
- Grammar Extension, page 20
- Language Excellence, pages 9–10

Digital Activities
- Student's Digital Material

How long …? with *for* and *since*

Present perfect with *for* and *since*

How long has she worked at the school?
She's worked at the school **since** 2013.
She's worked at the school **for** three years.

7 **Look at the sentences in the table and complete the rules. Write the correct words in your notebook.**

a) We use ***for*** / ***since*** with a period of time.
b) We use ***for*** / ***since*** with a point in time.

Exercise 7
a for
b since

8 **Copy and complete the table with the time expressions in the box.**

2010 2 pm a long time a month April I was born last night Saturday this morning three weeks two hours

for	*since*
three weeks	*2010*

Exercise 8
for: a long time, a month, three weeks (example), two hours
since: 2010 (example), 2pm, April, I was born, last night, Saturday, this morning,

9 **Complete the sentences with *for* or *since*.**

I've lived in Valencia *since* I was born.
1 Rob's been at home … two hours.
2 I haven't played tennis … last August.
3 He hasn't done a sponsored walk … he was 13.
4 My sister has known her best friend … a long time.

Exercise 9
1 for
2 since
3 since
4 for

10 **Write complete questions with *How long …?* in your notebook.**

you / be / at this school?
How long have you been at this school?
1 you / know / your best friend?
2 you / study / English?
3 you / have / your mobile phone?
4 you / live / in your flat?
5 you and your friends / play / football?

Exercise 10
1 How long have you known your best friend?
2 How long have you studied English?
3 How long have you had your mobile phone?
4 How long have you lived in your flat?
5 How long have you and your friends been at this school?

11 **In pairs, ask and answer the questions in exercise 10.**

How long have you been at this school?
I've been at this school for two years.

12 **Complete the text using *for* or *since*.**

My hero is my grandfather. He's 65 years old. He loves football and he has watched every Arsenal game [1]… 1955. He hasn't missed a game [2]… the day he got married – it was a Saturday. He's been married [3]… over 40 years and he and my grandma have lived with us [4]… five years. He loves music and he's been a fan of jazz [5]… he was a teenager. He's the coolest grandfather in the world.

Exercise 12
1 since
2 since
3 for
4 for
5 since

All Clear Grammar
1 2 3 4 5 6 7 8 9

13 **Write the correct words in your notebook.**

[1]**Do / Have** you know someone you really admire? I do. My best friend, Jenny. We've known each other since we [2]**start / started** primary school and we've been best friends [3]**for / since** ten years. Jenny loves [4]**help / helping** other people. She [5]**is raising / has raised** lots of money for charity in her life. She has washed cars and [6]**sells / has sold** cakes. I've done a sponsored swim with her to raise money for Save the Children. We think it's the [7]**more / most** important charity in the world. The only thing Jenny has [8]**never / ever** done is a sponsored walk, but she's going to do one this summer. She's fantastic!

Exercise 13
1 Do
2 started
3 for
4 helping
5 has raised
6 has sold
7 most
8 never

14 2.04 **Listen and check your answers.**

Vocabulary

make and *do*

Exercise 1
Students' own answers

1 Look at the words and phrases. How do you say them in your language?

a decision • a mistake • charity work • exercise • friends • homework • money • nothing • someone a favour • someone happy • someone laugh • your best

2 2.05 Copy and complete the table with the words in exercise 1 in your notebook. Listen and repeat the words.

do	make
charity work	

Exercise 2
do: charity work (example), exercise, homework, nothing, someone a favour, your best
make: a decision, a mistake, friends, money, someone happy, someone laugh

Exercise 3
1 do homework
2 do exercise
3 make friends
4 make money
5 do charity work
The expressions *make a decision, make a mistake, do nothing, do someone a favour, make someone happy, make someone laugh* and *do your best* are not in the pictures.

3 Match pictures 1–5 with *make* or *do* and a phrase from exercise 1 in your notebook. Which expressions are not in the pictures?

1 

2 

3 

4 

5 

Exercise 4
1 makes
2 make
3 made
4 do
5 do
6 made
7 do
8 make

4 Complete the questions with the correct form of *make* or *do*.

Have you ever *done* any charity work?

1 What … you happy?
2 Which people … you laugh?
3 Have you ever … a mistake?
4 How often do you … someone a favour?
5 How often do you … exercise?
6 Have you ever … a difficult decision?
7 Where do you usually … your homework?
8 What's the best way to … a lot of money?

Listening

Exercise 5
1 She's an actress and a pop singer.
2 Selena Gomez and The Scene

5 2.06 Listen to the programme and answer the questions in your notebook. Then check your answers.

1 Who is Selena Gomez?
2 What is her band called?

Exercise 6
1 since she was a child
2 Puerto Rico
3 2009
4 Ghana
5 a 14-year-old boy; because he wanted to go to school but couldn't

6 Listen again and answer the questions.

1 How long has Selena been famous?
2 Where is Island Dog?
3 What year did she become a UNICEF Goodwill Ambassador?
4 What country did she visit first with UNICEF?
5 Who does she remember from her first visit? Why?

Vocabulary Reference

Lesson Aims:

Students learn and practise collocations using *make* and *do*.
Students listen to a documentary about a UNICEF Goodwill Ambassador and identify general and specific information.

Vocabulary

make and *do*

Warmer

Ask students if they did any homework last night and how much they did. Once you've got some answers, write *do homework* on the board. Then ask a couple of students if they made their beds yesterday and write *make your bed* on the board. Elicit the translation of both expressions. Explain that the verbs *make* and *do* are often translated by the same verb in the students' own language. Tell students that they need to learn the expressions with *make* and *do* individually as there are no hard-and-fast rules.

1
- Students translate the words.

2 2.05
- In pairs, students decide whether we use *make* or *do* with the words and phrases in exercise 1.
- Students copy and complete the table.
- Check answers with the class.
- Play the audio. Students listen and repeat the words.

3
- Students look at the pictures and describe what they can see.
- Students match the pictures with *make* or *do* and a phrase from exercise 1. They then identify which expressions are not in the pictures.
- Check answers with the class.

4
- Look at the example with the class.
- Students complete the questions with the correct form of *make* or *do*.
- Check answers with the class.

Extra activity

Students ask and answer the questions in pairs.

Listening

Warmer

Introduce the idea of a UNICEF Goodwill Ambassador (see *Cultural note*).

5 2.06
- Students look at the picture and discuss the questions in pairs and write their answers.
- Play the audio. Students listen to the programme and check their answers.

6
- Students read the questions.
- Play the audio again. Students listen again for the answers to the questions.
- Check answers with the class.

Cultural note

UNICEF was originally called the United Nations International Children's Emergency Fund. Its name has since been shortened to United National Children's Fund but it generally known as UNICEF. It provides humanitarian aid to children and mothers in developing countries. UNICEF Goodwill Ambassadors are celebrities who use their fame to draw attention to important issues relating to children around the world. Their work may take the form of public appearances and talks, visits to troubled regions and use of their political access to support UNICEF causes.

Mixed-ability solutions

Students who need extra help: Exercise 6. Write the following options on the board.

1 *for three years / since she was a child*
2 *Puerto Rico / Ghana*
3 *2005 / 2009*
4 *Puerto Rico / Ghana*
5 *a 14-year-old boy / a 4-year-old boy; He didn't have enough food. / He couldn't go to school.*

Fast finishers: Exercise 4. Students write three more questions using the expressions from exercise 1.

Self-study and extra practice

Workbook
- Vocabulary, page 33
- Vocabulary Reference, page 88

Teacher's Resource File
- All Clear Basics, page 22
- Vocabulary Consolidation, page 17
- Vocabulary Extension, page 19
- Key Competences: Listening, page 10

Digital Activities
- Student's Digital Material

Lesson Aims:

Students learn and practise functional language to make requests and offers.

Speaking

Making requests and offers (2) / A fundraising event

Warmer

Ask students if they have ever participated in a fundraising event, eg by selling raffle tickets, helping out at a jumble sale, etc.

Model Dialogue

1 2.07

- Read the question with the class.
- Play the audio. Students listen to and read the dialogue.
- Elicit the answer to the question.

2
- Play the audio again. Students listen again and this time repeat the dialogue.
- Focus on and explain the expressions *Do you have a minute?*; *What can I do for you?*; *Would you like to … ?* and *I'll give you …* . Get the class to pay attention to stress and intonation.

Speaking Task

1 Talk about a fundraising event

Students read the information and choose one of the events. Alternatively, they use their own ideas.

2 Prepare a dialogue

Students look at the Model Dialogue and change the words in blue to make their own dialogue.

3 Speak

Students practise their dialogues in pairs.

Mixed-ability solutions

Students who need extra help: Speaking Task. Students write out their dialogue before they do step 3.

Fast finishers: Speaking Task. Students act out another dialogue about a different fundraising event. If possible, they do this without looking at the Model Dialogue.

Self-study and extra practice

Workbook
- Speaking, page 124

Teacher's Resource File
- Key Competences: Speaking, pages 27–8

Digital Activities
- Student's Digital Material

Speaking

Making requests and offers (2) / A fundraising event

Exercise 1
£1 a mile (£5 in total)

1 2.07 **Listen to the dialogue. How much money does Mr Moran offer Yasmin?**

Model Dialogue

Mr Moran: Hello, Yasmin.

Yasmin: Hi, Mr Moran. Do you have a minute?

Mr Moran: Sure. What can I do for you?

Yasmin: Well, I'm raising money for charity.

Mr Moran: Oh yes?

Yasmin: I've decided to do a sponsored walk for five miles.

Mr Moran: Sounds fun.

Yasmin: Would you like to sponsor me?

Mr Moran: Yes, OK. Which charity is it for?

Yasmin: Oxfam.

Mr Moran: OK. I'll give you £1 a mile.

Yasmin: Great. Thanks.

Mr Moran: And when is it?

Yasmin: Next Saturday.

Mr Moran: Well, good luck.

Yasmin: Thanks, Mr Moran.

2 **Listen again and repeat the dialogue.**

Speaking Task

1 Talk about a fundraising event

Choose one of the events below or use your own ideas.

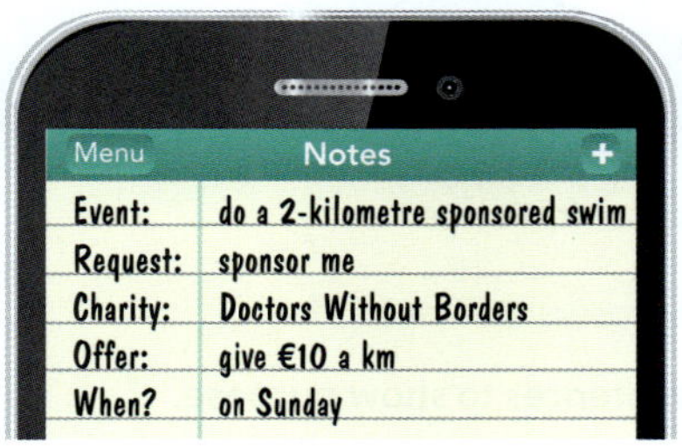

2 Prepare a dialogue

Look at the Model Dialogue and change the words in blue.

3 Speak

In pairs, practise your dialogue.

What can I do for you?

Well, I'm raising money for charity.

Useful Language

Making requests and offers (2)

Do you have a minute?
  Sure. **What can I do for you?**
Would you like to sponsor me?
  I'll give you £1 a mile.

Writing

A magazine article

1 2.08 **Read the Model Text and listen. Answer the questions in your notebook.**

1 How have they raised money?
2 Why did they decide on this fundraising idea?
3 Which charity have the students raised money for?
4 Why did they choose this charity?

Model Text

Students from Highbury School have donated over £1,500 to charity. Organizer Harriet Jones said, 'We all enjoy cycling so we did a 10km sponsored cycle ride at the local park to raise money.' Parents and friends were at the park to support the students.

The students have decided to donate the money to the WWF to help endangered animals. Student Ben Davies said, 'We are supporting this charity because many of us have studied endangered animals at school.'

Headteacher Marion Kemp said, 'This school has done charity work for years but we've never done a cycle ride before. I hope it becomes an annual event because it has been a real success.'

Exercise 1
1 by doing a sponsored cycle ride
2 because they all enjoy cycling
3 the WWF
4 because many of them have studied endangered animals at school

2 **Look at the All Clear Tips and translate the rule. Then find examples in the text. Write the rule in your notebook.**

All Clear Tips

Connectors of purpose:
***to* + infinitive**

*We did a 10km sponsored cycle race **to raise** money.*
We use *to* + infinitive to write sentences showing purpose.

Exercise 2
Students' own answers
… we did a 10km sponsored cycle ride at the local park **to raise** money.
Parents and friends were at the park **to support** the students.
The students have decided to donate the money to the WWF **to help** endangered animals.

3 **Rewrite the sentences to show purpose.**

I did a sponsored swim. I raised money for Oxfam.
I did a sponsored swim to raise money for Oxfam.
1 I'm going to Rome. I'm visiting my cousin.
2 Every day my sister goes to the sports centre. She plays basketball.
3 Andy went to the supermarket. He bought some milk.
4 My best friend has sent me a text. She has invited me to her party.

Writing Task

1 Plan
Make notes about a real or imaginary charity event and include:

Introduction: *the organizers, the amount of money raised, description of the event*
Description of charity: *which charity, reasons for choosing it*
Final comment: *the success of the event, any plans to repeat in the future*

2 Write
Use the Model Text, your notes and this structure:

Paragraph 1: Introduction
Paragraph 2: Description of charity
Paragraph 3: Final comment

3 Check
☑ present perfect, *for* and *since*
☑ fundraising ideas, *make* and *do*
☑ *to* + infinitive

Exercise 3
1 I'm going to Rome to visit my cousin.
2 Every day my sister goes to the sports centre to play basketball.
3 Andy went to the supermarket to buy some milk.
4 My best friend has sent me a text to invite me to her party.

Lesson Aims:

Students practise the use of *to* + infinitive to express purpose.
Students write a magazine article about a charity event.

Writing

A magazine article

Warmer

Students look at the picture in the Student's Book. Ask them what they can see and what they think the people in the picture have been doing.

1 2.08

- Students read the questions.
- Play the audio. Students read and listen to the article and answer the questions.
- Check answers with the class.

Extra activity

Students find examples of the following tenses in the article and to say why there are used: present perfect, past simple, present simple, present continuous.

All Clear Tips

2
- Read through the All Clear Tips with the class.
- Students translate the rule.
- Emphasize that we use *to* + infinitive to show purpose.
- Students find examples of *to* + infinitive in the Model Text.
- Students write the rule in their notebooks.

3
- Read the example with the class. Make sure they understand how the two sentences have been joined.
- Students rewrite the sentences using *to* + infinitive to show purpose.
- Check answers with the class.

Writing Task

1 Plan

Read the notes with the class. Students make notes about a real or imaginary charity event of their own.

2 Write

Look at the structure with the class. Students use their notes to write their article. Emphasize that they should try to use *to* + infinitive to show purpose.

3 Check

Encourage students to check their work, paying particular attention to the points mentioned.

Web info

Type these words in your search engine for more ideas for fundraising activities: 'CAFOD + fundraising ideas'

Mixed-ability solutions

Students who need extra help: Writing Task. Students just complete the notes in step 1.

Fast finishers: Writing Task. Students read their partner's article and ask them some follow-up questions about the event and the charity it was for.

Self-study and extra practice

Workbook

- Writing Guide, pages 110–1

Teacher's Resource File

- Key Competences: Writing, page 10

Lesson Aims:

Students learn about the British social reformer Elizabeth Fry and why she is considered a heroine.
Students practise the pronunciation of contractions.

Culture Reading

Famous heroes and heroines

Warmer

Write *Mother Teresa of Calcutta*, *Angelina Jolie* and *Shakira* on the board and ask students what they have in common. Elicit the fact that they are all women who are (or were) involved in helping people in need. Ask if they know what each of them has done. (Mother Teresa cared for the poorest of the poor and AIDS patients in India. Angelina Jolie is a UNHCR Special Envoy for refugee crises and Shakira, through her Pies Descalzos Foundation, helps poor and impoverished children in Colombia.)

2.09

- Students read the questions.
- Play the audio. Students read and listen to the text and answer the questions.
- Check answers with the class.

Extra activity

Ask students what the following numbers in the text refer to: 1780, 12, 1800, 1818, 1840.

Pronunciation

Contractions

a 2.10

- Play the audio. Students listen and repeat the sentences. If necessary, write the contractions on the board and isolate them for specific practice.

b 2.11

- Play the audio. Students listen and repeat the sentences. Once again, if necessary, write the contractions on the board and isolate them for specific practice.

Cultural note

There were several prominent social reformers in Victorian Britain. They campaigned against the appalling working conditions of the Industrial Revolution and the problems caused by the rapid emergence of large cities produced by the migration of people from the countryside to urban areas. One of the most famous reformers was the Earl of Shaftesbury, a politician who fought for the protection of children in factories and mines, public health legislation and for the proper treatment of the mentally ill.

Web info

Type these words in your search engine for an interactive page about Elizabeth Fry, including video and an interactive game: 'BBC schools primary history + Elizabeth Fry'

Mixed-ability solutions

Students who need extra help: Reading text.
Write the following options on the board:

1 *Because she had a good job / Because she worked to help other people*
2 *a banker / a prison officer*
3 *She helped them when they were ill. / She brought food and clothes for children in prison and taught their mothers to read.*
4 *1818: She became famous. / She became the first woman to talk to the British parliament.*
1840: She started a school for nurses. / She became a nurse.

Fast-finishers: Reading text. Students imagine they are Elizabeth Fry and have seen the children in prison. They write a diary entry describing what they have seen, how they feel and what they are going to do.

Self-study and extra practice

Workbook

- Culture: Reading and Listening, page 97

Culture Reading

EXTRA

FOLIO

Search

Main page
Contents
Help
Contact
Tools
Languages
English
Español
Français
Italiano

Download PDF
Create a book
Print Version

File Edit History View Navigate Tools Help

Folio home > Search > EDIT > SAVE > PRINT

Famous heroes and heroines

Elizabeth Fry

Elizabeth Fry is one of the most famous women in British history. All her life she worked to help the poor, especially poor people who were in prison.

Her early life

Elizabeth was born on 21st May 1780 into a family with 11 other siblings. Sadly, her mother died when Elizabeth was 12 years old and she had to look after her brothers and sisters. Elizabeth married Joseph Fry, a wealthy banker, in 1800 and they went to live in London.

Her prison work

When she was in London, Elizabeth visited Newgate Prison. There she met children who were living in prison because they had no home. The prison was dirty and terrible. She was so shocked by her visit that she went back with food and clothes for the children. She started a school and taught their mothers to read.

Fame

Elizabeth's work made her famous. In 1818, she became the first woman to talk to the British parliament. Queen Victoria gave her money. In 1840, she started a school for nurses which helped change the profession of nursing.

2.09 **Read and listen. Then answer the questions in your notebook.**

1 Why is Elizabeth Fry famous?
2 What did her husband do?
3 How did she help prisoners?
4 Why are 1818 and 1840 important dates in Elizabeth Fry's life?

Reading text exercise

1 because all her life she worked to help the poor
2 He was a banker.
3 She gave food and clothes to the children, started a school and taught the women to read.
4 1818: She became the first woman to talk to the British parliament.
1840: She started a school for nurses which helped change the profession of nursing.

Pronunciation

Contractions

a 2.10 **Listen and repeat.**

1 Elizabeth's a famous woman.
2 You haven't finished your homework.
3 She hasn't got a badge.
4 He's raised over €1,000.

b 2.11 **Listen and repeat the sentences.**

Unit 5 Language Reference

Vocabulary Fundraising ideas

collect money • do a sponsored swim • have a barbecue • have a bring and buy sale • make a charity CD • organize a jumble sale • sell badges • sell cakes • sell raffle tickets • wash cars

make and *do*

do your best • do charity work • make a decision • do exercise • do someone a favour • make friends • make someone happy • do homework • make someone laugh • make a mistake • make money • do nothing

Grammar Present perfect

Affirmative	Negative	Interrogative	Short answers
I / You **have** raise**d** the money.	I / You **have not** raise**d** the money.	**Have** I / you raise**d** the money?	Yes, I / you **have**.
He / She / It **has** raise**d** the money.	He / She / It **has not** raise**d** the money.	**Has** he / she / it raise**d** the money?	No, he / she / it **has not**.
We / You / They **have** raise**d** the money.	We / You / They **have not** raise**d** the money.	**Have** we / you / they raise**d** the money?	Yes, we / you / they **have**.

ever / *never*

Have you **ever** lived in France?
I have **never** lived in France.

How long…? with *for* and *since*

How long has she been a Goodwill Ambassador?
She's been a Goodwill Ambassador **since** August 2009. She's been a Goodwill Ambassador **for** more than a year.

for (a period in time)	*since* (a point in time)
a month a long time three weeks two hours	2010 2 pm April I was born last night Saturday this morning

Speaking Making requests and offers (2)

Do you have a minute? — Sure. **What can I do for you**?

Would you like to sponsor me? — **I'll give** you £1 a mile.

Unit 5 Progress Check

Vocabulary Fundraising ideas

1 Match 1–5 with a–e to make sentences. Write them in your notebook.

1 I bought a charity
2 Pop stars are making a
3 My friends are washing
4 There was a woman collecting
5 We've organized

a) money for the Red Cross.
b) charity CD to raise money for famine victims.
c) raffle ticket to help Syrian refugees.
d) a jumble sale for the RSPCA.
e) cars for charity.

Exercise 1
1 c
2 b
3 e
4 a
5 d

make and *do*

2 Complete the sentences with the correct form of *make* or *do*.

1 I've just … some exercise. I'm really tired.
2 I always … my homework before I watch TV.
3 I … lots of friends at the summer camp last year.
4 Can you … me a favour? I really need some help.
5 I think I failed the test. I … too many mistakes.

Exercise 2
1 done
2 do
3 made
4 do
5 made

Grammar Present perfect

3 Complete the sentences with the present perfect form of the verbs in brackets.

1 Dan … (raise) £200 for charity.
2 We … (decide) to do a sponsored walk next month.
3 … you … (sponsor) Luis for his charity bike ride?
4 I … (never / do) a sponsored skydive.
5 Jo … (not donate) any clothes to the bring and buy sale.

Exercise 3
1 's raised
2 've decided
3 Have (you) sponsored
4 've never done
5 hasn't donated

4 Correct the sentences.

1 Beth have never done a sponsored swim.
2 Have you raised ever money for charity?
3 I hasn't visited India, but I want to.
4 Have you see the new adventure film?
5 Alex was collected lots of money for charity.

Exercise 4
1 Beth ~~have~~ **has** never done a sponsored swim.
2 Have you **ever raised** money for charity?
3 I ~~hasn't~~ **haven't** visited India, but I want to.
4 Have you ~~see~~ **seen** the new adventure film?
5 Alex ~~was~~ **has** collected lots of money for charity.

for and *since*

5 Complete the sentences with *for* or *since*.

1 I've known my best friend … 2006.
2 Carla's done charity work … she was 12.
3 You've studied … three hours. Well done!
4 I haven't eaten … this morning. I'm hungry.
5 Tom's been here … a long time. He arrived early.

Exercise 5
1 since
2 since
3 for
4 since
5 for

Check your answers

Write your scores for exercises 1–5 in your notebook. What did you get for:

- fundraising ideas?
- *make* and *do*?
- present perfect?
- *for* and *since*?

Extra Practice

If you need extra practice, go to:

Unit 5 Grammar Reference
Unit 5 Vocabulary Reference
Unit 5 Grammar Exercises
Unit 5 Vocabulary Exercises

All Clear Self-Check

Correct the activities with the class. Students who need extra revision and practice can go to:

Workbook
- Unit 5 Revision, page 36
- Grammar Reference and Practice, pages 74–5
- Vocabulary Reference, page 88

Student's Digital Material
www.allclear.macmillan.es

6 Amazing journeys

Overview

Unit objectives and key competences

- Understand, memorize and correctly use vocabulary related to travel and extreme adjectives CLC, DC
- Identify the gist and main ideas in a text about a young disabled traveller CLC
- Learn about a man who has overcome physical difficulties to travel the world in a wheelchair CAE, SIE
- Understand, contrast and correctly use grammar structures related to the present perfect and past simple and quantity CLC, L2L
- Identify specific information through a listening activity about a young man who sailed around the world CLC
- Learn about a man who sailed solo around the world CAE, SIE
- Use appropriate functional language to talk about a journey CLC, SCC
- Write a description of a journey CLC, SIE, CAE
- Identify specific information in a text about the California gold rush CLC
- Learn about the California gold rush CAE
- Assimilate the All Clear Tips and study the Language Reference from the unit CLC, L2L, SIE
- Identify areas of language which need improvement and use ICT for extra practice DC, CLC, L2L

More information on Key Competences, page v

Linguistic content

Grammar

- Present perfect simple and past simple
- Quantity

Recycled grammar

- Comparatives and superlatives (Unit 4)
- *too* and *enough* (Unit 4)
- *for* and *since* (Unit 5)

Main vocabulary

- Travel: *arrive*, *buy a guidebook*, etc
- Extreme adjectives: *amazing*, *awful*, etc

Functional language

- Talk about a journey / At the station

Pronunciation

- The sounds /ɜː/ /iː/ /ʌ/

Skills: learning outcomes

- **Reading** Understand specific information in a profile of a young man in a wheelchair who travels around the world. The student can re-read the more difficult parts, page 63
- **Listening** Understand an informal conversation in which a person describes an event. Delivered slowly and with clarity, page 66
- **Speaking** Participate effectively in a face-to-face informal dialogue, talking about a journey, page 67
- **Writing** Write a description of a journey with the main points set out in a logical order, page 68
- **Reading** Understand specific information in a clearly structured text about the California gold rush. The student can re-read the more difficult parts, page 69

Lifelong learning skills and content-based learning

Life skills

- **Recognizing diversity** Different ways of travelling and seeing the world, pages 63 and 66
- **Social development** Write about favourite sports, page 68
- **Socio-cultural awareness** Learn about the California gold rush, page 69

Learning strategies

- Analyse examples to identify which tenses are used and with which function, page 64

Cross-curricular content

- Geography: countries and places around the world, throughout the unit
- Language: sequencing events in a narrative, page 68
- History: the California gold rush, page 69

Further materials and evaluation

Digital material

- Student's and Teacher's Resource Centres
- Teacher's Presentation Kit
- Student's Digital Material: interactive vocabulary and grammar activities
- Video *Literature* (Revision Units 4–6, page 74)

Student's website www.macmillansecondary.es

Workbook

- Vocabulary, pages 38–9
- Vocabulary Reference, page 89
- Grammar, pages 40–1
- Grammar Reference and Practice, pages 76–7
- Revision, page 42
- Culture: Reading and Listening, page 98
- Writing Guide, pages 112–3
- Speaking, page 125

Teacher's Resource File

Multi-level Materials Bank

- All Clear Basics, pages 26–30
- Vocabulary and Grammar Consolidation and Extension, pages 21–4
- Language Excellence, pages 11–2
- Translation and Dictation, pages 6 and 15

Lifelong Learning

- Digital Competence, pages 11–2
- Culture Video Material, pages 3–4
- Study Skills, pages 1–12

Evaluation and Key Competences

- Evaluation Rubrics, pages 1–7
- Key Competences, pages 11–2 and 29–30

Content-based Learning

- CLIL, pages 1–10
- Macmillan Readers, pages 1–7

Evaluation material

- Unit 6 end-of-unit test: Basic, Standard and Extra
- End-of-term test, Units 4–6: Basic, Standard and Extra
- CEFR Skills Exam Generator

Web info

Tips to find extra information on: Albert Casals' travels in a wheelchair, Mike Perham's round-the-world sail, bus tours in New York, the California gold rush, the classic Charlie Chaplin silent film *The Gold Rush* (about the gold rush in Alaska, not California)

Extra help for weaker students

Teacher's Resource File: All Clear Basics, pages 26–30

Material for fast finishers

Workbook: Grammar Extension, page 43
Teacher's Resource File: Vocabulary Extension, page 23
Teacher's Resource File: Grammar Extension, page 24
Teacher's Resource File: Language Excellence, pages 11–2

6 Amazing journeys

Objectives

Vocabulary	Travel; extreme adjectives
Grammar	Present perfect and past simple; quantity
Speaking	Talking about a journey
Writing	A description of a journey

Vocabulary

Travel

1 2.12 **Listen and repeat the words. Match them with pictures 1–12.**

arrive • buy a guidebook • buy souvenirs • come back home • get off a train • get on a train • have adventures • meet people • pack a suitcase • plan a trip • send postcards • set off

Exercise 1
1 get on a train
2 have adventures
3 send postcards
4 plan a trip
5 pack a suitcase
6 come back home
7 buy a guidebook
8 set off
9 get off a train
10 meet people
11 buy souvenirs
12 arrive

1 
2 
3 
4 
5 
6 
7 

8 
9 
10 
11 
12 

2 **Write the correct words in your notebook.**

Hi Sarah,

We're in Italy and it's really exciting! As usual, I (1) **packed / got on** my suitcase at the last minute. ☺ We (2) **set off / got on** from home on Sunday morning and we (3) **bought / planned** a guidebook at the airport. We (4) **arrived / set off** in Rome in the afternoon. Suzy and I have (5) **met / had** lots of adventures. On the first day, we (6) **met / sent** some Spanish boys at the hotel and we went to the Colosseum with them today. At the moment, we're (7) **getting off / planning** a trip to Naples. I've taken lots of photos to show you when we (8) **get off / come back** home next week. I've (9) **bought / had** you a great souvenir – a Roma football shirt!

Kate

Exercise 2
1 packed
2 set off
3 bought
4 arrived
5 had
6 met
7 planning
8 come back
9 bought

3 2.13 **Listen to Zoe and Chas. What souvenirs have they bought?**

Exercise 3
Chas bought a T-shirt.
Zoe bought a baseball cap.

4 **In pairs, ask and answer questions about travelling.**

Have you ever bought any souvenirs?

Yes, I bought a keyring in Paris.

Vocabulary Reference

Lesson Aims:

Students learn and practise vocabulary related to travel.
Students listen to two young people talking about what souvenirs they have bought and identify the souvenirs.

Vocabulary

Travel

Warmer

Ask students to think about when they go on holiday. Ask them what preparations they make before they go away and what they do while they are on holiday. Try to elicit some of the key vocabulary.

1 2.12

- Play the audio. Students listen and repeat the words.
- Draw attention to the silent letters in *g(u)idebook* and *su(i)tcase*.
- Check the class understands the vocabulary by asking them to translate each expression. (*Set off* may be the most problematic expression.)
- Students match the words with the pictures.
- Check answers with the class.

2

- Students choose the correct words to complete the email.
- Check answers with the class.

3 2.13

- Ask students to think of souvenirs that people often buy on holiday.
- Students listen and identify the souvenirs Zoe and Chas have bought.
- Check answers with the class.

4

- Model the pronunciation of the example in the speech bubbles.
- Elicit more questions using some of the expressions in exercise 1, eg *Have you ever sent a postcard?; Have you ever met any interesting people on a journey?; Have you ever bought a guidebook?*
- Students ask and answer questions about travelling in pairs.

Mixed-ability solutions

Students who need extra help: Exercise 3.
Write the following items on the board. Students choose the correct ones.
baseball cap, handbag, mug, T-shirt

Fast finishers: Exercise 2. Students answer the following questions.
Why didn't Kate prepare well? Give two reasons.
How did she travel?
Where is she now?
Name three things she has done.

Self-study and extra practice

- Vocabulary, page 38
- Vocabulary Reference, page 89

Teacher's Resource File

- All Clear Basics, page 26
- Vocabulary Consolidation, page 21
- Vocabulary Extension, page 23

Lesson Aims:

Students read an article about a disabled person who has travelled to many countries for general and specific information.

Reading

A personal profile

Warmer

Brainstorm with students why it is difficult to travel if you use a wheelchair.

Word Check

Check students understand the new words: *wheelchair*, *hitchhike*, *freedom*. Explain any they don't know.

1 • Students read the text quickly and make a list of the ways in which Albert isn't a typical young man.

2 2.14

- Play the audio. Students read and listen to the text in detail and check their answers.
- Check answers with the class and discuss them. Students may not all have the same opinion of what is typical and not typical.

3 • Students read the questions.
- Students read the text again and answer the questions.
- Check answers with the class.

4 • Students look at the numbers in pairs and try to say what they refer to from memory.
- Students refer back to the text to check and complete their answers.
- Check answers with the class.

All Clear Facts

Read the fact with the class. Ask the class if they would ever consider hitchhiking and why or why not.

Extra activity

In pairs, students write five questions to ask Albert. Ask a good student to come to the front of the class and play the role of Albert.

Cultural note

Albert Casals decided to go to New Zealand because one day, as he was looking at Google Earth, he decided to find out what was exactly on the other side of the world to his home village of Esparreguera. After doing some calculations, he found out that it was a farm in New Zealand.

Web info

Type these words in your search engine for more information about Albert Casals in English: 'Albert Casals + english as barxas'

Mixed-ability solutions

Students who need extra help: Exercise 3. Write the following options on the board:

1 *books / documentaries*
2 *more than 80 / he doesn't know*
3 *yes / no*
4 *by singing in the street / by working and doing tricks with his wheelchair*
5 *he can often travel free / it eliminates fear*
6 *love, freedom, luck and happiness / his girlfriend and his family*

Fast finishers: Exercise 3. Students write two or three sentences expressing their opinion of Albert Casals and why they have that opinion.

Self-study and extra practice

Teacher's Resource File

- Key Competences: Reading, page 11

Lesson Aims:

Students learn the difference in use between the present perfect and the past simple and practise using them.

Grammar

Present perfect and past simple

Warmer

Say and write on the board:
I have travelled to France many times.
I went to France last year.
Ask students which tense is used in each sentence and try to elicit why it is used. (The present perfect is used for an indefinite past time; the past simple is used for a definite past time.)

1 • Read the sentences in the grammar table with the class. Students identify the tenses.
• Ask students which of the verbs describes a condition that started in the past but continues in the present (*has been*).

2 • Students match the sentences with the uses.
• Check answers with the class.
• Ask students to translate the sentences in the table and compare them with their own language. Ask them if they use the same tenses in their language. Emphasize that in English we use the past simple for completed actions at a definite time in the past even if they happened very recently, eg *He left two minutes ago.*, not *He ~~has left~~ two minutes ago.*
• You might want to write some more examples on the board and ask students to identify the uses.

3 • Students choose the correct words to complete the sentences.
• To help them, write the following summary on the board.
action at a definite time in the past: past simple
action at an unspecified time in the past: present perfect
action that began in the past but continues in the present: present perfect
• As this is a challenging exercise, you may want students to do it in pairs.
• Check answers with the class, making sure that students understand why each option is correct.

4 • Look at the example with the class. Ask students why the correct tense is *I've lived* and not *I lived*.
• Again, you may want students to do the exercise in pairs as it is quite difficult.
• Check answers with the class. Ask students to explain why they have chosen a particular tense for their answer.

5 • Students complete the questions with the present perfect form of the verbs in brackets. Point out that we use the present perfect for these questions because we are asking about the past in general and not about a specific time.
• Check answers with the class.

6 • Students complete the questions with the past simple form of the verbs in brackets. Point out that we use the past simple here because we are asking about a specific time.
• Check the questions with the class.
• Students then match these questions with the questions in exercise 5.
• Check answers with the class.

Extra activity

Students ask and answer the questions in exercises 5 and 6 in pairs. Tell them to always answer *Yes, I have.* to the first question (*Have you ever … ?*) so that their partner can ask the second question.
Demonstrate the activity with one student before the rest of the class ask and answer the questions in pairs.

7 • Students read the dialogue carefully and decide which tense to use in each gap. They complete the dialogue with the correct form of the verbs in brackets.
• Check answers with the class and help with any problems students are having in correctly using the two tenses.

Mixed-ability solutions

Students who need extra help: Exercise 7.
Write the following summary on the board again.
action at a definite time in the past: past simple
action at an unspecified time in the past: present perfect
action that began in the past but continues in the present: present perfect

Fast finishers: Exercise 7. Students compare their answers in pairs.

Lesson Aims:

Students learn and practise using expressions of quantity.

Grammar

Quantity

Warmer

Students look back at the reading text on page 63 and find expressions related to quantity.

8
- Revise the concept of countable and uncountable with things to hand in the classroom, eg table, pen, water, air.
- Read the sentences in the grammar table with the class and ask students to translate them.
- Remind students of the rule for *some* and *any*.
- Make it clear that *a few* (for countable nouns) and *a little* (for uncountable nouns) are similar in meaning to *some* and do not mean *not much*.
- Elicit which expressions can be used with both countable and uncountable nouns and which can't.
- Students read the sentences in exercise 8 and choose the correct words from the box to complete them.
- Check answers with the class.

9
- Students choose the correct words to complete the text.
- Check answers with the class.

All Clear Grammar

10
- Tell students that this is a cumulative check of the grammar in Units 1 to 6.
- As this exercise is quite challenging, you may want students to do it in pairs.
- Students choose the correct words to complete the dialogue.

11 2.15
- Play the audio. Students listen and check their answers.
- Check answers with the class. This is a good moment to check they have understood the new grammar and to review the grammar from the previous units.

Extra activity

Books closed. Use part of the text as a dictation. Read out the sentences yourself or use the audio.

Mixed-ability solutions

Students who need extra help: Exercise 8. Write the following options on the board.

1 *a little / many*
2 *much / many*
3 *a little / any*
4 *much / many*
5 *a little / much*

Fast finishers: Exercise 9. Write the following prompts on the board.
do / homework, watch / films, drink / milk, eat / rice, buy / sweets
Students write true sentences about what they did yesterday, using an expression of quantity in each one. They then compare their sentences with a partner.

Self-study and extra practice

Workbook
- Grammar, pages 40–1
- Grammar Reference and Practice, pages 76–7

Teacher's Resource File
- All Clear Basics, pages 28–9
- Grammar Consolidation, page 22
- Grammar Extension, page 24
- Language Excellence, pages 11–2

Digital Activities
- Student's Digital Material

Quantity

	Countable nouns	Uncountable nouns
Affirmative	He had **a lot of** adventures.	He made **a lot of** money.
	He had **some** / **a few** adventures.	He made **some** / **a little** money.
Negative	He didn't have **many** / **any** adventures.	He didn't make **much** / **any** money.
Interrogative	**How many** adventures did he have?	**How much** money did he make?
	Did he have **many** / **any** adventures?	Did he make **much** / **any** money?

Exercise 8
1 a lot of
2 many
3 any
4 much
5 a little

8 **Complete the sentences with the words in the box.**

a little	a lot of	any	many	much

1 I've been to … European countries – almost all of them!
2 She didn't see … dolphins on the boat trip – only two in the end!
3 Are there … seats available on the next bus to Liverpool?
4 How … chocolate have you bought?
5 I was ill last week and only ate … food.

Exercise 9
1 some
2 any
3 any
4 a lot of
5 any
6 a little
7 a lot

9 **Write the correct words in your notebook.**

‹ reply | « reply all | delete | save | forward ›

Dear Parents,
Next week is the annual school trip to All Action Adventure Camp for all Year 10 students. All students need to bring (1)**some** / **any** warm clothes for the outdoor activities. They don't need to bring (2)**any** / **much** special equipment for the outdoor activities because the camp will provide everything they need. Students do not need to bring (3)**any** / **some** food. The camp provides all meals with (4)**a lot of** / **many** fresh fruit and vegetables. Most importantly, students shouldn't bring (5)**a little** / **any** gadgets such as mp3 players or mobile phones. The teachers have mobile phones for emergencies.
Students can bring (6)**a little** / **a few** money as there will be an excursion to the local town on the last day.
We're confident that all students will learn a lot and have (7)**a lot** / **a little** of adventures on the trip.
The Teachers

Eastview
HIGH SCHOOL

All Clear Grammar

1 2 3 4 5 6 7 8 9

Exercise 10
1 best
2 Have you ever been?
3 went
4 any
5 didn't like
6 for
7 any
8 too

10 **Write the correct words in your notebook.**

Hailey France is the (1)**best** / **better** country I've ever been to. (2)**Did you ever go** / **Have you ever been**?
Aiden Yes, I (3)**have been** / **went** two years ago.
Hailey Did you eat (4)**much** / **any** frogs' legs?
Aiden Yes, I did. They were awful. I (5)**didn't like** / **haven't liked** them.
Hailey How long did you stay there?
Aiden I was only there (6)**for** / **since** five days.
Hailey And did you buy (7)**any** / **much** souvenirs?
Aiden No, they were (8)**enough** / **too** expensive.

11 2.15 **Listen and check your answers.**

Grammar Reference

Vocabulary

Extreme adjectives

1 2.16 **Listen and repeat the words. How do you say them in your language? Match them with pictures 1–9.**

amazing • awful • boiling • delighted • enormous • exhausted • freezing • terrifying • tiny

Exercise 1

Students' own answers

1 exhausted
2 amazing
3 terrifying
4 boiling
5 tiny
6 enormous
7 awful
8 delighted
9 freezing

2 **Look at the extreme adjectives in exercise 1 and match them with the adjectives in the box.**

bad	big	cold	frightening	good	happy	hot	small	tired

Exercise 2

amazing – good
awful – bad
boiling – hot
delighted – happy
enormous – big
exhausted – tired
freezing – cold
terrifying – frightening
tiny – small

3 **Write the extreme adjective for each sentence in your notebook.**

I don't like flying. It's frightening.
terrifying

1 The journey was really bad.
2 I love Greek food. It's good.
3 It's hot on this bus. Can I open a window?
4 There were 300 people on our flight. The plane was big.
5 Put your coat on. It's cold outside.

Exercise 3

1 awful
2 amazing
3 boiling
4 enormous
5 freezing

4 **Write the correct words in your notebook.**

1 I'm **tiny** / **exhausted** / **freezing**. I'm going to bed early.
2 I'm wearing too many clothes. I'm **boiling** / **freezing** / **awful**.
3 Julie was **delighted** / **tiny** / **exhausted** with her present.
4 That horror film was **terrifying** / **amazing** / **tiny**. I'm never watching it again.
5 The journey was **enormous** / **terrifying** / **awful**. We arrived three hours late.

Exercise 4

1 exhausted
2 boiling
3 delighted
4 terrifying
5 awful

Listening

5 2.17 **Listen to the dialogue about adventurer, Mike Perham. How long did it take Mike to sail around the world?**

Exercise 5

nine months

6 **Listen again. Write true or false in your notebook.**

1 Mike was the youngest person to travel around the world.
2 Mike celebrated his 17th birthday at sea.
3 He had really bad weather in the Indian Ocean.
4 He stopped three times to make repairs to his yacht.
5 He had a terrifying experience with a shark.
6 His ambition is to be the first person to travel around the world by land, sea and air.

Exercise 6

1 false (He was the youngest person to travel around the world *alone*.)
2 true
3 false
4 true
5 false
6 true

Vocabulary Reference

Lesson Aims:

Students learn and practise some extreme adjectives.
Students listen to a conversation about a young adventurer and identify general and specific information.

Vocabulary

Extreme adjectives

Warmer

On the board write *very good*. Ask students if they can think of one adjective which means *very good*. Elicit adjectives such as *great, fantastic, excellent*. Repeat the process with *very bad*.
Explain that we call adjectives such as *great* or *terrible* extreme adjectives.

1 2.16

- Play the audio. Students listen and repeat the words. Make sure that they say them with the correct stress. Also, point out the /aɪ/ in *tiny*.
- Elicit the translation of each adjective and tell students any they don't know.
- Students match the extreme adjectives with the pictures.
- Check answers with the class.

2
- Students match the extreme adjectives in exercise 1 with the adjectives in the box.
- Check answers with the class.

3
- Read the example with the class.
- Students read the sentences and write the extreme adjective for each sentence.
- Check answers with the class.

4
- Students read the sentences and choose the correct words to complete them. You may want to do the first one with the class as an example.
- Check answers with the class.

Extra activity

Students work in pairs. One mimes one of the extreme adjectives and his/her partner says which one it is.

Listening

Warmer

Students tell you what they can see in the picture.

5 2.17

- Students read the question.
- Play the audio. Students listen for the answer to the question.
- Check the answer with the class.

6
- Students read the statements.
- They try to decide if they are true or false from the first time they listened.
- Play the audio again. Students listen again and decide if each statement is true or false.
- Check answers with the class.

Web info

Type these words in your search engine for more information about Mike Perham's round-the-world sail: 'mailonline + british teenager Mike Perham'

Mixed-ability solutions

Students who need extra help: Exercise 3. Write the following options on the board.

1 *awful / delighted*
2 *amazing / enormous*
3 *boiling / exhausted*
4 *enormous / tiny*
5 *freezing / terrifying*

Fast finishers: Exercise 3. Students write three true sentences about themselves using three of the extreme adjectives from exercise 1. Ask some students to read their sentences to the class.

Self-study and extra practice

Workbook
- Vocabulary, page 39
- Vocabulary Reference, page 89

Teacher's Resource File
- All Clear Basics, page 27
- Vocabulary Consolidation, page 21
- Vocabulary Extension, page 23
- Key Competences: Listening, page 12

Digital Activities
- Student's Digital Material

Students learn and practise functional language to describe a journey.

Speaking

Talk about a journey / At the station

Warmer

Ask some students about the last time they took a train, eg where they travelled to and from, why they made the journey, how long it took, whether they travelled alone, etc.

Model Dialogue

1 2.18

- Students read the question.
- Play the audio. Students listen to and read the dialogue.
- Elicit the answer to the question.

2
- Play the audio again. Students listen again and this time repeat the dialogue.
- Focus on and explain the expressions *How was the journey?*; *Did you get a good seat?*; *I had to stand.*; *Did you change trains?*; *Did you have anything to eat?*. Get the class to pay attention to stress and intonation.

Extra activity

Practice the pronunciation of the questions and answers in the Useful Language box. Students say the four exchanges in pairs.

Speaking Task

1 Talk about a journey

Students look at the information about the two journeys and decide which one they want to talk about. Alternatively, they can use their own ideas.

2 Prepare a dialogue

Students look at the Model Dialogue and change the words in blue to make their own dialogue.

3 Speak

Students practise their dialogues in pairs.

Cultural note

On UK trains, you are not guaranteed a seat unless you reserve one. At busy times of the day you may have to stand the whole way, even on long journeys.

Mixed-ability solutions

Students who need extra help: Speaking Task. Students write out their dialogue before they do step 3.

Fast finishers: Speaking Task. Students act out another dialogue about a different journey. If possible, they do this without looking at the Model Dialogue.

Self-study and extra practice

Workbook
- Speaking, page 125

Teacher's Resource File
- Key Competences: Speaking, pages 29–30

Digital Activities
- Student's Digital Material

Speaking

Talking about a journey / At the station

Exercise 1
No, she didn't.

1 2.18 Listen to the dialogue. Did Lizzie have a good train journey?

Model Dialogue

Tanya

Lizzie

Tanya: You've arrived at last! Welcome to Oxford!

Lizzie: Hi! Thanks for coming to meet me.

Tanya: No problem. So, how was the journey?

Lizzie: It was terrible. The train from Edinburgh left 30 minutes late.

Tanya: Did you get a good seat?

Lizzie: No, I had to stand.

Tanya: What? Did you change trains?

Lizzie: Yes, I changed in Birmingham.

Tanya: Did you have anything to eat?

Lizzie: No, there wasn't any food on the train, so I haven't eaten all day.

Tanya: Oh, no. How terrible!

2 Listen again and repeat the dialogue.

Speaking Task

1 Talk about a journey

First, choose a journey. Use the ideas below or your own ideas.

Cambridge – Edinburgh

Journey:	*Great. Train left on time.*
Seat:	*Yes. By the window. Very comfortable.*
Change:	*Yes. Newcastle.*
Food:	*Yes. Some sandwiches and crisps.*

Liverpool – Leeds

Journey:	*Terrible. Train left late.*
Seat:	*No. Had to stand.*
Change:	*No. Direct.*
Food:	*No. No food.*

2 Prepare a dialogue

Look at the Model Dialogue and change the words in blue.

3 Speak

In pairs, practise your dialogue.

You've arrived at last! Welcome to Edinburgh!

Thanks for coming to meet me.

Useful Language

Talking about a journey

How was the journey?
It was terrible.
Did you get a good seat?
No, I had to stand.
Did you change trains?
No, it was a direct train.
Did you have anything to eat?
No, there wasn't any food on the train.

Writing

A description of a journey

1 2.19 **Read the Model Text and listen. Order the events in your notebook.**

Exercise 1
The correct order is d (example), a, c, f, e, b.

a) flew to Washington DC
b) arrived at the hotel
c) waited to get off the plane
d) the plane left London *1*
e) waited for a bus
f) queued at the immigration desk

Model Text

Hi Nick,
Well, we've arrived in the USA but it was an awful journey!
We set off from London on time, but we couldn't land in New York because of bad weather. **First**, we flew to Washington DC. **Then**, we waited for three hours to get off the plane. **Next**, we queued for two hours at the immigration desk. **After that**, we waited 45 minutes for the bus. **Finally**, we arrived at the hotel at midnight – we were exhausted! Look at the picture of my little sister!
We've booked another flight to New York for tomorrow. I'll send an email when we get there.
Liv

2 **Look at the All Clear Tips and complete the rules below with the words in bold.**

All Clear Tips

Linkers

First, we flew to Washington DC.
Then, we waited for three hours.
Next, we queued for two hours at the immigration desk.
After that, we waited 45 minutes for the bus.
Finally, we arrived at the hotel at midnight.

Exercise 2
a first
b then; next; after that
c finally

a) We use … to show the beginning of an event.
b) We use …, …, and … to show the order of events.
c) We use … to show the end of an event.

3 **Write the correct words in your notebook.**

Exercise 3
1 First
2 Then
3 Next
4 After that
5 Finally

We went on a bus tour in New York last year. (1)**Next / First**, we went to Times Square in the centre of Manhattan. (2)**Then / Finally**, we drove up one side of Central Park and saw the Museum of Natural History. (3)**First / Next**, we went to Harlem and saw the Apollo Theatre. (4)**After that / Finally**, we drove down Park Avenue. (5)**Then / Finally**, we got off the bus by the Guggenheim Museum. It was brilliant!

Writing Task

1 Plan

Make notes about a real or imaginary journey and include:

Introduction: *where you were going, what the journey was like (good or bad)*
Description: *what happened and in what order*
Closing phrase: *how the journey ended*

2 Write

Use the Model Text, your notes and this structure:

Paragraph 1: Introduction
Paragraph 2: Description
Paragraph 3: Closing phrase

3 Check

☑ present perfect and past simple, quantity
☑ travel, extreme adjectives
☑ linkers: *first, then, next, after that* and *finally*

Lesson Aims:

Students practise using linkers to sequence events.
Students write a description of a journey.

Writing

A description of a journey

Warmer

Students imagine all the things that could go wrong on a plane journey. Have some prompts ready if the class doesn't come up with many ideas, eg *passport*, *delay*, *suitcase*, *overbooking*, etc.

1 2.19

- Students look at the picture and read the statements.
- Play the audio. Students read and listen to the email and order the events.
- Check the answer with the class.

All Clear Tips

2
- Read the All Clear Tips with the class.
- Check students understand the linkers in bold.
- Students read and complete the rules with the words in bold.
- Check answers with the class.

3
- Check students understand what a *bus tour* is.
- Students read the text and choose the correct linkers to complete it.
- Check answers with the class.

Extra activity

Students practise using the linkers orally. Start a sequence of events by saying *First, I went to the supermarket.* Choose a student to repeat and continue the sequence, eg *First, I went to the supermarket. Then, I went to the post office.*, and so on, with two more students adding an event with *Next* and an event with *After that*. A fourth student ends the sequence with *Finally*.

Writing Task

1 Plan

Read the notes with the class. Students make notes about a real or imaginary journey of their own.

2 Write

Look at the structure with the class. Students use their notes to write an email about their journey. Emphasize that they should try to use some of the linkers to order the events in their description.

3 Check

Encourage students to check their work, paying particular attention to the points mentioned.

Web info

Type these words in your search engine for more information about bus tours in New York: 'New York sightseeing bus tours'

Mixed-ability solutions

Students who need extra help: Writing Task. Students just complete the notes in step 1.

Fast finishers: Writing Task. Students read their partner's text and try to decide if the journey is real or imaginary.

Self-study and extra practice

Workbook
- Writing Guide, pages 112–3

Teacher's Resource File
- Key Competences: Writing, page 12

Lesson Aims:

Students read and learn about the gold rush in California in the 19th century.
Students practise the pronunciation of the /ɜː/ /iː/ and /ʌ/ sounds.

Culture Reading

American history

Warmer

Write on the board *California*, *gold*, *1848*, *San Francisco*. Tell students that these are the key words in the text. Ask them to speculate about what the text might be about.

2.20

- Students look at the pictures and read the questions. Explain what *gold rush* means.
- Play the audio. Students read and listen to the text.
- Students answer the questions.
- Check answers with the class.

Pronunciation

/ɜː/ /iː/ /ʌ/

a 2.21

- Play the audio. Students listen and repeat the words.

Extra activity

Ask students to think of two or three more words with each sound. If they can't think of any, give them hints to elicit the words *bird*, *word*, *third*; *week*, *meet*, *seat*; *lucky*, *sun*, *won*.
Write students' words on the board if they are correct, putting them in three columns according to the sound they contain.
Practise the pronunciation of the new words.

b 2.22

- Play the audio. Students listen and repeat the sentences.
- Check the pronunciation of the key words.

Web info

Type these words in your search engine

- for more information about the California gold rush: 'ducksters + California gold rush'
- to see the classic Charlie Chaplin silent film *The Gold Rush* (about the gold rush in Alaska, not California): 'Charlie Chaplin + gold rush'

Mixed-ability solutions

Students who need extra help: Reading text. Write the following options on the board.

1 *James W Marshall / Stutter Mill*
2 *December 1848 / 1849*
3 *by horse / by ship or on foot*
4 *The population got bigger and trains began to arrive. However, the Native Americans suffered. / It became more dangerous.*

Fast-finishers: Reading text. Students read the text again and answer the following questions.

1 *How did people hear about the gold rush?*
2 *Who were the forty-niners?*
3 *How many people walked across America?*

Self-study and extra practice

Workbook

- Culture: Reading and Listening, page 98

Culture Reading

EXTRA

AMERICAN HISTORY ONLINE

HOME | ARCHIVE | COMMENTS | CONTACT

THE CALIFORNIA GOLD RUSH

The California gold rush started on 24th January 1848 when James W Marshall discovered gold at Sutter's Mill in California. Soon, people in San Francisco heard stories about gold. In December 1848, the president of the USA told the world that there was gold in California.

THE FORTY-NINERS

The early gold-seekers were called 'forty-niners' because they started their journey to California in 1849. A lot of the 'forty-niners' arrived by ship but 150,000 walked to California from other parts of the USA.

EFFECTS OF THE GOLD RUSH

The gold rush changed California. The population of San Francisco grew from 1,000 in 1848 to 150,000 in 1870. A railway line was built to join California to the rest of the USA. But not all the changes were good. The Native Americans lost their lands and many died from diseases which the Europeans brought with them.

2.20 **Read and listen. Then answer the questions in your notebook.**

1 Who was the first man to find gold in California?
2 When did the world hear that there was gold in California?
3 How did people travel to California?
4 How did the gold rush change California?

Pronunciation

/ɜː/ /iː/ /ʌ/

a 2.21 **Listen and repeat the words.**

/ɜː/ heard, world, were, work
/iː/ seek, between, seen, been
/ʌ/ rush, just, but, country, love

b 2.22 **Listen and repeat the sentences.**

Reading text exercise

1 James W Marshall
2 in December 1848
3 by ship or on foot
4 The population grew, a railway was built, the Native Americans lost their lands and many of them died from diseases brought by the Europeans.

Unit 6 Language Reference

Vocabulary Travel

arrive • buy a guidebook • buy souvenirs • come back home • get off a train • get on a train • have adventures • meet people • pack a suitcase • plan a trip • send postcards • set off

Extreme adjectives

amazing / good • awful / bad • boiling / hot • delighted / happy • enormous / big • exhausted / tired • freezing / cold • terrifying / frightening • tiny / small

Grammar Present perfect and past simple

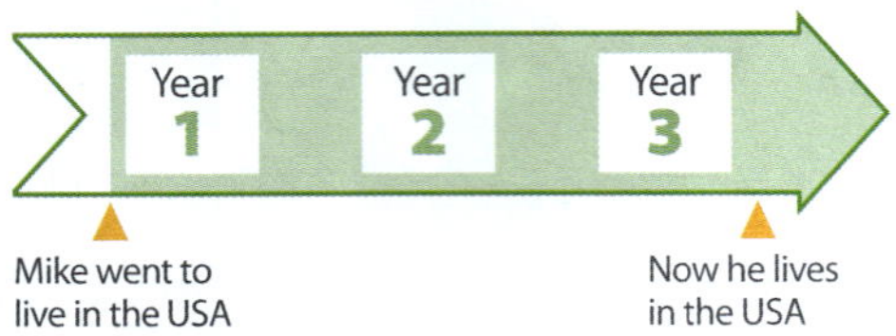

Mike has lived in the USA for three years.

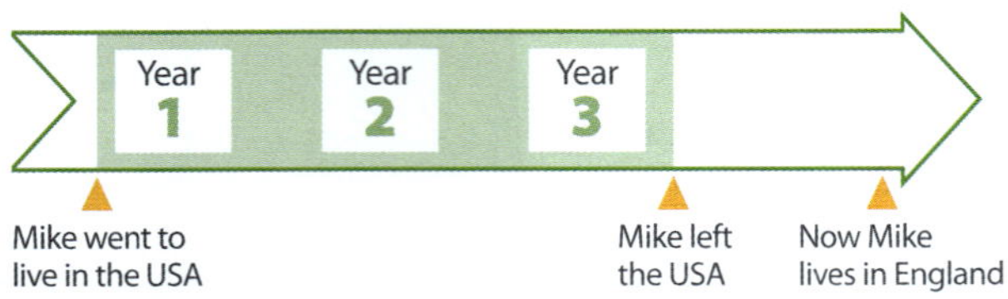

Mike has lived in the USA.

Mike lived in the USA for three years.

Quantity

	Countable nouns	Uncountable nouns
Affirmative	He had **a lot of** adventures. He had **some / a few** adventures.	He made **a lot of** money. He made **some / a little** money.
Negative	He didn't have **many** adventures. He didn't have **any** adventures.	He didn't make **much** money. He didn't make **any** money.
Interrogative	**How many** adventures did he have? Did he have **many / any** adventures?	**How much** money did he make? Did he make **much / any** money?

Speaking Talking about a journey

How was the journey? — **It was** terrible.

Did you get a good seat? — **No, I had to** stand.

Did you change trains? — **No, it was** a direct train.

Did you have anything to eat? — **No, there wasn't** any food on the train.

Unit 6 Progress Check

Vocabulary Travel

1 Complete the sentences with the words in the box.

adventures home postcard suitcase trip

1 Paula sent me a … from Sydney.
2 You haven't packed your … . You're going to be late!
3 I planned a … with my guidebook.
4 Lucy had lots of … when she went to Japan.
5 I had such a great holiday that I didn't want to come back …!

Exercise 1
1 postcard
2 suitcase
3 trip
4 adventures
5 home

Extreme adjectives

2 Match adjectives 1–5 with extreme adjectives a–e. Write them in your notebook.

1 small	a) awful
2 cold	b) exhausted
3 tired	c) amazing
4 good	d) tiny
5 bad	e) freezing

Exercise 2
1 d
2 e
3 b
4 c
5 a

Grammar Present perfect and past simple

3 Write the correct words in your notebook.

1 Has Sarah seen / Did Sarah see the Taj Mahal when she was in India?
2 I 've set off / set off on my travels a year ago. So far I 've been / went to 30 countries.
3 I bought / 've bought a guidebook for Istanbul yesterday.
4 The postcard hasn't arrived / didn't arrive. When did you send it?
5 Have you ever visited / Did you ever visit Greece? – No, but I'd love to go one day.

Exercise 3
1 Did Sarah see
2 set off; 've been
3 bought
4 hasn't arrived
5 Have you ever visited

4 Complete the sentences with the correct form of the present perfect or past simple.

1 I've been to lots of countries. Last summer I … (go) to Greece.
2 I … (pack) my suitcase last night.
3 She … (have) many adventures over the years. Last year she … (write) a book about them.
4 When … he … (come) back home? A week ago.
5 They … (plan) their trip very carefully. They would like to go next summer.

Exercise 4
1 went
2 packed
3 's had; wrote
4 did (he) come
5 've planned

Quantity

5 Write the correct words in your notebook.

1 I haven't packed any / much socks.
2 Nick's bought much / a lot of souvenirs.
3 I haven't got many / much time.
4 Did you meet many / much people on holiday?
5 I only spent a little / a few money yesterday.

Exercise 5
1 any
2 a lot of
3 much
4 many
5 a little

Correct the activities with the class. Students who need extra revision and practice can go to:
Workbook
- Unit 6 Revision, page 42
- Grammar Reference and Practice, pages 76–7
- Vocabulary Reference, page 89

Student's Digital Material
www.allclear.macmillan.es

Check your answers

Write your scores for exercises 1–5 in your notebook. What did you get for:

- travel?
- extreme adjectives?
- present perfect and past simple?
- quantity?

Extra Practice

If you need extra practice, go to:

- Unit 6 Grammar Reference
- Unit 6 Vocabulary Reference
- Unit 6 Grammar Exercises
- Unit 6 Vocabulary Exercises

Revision Units 4–6

Vocabulary

- Places to visit
- Adverbs
- Fundraising ideas
- *make* and *do*
- Travel
- Extreme adjectives

Work with a partner to complete the sentences with the correct word in your notebooks. Who finishes first?

START

What … you laugh? (5)

I play the guitar very … . (4)

Have you ever sold … tickets for charity? (6)

Have you seen any Roman …? (5)

What do you wear when the weather is …? (8)

Do you do some … every day? (8)

When did you last send a …? (8)

Have you ever done a … swim for charity? (9)

Have you been to the Great Barrier …? (4)

How often do you buy …? (9)

FINISH

Revision Units 4–6 Vocabulary

makes
well
raffle
ruins
freezing
exercise
postcard
sponsored
Reef
souvenirs

Lesson Aims:

Students revise and practise vocabulary from Units 4 to 6.

Revision Units 4–6

Vocabulary

Warmer

Students look through Units 4 to 6 and tell you what vocabulary areas they have seen. Alternatively, you could get the class to do this from memory and then to check by looking in the Student's Book.

- Do the board game as a competition. Explain these rules to the class before you start.
- Students work in pairs. They write the words to complete the sentences. The numbers in brackets show the number of letters in each word.
- When they have finished, they shout *Stop!* All the other teams must stop writing.
- Check answers with the class and write them on the board.
- Teams get two points for each correct answer and minus one point for each wrong answer. For a blank, they get zero points.
- Ask how many points the teams have, starting at 20 (the maximum) and working down.

Extra activity

Students ask and answer the questions in the board game in pairs.

Lesson Aims:

Students revise and practise the grammar from Units 4 to 6.

Revision Units 4–6

Grammar

Comparatives and superlatives

Warmer

Write *history*, *geography*, *easy*, *difficult*, *interesting* on the board. Students compare the two subjects using the adjectives. Write the key language on the board after they have answered and use it to revise comparatives.

Repeat the process with *London*, *Valencia* and *Toledo* and the adjectives *big*, *small* and *interesting* to revise superlatives.

1
- Students choose the correct words to complete the sentences.
- Check answers with the class.
- If you detect any major problems, you might want to read through the grammar section of the Language Reference on page 50 with the class.

Present perfect

Warmer

Write on the board:

I've lived in my flat for three years.

Maria's listened to all of Rihanna's songs.

Ask students which tense this is, how it is formed, and why it is used in each sentence. (In the first sentence, the action started in the past and continues in the present; in the second, the action happened at an indefinite time in the past.)

2
- Students complete the sentences with the correct form of the verbs in brackets.
- Check answers with the class.
- If you detect any major problems, you might want to read through the grammar section of the Language Reference on page 60 with the class.

for and *since*

Warmer

Write on the board:

I've lived in Bilbao for / since two years.

Ask the class which is correct, *for* or *since*, and why.

3
- Students complete the sentences with *for* or *since*.
- Check answers with the class.
- If you detect any major problems, you might want to read through the grammar section of the Language Reference on page 60 with the class.

Present perfect and past simple

Warmer

Write on the board:

I bought a new smartphone yesterday.

I have bought a lot of things this year.

Elicit which tense is used in each sentence and why. (The first sentence uses the past simple because the action happened at a definite time in the past; the second uses the present perfect because the action happened at an indefinite time in the past.)

Ask students to translate the sentences.

4
- Students choose the correct words to complete the sentences.
- Check answers with the class.
- If you detect any major problems, you might want to read through the grammar section of the Language Reference on page 70 with the class.

Grammar check

5
- Tell students that this exercise revises the rest of the grammar they have seen in Units 4 to 6 and it will give them a good idea of how well they have learnt it.
- Explain any potentially difficult vocabulary in the text such as *fresh water*, *farmers*, *government employees*, *survive*.
- Students choose the correct words to complete the text.
- Check answers with the class.

Grammar

- Comparatives and superlatives
- (*not*) *as* … *as*
- *too*, *enough* and *not enough*
- Present perfect
- *ever* and *never*
- *How long* …? with *for* and *since*
- Present perfect and past simple
- Quantity

Comparatives and superlatives

1 **Write the correct words in your notebook.**

1 My mum is older / oldest than my dad.
2 I think English is the more / most difficult subject at school.
3 The Alhambra is the most beautiful / beautifulest building in Spain.
4 The Amazon rainforest is the biggest / bigest rainforest in the world.
5 Watching a football match in a stadium is more good / better than watching it on TV.

Exercise 1
1 older
2 most
3 most beautiful
4 biggest
5 better

Present perfect

2 **Complete the sentences with the correct form of the verbs in brackets.**

1 How long … you … (have) your mobile phone?
2 I … (not visit) Paris.
3 He … (eat) a lot of chocolate today.
4 … your brother … (make) many friends in his new school?
5 I … (listen) to the new Lorde album twice today.

Exercise 2
1 have (you) had
2 haven't visited
3 's eaten
4 Has (your brother) made
5 've listened

for and *since*

3 **Complete the sentences with *for* or *since*.**

1 My sister has lived in China … two years.
2 My cousin has been a mechanic … he left school.
3 I've been on holiday … last Friday.
4 They've lived in London … a long time.
5 She's been at home … 6 pm.

Exercise 3
1 for
2 since
3 since
4 for
5 since

Present perfect and past simple

4 **Write the correct words in your notebook.**

1 Did you buy / Have you bought any new clothes last weekend?
2 I'm interrailing round Europe. I visited / 've visited ten countries.
3 My mum travelled / 's travelled to Barcelona on business last week.
4 He didn't eat / hasn't eaten kangaroo when he was in Australia.
5 I 've bought / bought a new laptop last month. It was / has been very cheap.

Exercise 4
1 Did you buy
2 've visited
3 travelled
4 didn't eat
5 bought; was

Grammar check

5 **Write the correct words in your notebook.**

(1) Have you ever heard / Did you ever hear of Tuvalu? It's an island in the Pacific Ocean and it's the (2) smaller / smallest English-speaking country in the world. All Tuvaluans speak Tuvaluan, but (3) a lot of / much people can speak English too. Tuvalu only has 12,373 inhabitants but the population is not as (4) small / smaller as the Vatican City.
Europeans (5) have known / knew about the islands (6) for / since over 400 years. The islands (7) became / have become part of the British Empire in 1892 but Tuvalu (8) was / has been an independent country (9) since / for 1978.
Tuvalu is a very poor country. There is no fresh water, so sometimes there is (10) not enough / enough water to drink. Not (11) many / much tourists visit Tuvalu because it is (12) enough / too difficult to travel there. A lot of Tuvaluans work as fishermen, farmers or government employees, but the country needs (13) a lot of / many help from other countries to survive.

Exercise 5
1 Have you ever heard
2 smallest
3 a lot of
4 small
5 have known
6 for
7 became
8 has been
9 since
10 not enough
11 many
12 too
13 a lot of

Cultural Awareness: Literature

Multimedia

1 How much do you know about literature in Britain? Do the quiz.

Exercise 1
1 b
2 a
3 a
4 c
5 c
6 c

QUIZ

1 Shakespeare wrote … plays.
   a 28
   b 38
   c 48

2 Shakespeare's Globe Theatre is in …
   a London.
   b Stratford-upon-Avon.
   c Bath.

3 What year was Charles Dickens born?
   a 1812
   b 1821
   c 1870

4 Charles Dickens wrote books about …
   a politics and economics.
   b relationships and romance.
   c poverty and social issues.

5 Jane Austen wrote just … novels.
   a four
   b five
   c six

6 Many of Britain's most popular books have been turned into …
   a comic books.
   b theme parks.
   c films.

WATCH

2 Watch the documentary about literature and answer the questions.

1 How many of Shakespeare's plays are named in the documentary?
2 Where are many of Dickens' novels based?
3 What can you visit in Bath if you're interested in literature?

Exercise 2
1 three
2 London
3 Jane Austen's house

Lesson Aims:

Students do a quiz to see how much they know about literature in Britain.
Students watch a video about literature in Britain.

Cultural Awareness:

Literature

Warmer

Brainstorm with the class the names of famous British writers and works of English literature.

1
- Tell students they are going to do a quiz about literature in Britain. Read through the questions with the class and clear up any vocabulary problems.
- Students do the quiz individually.
- Students compare answers in pairs.
- Check answers with the class.

Extra activity

Books closed. Read out the questions in the quiz without the options. Students try to answer from memory.

2
- Tell students that they are going to watch a documentary about literature in Britain.
- Read the questions with the class.
- Play the video. Students watch and listen.
- Students answer the questions.
- Check answers with the class. Replay the video if necessary.

Web info

Type these words in your search engine for more information about Shakespeare:
'youtube + Shakespeare biography misswezeman'

Culture Video: *Literature*

This Culture video and accompanying worksheet, teaching notes, videoscript and answer key are in the Teacher's Resource Centre.
The worksheet, teaching notes, videoscript and answer key can also be found in the Teacher's Resource File.

Lesson Aims:

Students read a blog post about a book and then write one.

Digital Competence:

Blog posts

Warmer

Ask the class what kind of things people usually write blogs about. Find out if any students read blogs regularly or if they write a blog. If so, encourage them to tell the class about them.

Read the question with the class.
Students look at the blog and identify which book Pablo has written about.

Extra activity

Ask students what Pablo devotes most space to: the author, the plot or his opinion.
Ask the class if they think it is a good book review and why or why not.

Task

Tell the class that they are going to write a blog post about a book they've read. Read through the steps with the class.

Step 1 Think about a book they have read and make notes about it using the prompts in the Student's Book.

Step 2 Students write about the book for a blog. Emphasize that they should plan the structure of their blog post before they start. Students check what they have written.

Step 3 Students show their blog post to the other students in the class and ask them to comment.

Step 4 Students read their classmates' blog posts and decide which books they want to read. They comment on their classmates' blog posts.

Web info

Type these words in your search engine for more information about blog posts: 'blog posts for teenagers'

Term Project

For a different type of project, see the Life Skills Collaborative Project in the Workbook, pages 132–3.

Digital Competence: Blog posts

Look at the blog. Which book has Pablo written about?

The Man in the Iron Mask

4:16 PM

Back www.pablosbookblog.com

Pablo's Book Blog

Wednesday, 11 December

Hi everyone! Welcome to my book blog.

I read *The Man in the Iron Mask* by Alexandre Dumas last week. It is the story of a man called d'Artagnan and the last adventure of the Three Musketeers – Athos, Porthos and Aramis.

The story is set in 1661 in France. Louis XIV is King. He is young, clever and powerful, but not everyone likes him. He spends a lot of money on himself, but he doesn't look after the poor people. However, unknown to Louis, he has a kind brother, Philippe, who is locked in the Bastille Prison. The Three Musketeers decide to make Philippe the king and put Louis in prison. First, they have to teach Philippe how to behave like a king. Will they succeed or will King Louis find out and kill them all?

The story is exciting and the ending is very dramatic.

Recommendation ★★★★☆

Posted by Pablo, 07:43

About Me

My Posts

Blog Archive

➔ October (3)
➔ November (5)
↓ December (1)
Hi everyone! Welcome to my book blog. I read *The Man* …

Post a comment

This book sounds really interesting!

Carlos

Thursday, 13 December, 18:22

TASK Write a blog post about a book. Follow the steps below.

Step 1
Think about a book you have read. Make notes:
- The title and author
- Information about the plot and characters
- Where and when the book is set
- If you recommend the book or not

Step 2
Write about the book for a blog. Check your grammar and spelling.

Step 3
Show your blog post to the other students in your class. Ask them to comment!

Step 4
Read your classmates' blog posts. Which books do you want to read? Comment on your classmates' blog posts.

7 Films

Overview

Unit objectives and key competences

- Understand, memorize and correctly use vocabulary related to films CLC, DC
- Learn and use some common suffixes for the formation of nouns CLC, L2L
- Identify the main ideas in a text about films in the future CLC
- Learn about possible future developments in film making CAE, CMST
- Understand, contrast and correctly use grammar structures to express the future (*will*, *be going to* and present continuous) and the first conditional CLC, L2L
- Identify specific information through a listening activity about a film project for teenagers CLC

More information on Key Competences, page v

- Learn about an interesting film project for teenagers CAE, SIE
- Use appropriate functional language to ask for and give opinions about films CLC, SCC
- Identify the paragraph content in a review of the film *Gravity* CLC, L2L
- Write a film review CLC, SIE, CAE
- Find specific content in a text about Alfred Hitchcock and his films CAE
- Learn about Alfred Hitchcock and his films CAE
- Assimilate the All Clear Tips and Rules and study the Language Reference from the unit CLC, L2L, SIE
- Identify areas of language which need improvement and use ICT for extra practice DC, CLC, L2L

Linguistic content

Grammar

- Future tenses: *will*, *be going to*, present continuous
- First conditional

Recycled grammar

- Past simple (Unit 2)
- Present perfect (Unit 5)

Main vocabulary

- Films: *director*, *film a scene*, etc
- Noun suffixes: *-ion* and *-ment*: *suggestion*, *development*, etc

Functional language

- Asking for and giving opinions / Talking about a film

Pronunciation

- Sentence stress and weak forms

Skills: learning outcomes

- **Reading** Understand specific information in a clearly structured online magazine about the future of film. The student can re-read the more difficult parts, page 77
- **Listening** Extract the main ideas and relevant information from a report about a special film programme for teenagers, page 80
- **Speaking** Participate effectively in a face-to-face informal dialogue, asking for and giving opinions about a film, page 81
- **Writing** Write a film review with the main points set out in a logical order, page 82
- **Reading** Understand specific information from a clearly structured biography of Alfred Hitchcock. The student can re-read more the difficult parts, page 83

Lifelong learning skills and content-based learning

Life skills

- **Socio-cultural awareness** Critical appreciation of cinema and culture, pages 77, 81 and 82
- **Social development** Appreciation of the entrepreneurial spirit of young film-makers, page 79
- **Communication** Awareness of the function of paragraphs to convey different information, page 81

Learning strategies

- Grouping vocabulary by category, page 76
- Use topic sentences in paragraphs to infer the general content, page 77
- Using suffixes to form words, page 79

Cross-curricular content

- Technological advances in films, page 77
- Language: word formation, page 79

Further materials and evaluation

Digital material

- Student's and Teacher's Resource Centres
- Teacher's Presentation Kit
- Student's Digital Material: interactive vocabulary and grammar activities
- Video *Music* (Revision Units 7–9, page 108)

Student's website www.macmillansecondary.es

Workbook

- Vocabulary, pages 44–5
- Vocabulary Reference, page 90
- Grammar, pages 46–7
- Grammar Reference and Practice, pages 78–9
- Revision, page 48
- Culture: Reading and Listening, page 99
- Writing Guide, pages 114–5
- Speaking, page 126

Teacher's Resource File

Multi-level Materials Bank

- All Clear Basics, pages 31–5
- Vocabulary and Grammar Consolidation and Extension, pages 25–8
- Language Excellence, pages 13–4
- Translation and Dictation, pages 7 and 16

Lifelong Learning

- Digital Competence, pages 13–4
- Culture Video Material, pages 5–6
- Study Skills, pages 1–12

Evaluation and Key Competences

- Evaluation Rubrics, pages 1–7
- Key Competences, pages 13–4 and 31–2

Content-based Learning

- CLIL, pages 1–10
- Macmillan Readers, pages 1–7

Evaluation material

- Unit 7 end-of-unit test: Basic, Standard and Extra
- CEFR Skills Exam Generator

Web info

Tips to find extra information on: Andy Serkis and cyber acting, Fresh Films, reviews about *Gravity*, Alfred Hitchcock and his films

Extra help for weaker students

Teacher's Resource File: All Clear Basics, pages 31–5

Material for fast finishers

Workbook: Grammar Extension, page 49
Teacher's Resource File: Vocabulary Extension, page 27
Teacher's Resource File: Grammar Extension, page 28
Teacher's Resource File: Language Excellence, pages 13–4

7 Films

Objectives

Vocabulary Films; suffixes
Grammar Future forms: *will*, *be going to*, present continuous; first conditional
Speaking Asking for and giving opinions
Writing A film review

Vocabulary

Films

1 2.23 **Listen and repeat the words and phrases. Match them with pictures 1–14.**

director • film a scene • film star • plot • producer • release a film • screen • script • soundtrack • special effects • star in a film • stunt • stuntman / stuntwoman • win an award

1 
2 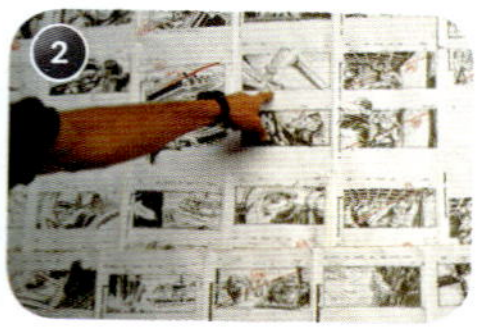
3 
4 
5 
6 
7 
8 
9 
10 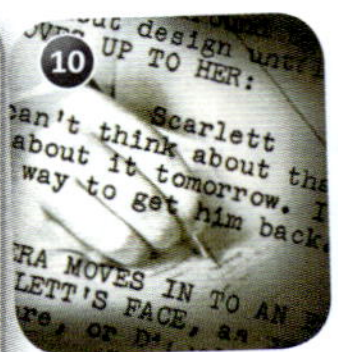
11 
12 
13 
14 

Exercise 1
1 stunt
2 plot
3 release a film
4 film star
5 soundtrack
6 producer
7 star in a film
8 director
9 stuntman / stuntwoman
10 script
11 special effects
12 screen
13 win an award
14 film a scene

2 **Copy and complete the table with all the words and phrases in exercise 1.**

people	verbs related to films	other film words
director	*star in a film*	*stunt*

Exercise 2
People: director (example), film star, producer, stuntman / stuntwoman
Verbs related to films: film a scene, release a film, star in a film (example), win an award
Other film words: plot, screen, script, soundtrack, special effects, stunt (example)

3 **Complete the sentences with the correct form of words and phrases from exercise 1.**

1 The … is wonderful – the dialogues are great.
2 The music is great, too – I love the … .
3 Johnny Depp … in the film. I hope he wins an … at the next Oscars.
4 A … does all the dangerous scenes in a film instead of the actor.
5 The … in that science-fiction film are wonderful. They look really realistic.

Exercise 3
1 script
2 soundtrack
3 stars; award
4 stuntman / stuntwoman
5 special effects

4 2.24 **Listen to Isabel and Xavi. What are their favourite films? Why?**

5 **In pairs, ask and answer questions about films.**

What's your favourite film?

Chef.

Exercise 4
Xavi's favourite film is *Gravity* because he likes the script and the special effects. Isabel's favourite film is *The Hobbit* because she loves fantasy films.

Vocabulary Reference

Lesson Aims:

Students learn and practise some words and expressions related to films.
Students listen to two young people talking about their favourite films and identify the films.

Vocabulary

Films

Warmer

Revise words for different types of film: *action*, *comedy*, *horror*, etc. Ask students if they have seen any good films recently. What type of film was it? Why did they like it?

1 2.23

- Students listen and repeat the words and phrases. Get the class to pay attention to word stress.
- Ask students to translate the expressions, helping as necessary.
- Students match the words and phrases with the pictures.
- Check answers with the class.

2
- Look at the table with the class and make sure they understand the three categories.
- Students copy the table into their notebooks.
- Students complete the table.
- Check answers with the class.

3
- Students complete the sentences with the correct form of words and phrases from exercise 1.
- Check answers with the class.

4 2.24

- Read the questions with the class.
- Play the audio. Students listen and identify the speakers' favourite films and why they like them.
- Check answers with the class.

5

- Ask the question in the speech bubble to a student.
- Students ask and answer the question in pairs. They should give a reason for their answer.
- Ask some students to report their partner's answer.

Extra activity

Play a guessing game. A student thinks of a film and the others have to guess the film by asking questions, eg *Who is the director?;Who stars in the film?; Are there any special effects?; Is it an action film?*. Do an example first and then students can play in groups.

Mixed-ability solutions

Students who need extra help: Exercise 3. Write the following options on the board.

1 *screen / script*
2 *plot / soundtrack*
3 *stars / stunts; award / effect*
4 *director / stuntman*
5 *screens / special effects*

Fast finishers: Exercise 2. In pairs, students add two more words to each column. When they finish, they read out their words. Write them on the board.

Self-study and extra practice

Workbook
- Vocabulary, page 44
- Vocabulary Reference, page 90

Teacher's Resource File
- All Clear Basics, page 31
- Vocabulary Consolidation, page 25
- Vocabulary Extension, page 27

Lesson Aims:

Students read and listen to an online film magazine about the future of film.
Students identify the paragraph topic and find specific information in the text.

Reading

Online film magazine

Warmer

Ask students if they have ever seen a film in 3D? If any of them have, ask them to tell the class about it, eg what the film was, what the experience was like, how it was different from a normal film, etc.

Word Check

Check students understand the new words: *smoke*, *rollercoaster*, *headsets*, *sensors*. Explain any they don't know.

1
- Students look at the pictures and describe what they can see.
- Students read the text quickly and choose the best title.
- Check the answer with the class.

2 2.25
- Students read the beginning of the sentences and the multiple-choice options. Encourage them to note the answers they think are correct.
- Play the audio. Students read and listen to the text and check and complete their answers.
- Check answers with the class, asking students to explain why they chose each answer.

3
- Read the question with the class.
- Write the words and phrases *I think*, *will be* and *because* on the board and explain that these are useful words and phrases for discussing the question.
- Give students a minute to decide on their own opinion.
- Students discuss the question in groups of four.

All Clear Facts

Read the fact with the class. Ask the class if they can remember any other gender-neutral words to describe jobs from Unit 2, eg *firefighter*, *police officer*, *postal worker*.

Extra activity

Students find film-related words in the text.

Cultural note

4DX cinema started in South Korea in 2009 when the film *Journey to the Center of Earth* was shown in this format. You can watch films in 4DX format in over 20 countries, including Chile, Brazil, Hong Kong, Japan and Russia.

Web info

Type these words in your search engine for more information about Andy Serkis and cyber acting: 'bbc newsbeat + Andy Serkis'

Mixed-ability solutions

Students who need extra help: Exercise 2. Read out the following extracts.

1 *… actors won't disappear because digital characters need good actors.*
2 *4DX cinemas already exist, but they will probably become more common.*
3 *… it's clear that VR films are going to be very different.*
4 *During the film, sensors will detect our emotions.*
5 *Technology will change, but people are never going to stop watching films!*

Fast finishers: Exercise 2. Students write two or three sentences about what film they would like to see in a 4DX cinema and why. They then compare their ideas in pairs.

Self-study and extra practice

Teacher's Resource File
- Key Competences: Reading, page 13

Reading

Online film magazine

Word Check
smoke rollercoaster headsets sensors

Exercise 1
b) The future of film

1 Read the text quickly and choose the best title.

a) Cinema today b) The future of film c) A film review

Film

Do you remember Gollum from The Hobbit? The film's creators used motion-capture to transform the human actor into the digital character. In the future, more films will use this technology and soon, many films will only have digital characters. But actors won't disappear, because digital characters need good actors. Being a 'cyber-actor' is a skill that many film stars will learn in the future.

4DX cinemas already exist, but they will probably become more common. Audiences will experience real special effects. If there's an explosion, there will be real **smoke**. If it rains in the film, you will get wet! Seats will move to match the action in the film. Imagine a scene on a **rollercoaster** or on a boat!

Virtual Reality (VR) already exists in the world of gaming but some people predict that it will transform our experience of films. VR **headsets** will put audiences *inside* the film and we will experience the characters' lives first-hand. But will VR affect the development of scripts and plots? We aren't sure, but it's clear that VR films are going to be very different.

Have you ever been disappointed by a film's ending? In the future, film plots will change while we are watching them. During the film, **sensors** will detect our emotions. Then, software will choose the best scene to play next depending on our emotions.

Audiences have always wanted enjoyment and excitement. Technology will change, but people are never going to stop watching films!

All Clear Facts
In the past, people used the word *actor* for men and *actress* for women. Now, we usually say *actor* for men and women.

Exercise 2
1 b
2 c
3 b
4 a
5 c

2 2.25 Read and listen. Write the correct answers in your notebook.

1 In the future, human actors will …
  a) disappear.
  b) still exist.
  c) work with robots.

2 In the future, there …
  a) won't be as many 4DX cinemas as now.
  b) will be real special effects in all cinemas.
  c) will be more 4DX cinemas than now.

3 Films developed for VR …
  a) are going to be quite similar to 4DX films.
  b) aren't going to be like today's films.
  c) are going to have more complicated plots.

4 Technology will detect how we feel about a film …
  a) while it is playing.
  b) before it begins.
  c) when it ends.

5 People in the future …
  a) will watch more films.
  b) won't need cinemas.
  c) will continue to watch films.

Exercise 3
Students' own answers

3 Which idea do you think will become the most common in the future?

Grammar

Future forms

will	
Affirmative	She**'ll go**
Negative	We **won't go**
Interrogative	**Will** you **go** …?

Language Reference p84

1 **Complete the sentences with the correct form of *will* and the verbs in brackets.**

In the future, there *will be* (be) more 4DX cinemas.

1 I don't think Spielberg … (direct) that new film.
2 How many people … (see) the film?
3 My friend … probably … (not enjoy) that film.
4 … they … (release) a CD of the soundtrack?
5 That film … probably … (win) awards.

Exercise 1
1 will direct
2 will see
3 won't enjoy
4 Will they release
5 will (probably) win

2 **Look at the sentences in exercise 1 and complete the rules below.**

probably   definitely   *will*   predictions

a) We use *will* and *won't* to make … about the future.
b) We use … when we are sure about something in the future and … when we think something is likely.
c) In the affirmative, *probably* and *definitely* come after … but in the negative they come before *won't*.

Exercise 2
a) predictions
b) definitely; probably
c) *will*

3 **Write complete questions using *will* in your notebook.**

Spain / win / the next World Cup?
Will Spain win the next World Cup?

1 you / pass / all your exams?
2 you / go / to England / next year?
3 Which / bands / be / popular / next year?
4 your teacher / give / you / a lot of homework?

Exercise 3
1 Will you pass all your exams?
2 Will you go to England next year?
3 Which bands will be popular next year?
4 Will your teacher give you a lot of homework?

4 **In pairs, ask and answer the questions in exercise 3.**

be going to	
Affirmative	She**'s going to go**
Negative	We **aren't going to go**
Interrogative	**Are** you **going to go** …?

Language Reference p84

5 **Match rules 1 and 2 with sentences a) and b). Write them in your notebook.**

1 We use *be going to* to talk about future plans and intentions.
2 We use *be going to* when there is evidence in the present for future events or actions.

a) The actress has broken her leg so she isn't going to star in the film.
b) They are going to make this book into a film next year.

Exercise 5
1 b
2 a

6 **Complete the sentences with the correct form of the verbs in the box. Use *be going to*.**

not ask   not celebrate
download   finish   invite

1 I love that song! I … it to my phone now.
2 They … him to sing because he's got a terrible voice.
3 Jim … because he didn't get the new job.
4 … you … your homework before class?
5 I … Paul to my birthday party.

Exercise 6
1 'm going to download
2 aren't going to ask
3 isn't going to celebrate
4 Are (you) going to finish
5 'm going to invite

All Clear Rules

We use the present continuous for definite future arrangements.
*I'm **meeting** my friends at 7 pm.*

7 **Complete the sentences with the correct form of the words in brackets. Use the present continuous.**

1 Tomorrow I … (travel) to the festival by train.
2 … you … (give) me a lift to the station?
3 My friend Alex … (meet) me at 11 am.
4 I … (not / take) the 10 am train.
5 … we … (eat) before we leave?

Exercise 7
1 'm travelling
2 Are (you) giving
3 is meeting
4 'm not taking
5 Are (we) eating

Lesson Aims:

Students learn and practise three ways to talk about the future: *will*, *be going to* and the present continuous.

Grammar

Future forms

Warmer

Say and write the following sentences on the board.
I'll probably go to a 4DX cinema some time this year.
Virtual reality video games will become popular very soon.
Ask the class if they think the statements are true.
Ask the students which form of the verb is used and why (*will*, for predictions).

1
- Look at the grammar table with the class.
- Emphasize that we use *will* to predict the future when we don't have any firm evidence that the events will happen. Point out that we often start these predictions with *I think …*, *I don't think …* or *Perhaps …* .
- Look at the example in exercise 1 with the class.
- Students complete the sentences with the correct form of *will* and the verbs in brackets.
- Check answers with the class.

2
- Students complete the rules with the words in the box.
- Emphasize that they need to look at the sentences in exercise 1 carefully to complete the rules, especially in the case of the last rule.
- Check answers with the class.

Extra activity

Students write five predictions about their future using *will / won't* and *probably* or *definitely*. If they have problems coming up with ideas, write the following prompts on the board.
go to university; become a teacher; be rich and famous; leave school when I'm 26; go abroad this summer

3
- Look at the example with the class.
- Students write questions using *will* and the prompts.
- Check answers with the class.

4
- Practise the pronunciation of the questions in exercise 3. Pay particular attention to stress and intonation.
- Teach or suggest the following possible short answers, which can be used in response to questions 1, 2 and 4: *I hope so. / I hope not.*; *I think so. / I don't think so.*; *I don't know.*
- Ask different students the questions and encourage the use of the short answers when appropriate.
- Students ask and answer the questions in exercise 3 in pairs.

5
- Look at the second grammar table with the class.
- Students read the sentences in exercise 5 and match them with the rules.
- Check answers with the class.

6
- Students complete the sentences with the correct form of *be going to* and the verbs in the box.
- Check answers with the class.

All Clear Rules

Read through the All Clear Rules with the class. Students may be confused because they think the present continuous is only used to talk about an action in the present. Make it clear that it can also be used to describe definite future arrangements.

7
- Students complete the sentences with the present continuous form of the verbs in brackets.
- Check answers with the class.
- By way of a round-up, elicit from the class the different future situations in which we use *will*, *be going to* and the present continuous.

Mixed-ability solutions

Students who need extra help: Exercise 6. Tell students the verb they need to use in each sentence.

Fast finishers: Exercise 6. Students write three sentences with *be going to* about their plans and intentions for the future. When they finish, they compare their plans in pairs.

Lesson Aims:

Students learn and practise the first conditional.

Grammar

First conditional

Warmer

Write on the board:
If I don't have any homework tonight …
and elicit possible ways of ending the sentence. Write a couple on the board and then point out the tenses used.

8
- Students look at the sentences in the grammar tables. Make sure they understand the notion of *if clause* and *consequence*. Ask them to translate the sentences into their language.
- Students choose the correct options to complete the rules.
- Check answers with the class.

9
- Students choose the correct words to complete the sentences.
- Check answers with the class.

10
- Look at the example with the class. Point out that if we start the sentence with an *if* clause, we need a comma before the clause with the consequence, eg *If we don't hurry, we'll be late.*
- Students write first conditional sentences and questions.
- As this exercise is quite challenging, ask students to compare answers in pairs to allow the possibility of peer teaching before you check answers with the class.

All Clear Grammar

11
- Tell students that this is a cumulative check of the grammar in Units 1 to 7.
- Point out that students will need to be careful in this exercise because they will need to decide which of the three future forms (*be going to*, *will* or the present continuous) to use in many of the gaps. To prepare the class, elicit when we use each of the three future forms and write the following on the board:
  will: to predict the future when there is **no** clear evidence that something will happen
  be going to: for future plans and intentions and to predict the future when there **is** clear evidence that something will happen
  present continuous: for definite future arrangements
- As this exercise is quite challenging, you may want students to do it in pairs.
- Students complete the dialogue with the correct form of the verbs in brackets.

12 2.26
- Play the audio. Students listen and check their answers.
- Check answers with the class.
- Encourage questions if they are not sure why they have got one of the answers wrong. For gap 5, make it clear that either *'m starting* or *'m going to start* is acceptable because it's a definite arrangement but it's also a plan.

Mixed-ability solutions

Students who need extra help: Exercise 11. Write the following options on the board.

1 *it wins / it will win*
2 *you will do / will you do*
3 *win / will win*
4 *will you do / are you going to do*
5 *'m starting / 'll start*
6 *'ll have / 'm having*
7 *went / been*
8 *have gone / went*

Fast finishers: Exercise 10. Students complete the following sentence stems.
If I get a lot of money for my next birthday, …
If it rains tomorrow, …
If I get good marks in my next English exam, …
I'll get some new jeans next month if …

Self-study and extra practice

Workbook
- Grammar, pages 46–7
- Grammar Reference and Practice, pages 78–9

Teacher's Resource File
- All Clear Basics, pages 33–5
- Grammar Consolidation, page 26
- Grammar Extension, page 28
- Language Excellence, pages 13–4

Digital Activities
- Student's Digital Material

First conditional

If clause	Consequence
If I **win**,	I'**ll go** to film school next year.
If I **don't win**,	I **will try** again.

Consequence	*If* clause
I'**ll go** to film school next year	if I **win**.
I **will try** again	if I **don't win**.

Exercise 8
a) future
b) can
c) use

8 **Look at the tables then write the correct words to complete the first conditional rules.**

a) We use the first conditional to talk about **future / past** possibility.
b) We **can / can't** change the order of the clauses.
c) When the *if* clause comes first, we **use / don't use** a comma.

Exercise 9
1 will enjoy
2 don't take
3 have
4 finish
5 will you do

9 **Write the correct words in your notebook.**

1 If you go to the cinema, you **enjoy / will enjoy** the film.
2 It's raining. You will get wet if you **don't take / won't take** an umbrella.
3 If I **have / will have** enough money, I'll buy the film soundtrack.
4 We'll watch a film later if we **finish / will finish** our homework.
5 What **do you do / will you do** if you don't pass your exams?

Exercise 10
1 If I go to bed late, I'll be tired tomorrow.
2 Will they miss the train if they leave after 6 pm?
3 If they study a lot, they won't fail the exam.
4 You will see lots of film stars at the ceremony if you're lucky.
5 If we go to the cinema tonight, will Sarah come with us?

10 **Write first conditional sentences and questions. Use a comma where necessary.**

we / be late / if / we / not hurry.
We'll be late if we don't hurry.
1 if / I / go to bed late / I / be tired tomorrow.
2 they / miss the train / if / they / leave after 6 pm?
3 if / they / study a lot / they / not fail the exam.
4 you / see / lots of film stars at the ceremony / if / you / be lucky.
5 if / we / go to the cinema tonight / Sarah / come / with us?

All Clear Grammar
1 2 3 4 5 6 7 8 9

Exercise 11
1 it'll win
2 will you do
3 win
4 are you going to do
5 'm starting / 'm going to start
6 'll have
7 been
8 went

11 **Complete the interview with the correct form of the verbs in brackets.**

Interviewer Congratulations on your new film. Do you think [1]… (it / win) an award?
Rachel Thanks. I hope it will get a nomination.
Interviewer What [2]… (you / do) if you win?
Rachel If I [3]… (win), I will celebrate with my friends.
Interviewer And what about your plans for the future? What [4]… (you / do) next?
Rachel I [5]… (start) work on a new film next week. After that, I'm not sure. Perhaps I [6]… (have) a holiday!
Interviewer Have you [7]… (go) on holiday this year?
Rachel Yes. I [8]… (go) to Australia in March.

12 2.26 **Listen and check your answers.**

Grammar Reference

Vocabulary

Suffixes

Exercise 1
Students' own answers

1 2.27 **Listen and repeat the verbs. How do you say them in your language?**

advertise • argue • celebrate • connect • decorate • develop • educate • enjoy • equip • excite • move • possess • predict • suggest

2 **Copy and complete the table with verbs from exercise 1. Then use the suffixes *-ion* or *-ment* to make the noun forms.**

Verbs	Nouns
advertise	*advertisement*
argue	*argument*

Exercise 2

Verbs	Nouns
advertise	*advertisement*
argue	*argument*
celebrate	celebration
connect	connection
decorate	decoration
develop	development
educate	education
enjoy	enjoyment
equip	equipment
excite	excitement
move	movement
possess	possession
predict	prediction
suggest	suggestion

3 2.28 **Listen and check your answers.**

4 **Complete the sentences with nouns from the table in exercise 2.**

We think the d*ecoration* on this cake is really colourful.

1 You need a lot of e… to make a film.
2 What is the c… between these two things?
3 I think e… is important. I want to get a good job, so I study a lot.
4 My parents are having a big c… for their wedding anniversary.
5 I get a lot of e… from reading – I love it!

Exercise 4
1 equipment
2 connection
3 education
4 celebration
5 enjoyment

Listening

5 2.29 **Listen and look at the pictures. Write the correct words in your notebook.**

Fresh Films makes films **about teenagers / using teenage film-makers.**

Exercise 5
using teenage film-makers

6 **Listen again. Write true or false in your notebook.**

1 The Fresh Films programme started more than ten years ago.
2 Some participants who have been on the programme now work in the film industry.
3 You need to have some experience to apply for the programme.
4 Fresh Films has only made short films.

Exercise 6
1 true
2 true
3 false
4 false

Vocabulary Reference

Lesson Aims:

Students learn about noun suffixes and practise forming nouns from verbs.
Students listen to a report about a programme that gives young people experience in film-making and identify general and specific information from it.

Vocabulary

Suffixes

Warmer

Write on the board *calculate* and *calculation*. Ask what they mean and which one is the verb and which one is the noun. Then ask how we change the verb to the noun. Explain that *-ion* is what is called a *suffix* in English. Explain also that suffixes are letters that we can add to words to change their grammatical function, eg from a verb to a noun, but that they do not usually change their basic meaning.
Ask students if they can think of any words in their own language that change from being a verb to a noun through the addition of a suffix, or give some examples.

1 2.27

- Play the audio. Students listen and repeat the verbs. Make sure that they stress the words correctly.
- Elicit or give a translation of each word.

2
- Students look at and copy the table.
- Point out the two noun suffixes, *-ion* and *-ment*, and the examples.
- Students complete the table with the verbs from exercise 1 and decide whether to add *-ion* or *-ment* to make nouns. Allow students to use dictionaries to help them.

3 2.28

- Play the audio. Students listen and check their answers to exercise 2. Check they have spelt each of the nouns correctly, especially in the case of the nouns that lose the final *e* of the verb.
- Point out that *argument* can never mean the plot of a film. (It is a false friend in many Latin-based languages.)

4
- Read the example with the class.
- Students complete the sentences with nouns from the table in exercise 2.
- Check answers with the class.

Listening

Warmer

Brainstorm with the class what you need to do if you want to make a short film, eg, have a good storyline, have a good script, hire the right actors, have the right equipment, etc.

5 2.29

- Students look at the pictures and read the sentence with the two possible options.
- Play the audio. Students listen to the documentary and choose the correct words to complete the sentence.
- Check the answer with the class.

6
- Students read the statements. They try to decide whether they are true or false based on their first listening.
- Play the audio again. Students listen and check and complete their answers.
- Check answers with the class.

Web info

Type these words in your search engine for more information about Fresh Films: 'Fresh Films FAQs'

Mixed-ability solutions

Students who need extra help: Exercise 2. Tell students that all the verbs that end in consonant + *-t* or *-ate* take the *-ion* suffix.

Fast finishers: Exercise 2. Students underline where the stress comes in both the verbs and the nouns.

Self-study and extra practice

Workbook
- Vocabulary, page 45
- Vocabulary Reference, page 90

Teacher's Resource File
- All Clear Basics, page 32
- Vocabulary Consolidation, page 25
- Vocabulary Extension, page 27
- Key Competences: Listening, page 14

Digital Activities
- Student's Digital Material

Lesson Aims:

Students learn and practise functional language to ask for and give opinions.

Speaking

Asking for and giving opinions / Talking about a film

Warmer

Ask students what the last very good and very bad film was that they have seen. Then elicit why it was very good or very bad.

Model Dialogue

1 2.30

- Students read the question.
- Play the audio. Students listen to and read the dialogue.
- Students answer the question.
- Check the answer with the class.

2
- Play the audio again. Students listen again and this time repeat the dialogue.
- Focus on the use of *What did you think of … ?*; *What about … ?*; and *Did you like … ?* to ask for opinions. Get the class to pay attention to stress and intonation.

Extra activity

Students look at what Ruby says and find all the verbs she uses to express her opinion (*thought*, *suppose*, *liked*, *agree*).

Speaking Task

1 Talk about a film

Students look at the information and choose a film. Alternatively, they can use their own ideas.

2 Prepare a dialogue

Students look at the Model Dialogue and change the words in blue to make their own dialogue.

3 Speak

Students practise their dialogues in pairs.

Mixed-ability solutions

Students who need extra help: Speaking Task. Students write out their dialogue before they do step 3.

Fast finishers: Speaking Task. Students act out another dialogue about a different film or about a series on TV. If possible, they do this without looking at the Model Dialogue.

Self-study and extra practice

Workbook
- Speaking, page 126

Teacher's Resource File
- Key Competences: Speaking, pages 31–2

Digital Activities
- Student's Digital Material

Speaking

Asking for and giving opinions / Talking about a film

Exercise 1
She liked the soundtrack and the special effects were OK.

1 2.30 **Listen to the dialogue. What did Ruby like about the film?**

Model Dialogue

Paul

Ruby

Paul: What did you think of *After Earth*?

Ruby: I thought it was rubbish.

Paul: Really? I thought it was brilliant! The special effects were amazing.

Ruby: I suppose they were OK but the plot was terrible.

Paul: What about the actors? I thought they were brilliant!

Ruby: No, they weren't. They were awful and the script was really bad.

Paul: Did you like anything?

Ruby: Yes, I liked the soundtrack.

Paul: Me too. It was incredible.

Ruby: At least we agree about something …

2 **Listen again and repeat the dialogue.**

Speaking Task

1 Talk about a film

Choose a film and read the opinions. You can use the ideas below or your own.

Student A

Mockingjay	*Guardians of the Galaxy*
special effects: incredible	*action scenes: very exciting*
soundtrack: great	*stunts: amazing*

Student B

Mockingjay	*Guardians of the Galaxy*
stunts: terrible	*script: awful*
plot: really boring	*plot: a bit silly*
liked the acting	*enjoyed the ending*

2 Prepare a dialogue

Look at the Model Dialogue and change the words in blue.

3 Speak

In pairs, practise your dialogue.

What did you think of *Mockingjay*?

I thought it was rubbish.

Useful Language **Asking for and giving opinions**

What did you think of *After Earth*?	**I thought it was** rubbish.
What about the actors?	**They were** awful and the script was really bad.
Did you like anything?	Yes, **I liked** the soundtrack.

Writing

A film review

1 2.31 **Read the Model Text and listen. Match descriptions 1–4 with paragraphs A–D. Write them in your notebook.**

1 Conclusion and recommendation
2 Personal opinions about the film
3 Basic information about the film
4 Description of the plot

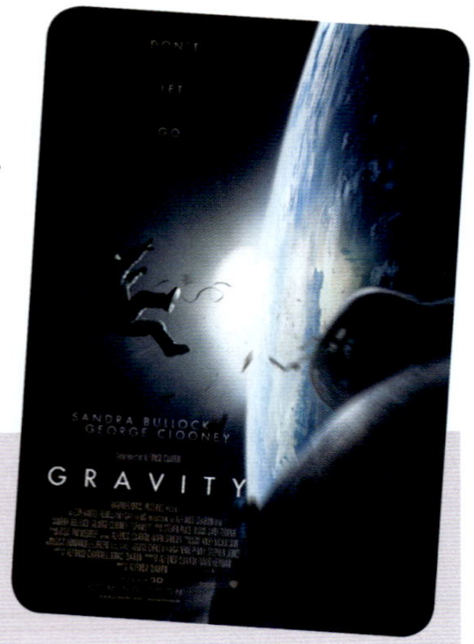

Exercise 1
1 D
2 C
3 A
4 B

Model Text

Film of the week

A *Gravity* is a thriller set in space. The director is Alfonso Cuarón and the main actors are Sandra Bullock and George Clooney.

B Sandra Bullock plays a scientific engineer on a mission with George Clooney, a veteran astronaut. An accident destroys their space shuttle and they are alone in space, desperately trying to return to Earth.

C **In my opinion**, *Gravity* is a fantastic film. The action scenes are terrifying, the special effects are amazing and the actors are brilliant. Sandra Bullock has always been **one of my favourite** actors. **For me**, this is her best film.

D If you like excitement, tension and horror, you will love *Gravity*. **I think** it will become a classic and I would recommend it to everyone.

2 **Look at the All Clear Tips and translate the words in bold.**

Exercise 2
Students' own answers

All Clear Tips

Giving opinions

Sandra Bullock has always been **one of my favourite** actors.
For me, this is her best film.
I think it will become a classic.
In my opinion, *Gravity* is a brilliant film.

3 **Order the words to make sentences giving opinions.**

1 I / really / the / is / script / funny / think / .
2 special effects / In / the / my / are / opinion, / terrible / .
3 is / worst / me, / it / For / film / his / .
4 of / one / my / favourite / is / directors / Amenábar / .
5 it / an / awful / In / opinion, / film / my / is / .

Writing Task

1 Plan

Make notes about a film and include:

Basic information: *the title, the type of film, the actors, the director*
The plot: *where the film is set, the main characters, the general story*
Your opinions: *actors, special effects, soundtrack, plot, script*
Conclusion: *a final opinion and a recommendation*

2 Write

Use the Model Text, your notes and this structure:

Paragraph 1: Basic information
Paragraph 2: The plot
Paragraph 3: Your opinions
Paragraph 4: Conclusion

3 Check

☑ future tenses, first conditional
☑ films, suffixes
☑ giving opinions

Exercise 3
1 I think the script is really funny.
2 In my opinion, the special effects are terrible.
3 For me, it is his worst film.
4 Amenábar is one of my favourite directors.
5 In my opinion, it is an awful film.

Lesson Aims:

Students learn and practise ways of giving an opinion.
Students write a film review.

Writing

A film review

Warmer

Ask students what type of film they like most, eg horror, action, romance, etc, and why.

1 2.31

- Students look at the picture and identify the film. Ask them if they have seen it and whether they liked it.
- Ask students how many paragraphs there are in the review.
- Read the paragraph descriptions with the class.
- Play the audio. Students read and listen to the Model Text.
- Students match the descriptions with the paragraphs.
- Check answers with the class.
- Point out that when we write a film review it is important to structure it in an orderly way and to discuss different points in different paragraphs.

All Clear Tips

2
- Read the All Clear Tips with the class.
- Students translate the words in bold into their language.

3
- Students write the words in the correct order to make sentences.
- Check answers with the class.

Writing Task

1 Plan

Read the notes with the class. Students make notes about a film of their choice.

2 Write

Look at the structure with the class. Students use their notes to write a film review. Emphasize that they should use some of the expressions for giving opinions that they have just learnt.

3 Check

Encourage students to check their work, paying particular attention to the points mentioned.

Extra activity

Play *Guess the film*. Ask a student to start reading his / her review without mentioning the name of the film. The rest of the class have to see how quickly they can guess the film.

Web info

Type these words in your search engine to read a range of reviews about *Gravity*: 'Gravity + IMDB'

Mixed-ability solutions

Students who need extra help: Writing task. Students just complete the notes in step 1.

Fast finishers: Writing task. Students read their partner's review. If they have also seen the film, they compare their opinions.

Self-study and extra practice

Workbook
- Writing Guide, pages 114–5

Teacher's Resource File
- Key Competences: Writing, page 14

Lesson Aims:

Students read a short biography of the film director Alfred Hitchcock.
Students practise sentence stress and the pronunciation of weak forms

Culture Reading

Famous films and film-makers

Warmer

Books closed. Ask if students like mystery and suspense films. Teach the word *thriller*. Ask them if they have seen any good thrillers. Then ask if they know which director is famous for the thrillers he made.

2.32

- Students look at the picture of Hitchcock and the poster for the film *The Birds*. Ask them if they have seen any of Hitchcock's films. Write some of the names of his films on the board in English, eg *The Birds*, *Psycho*, *Vertigo*, *Rear Window*, *North by Northwest*.
- Read the questions with the class.
- Play the audio. Students read and listen to the text to find the answers to the questions.
- Check answers with the class.

Extra activity

Tell students the plot of the Hitchcock film *Rear Window*. *Jeff is a professional photographer. He breaks his leg while he is taking photos at a car race. As a result, he has to rest in his flat in New York. He is bored so he spends a lot of time looking out of the window and observing his neighbours. He begins to think that the man who lives opposite him has killed his wife. His friend, fashion designer Lisa Fremont, helps him to investigate.*

In groups, students invent a slogan and design a poster advertising the film.

When they have finished, ask the different groups to share their ideas.

Finally, you may want to show the original poster for the film (see *Web info*).

Pronunciation

Sentence stress and weak forms

a 2.33

- Play the audio. Students listen and repeat the sentences.
- Ask students which words have the main stress and why they have them. (*The most important words have the main stress.*)
- Then ask the class what happens to the words in blue. (*They are unstressed and the short vowel sounds are pronounced /ə/.*) Explain that in informal speech *going to* can be pronounced /ˈgʌnə/. In more correct speech, *going* is pronounced normally and *to* takes the weak form /tə/ before a consonant or /tʊ/ before a vowel.

b 2.34

- Play the audio. Students listen and repeat the sentences.
- Check that they are placing the stress on the correct words.

Web info

Type these words in your search engine for

- more information about Alfred Hitchcock: 'alfredhitchcock.com'
- the original poster for *Rear Window*: 'rear window original movie poster'
- the original trailer for *Vertigo*: 'youtube + vertigo original trailer'

Mixed-ability solutions

Students who need extra help: Reading text. Tell students in which paragraph the answer to each question is to be found.

1 *paragraph 1*
2 *paragraph 2*
3 *paragraph 2*
4 *paragraph 3*

Fast finishers: Reading text. Students read the text again and write down all the numbers and what they refer to.

Self-study and extra practice

Workbook

- Culture: Reading and Listening, page 99

Culture Reading

EXTRA

FAMOUS FILMS AND FILM-MAKERS

Alfred Hitchcock

Hitchcock was born in the UK in 1899 and he became one of the most famous and influential directors in the world. He started his career as a director in 1925. He moved to Hollywood in 1939 and continued to make films until he died.

Hitchcock never won an Oscar for Best Director, although he was nominated five times. However, he received a Life Achievement Award from the American Film Institute (AFI). Four of his films appear in AFI's list of *Top 10 Mystery Films of All Time*. In 1980, he was given a special award by Queen Elizabeth II and became Sir Alfred Hitchcock.

Hitchcock's films

Hitchcock made 53 films altogether. Many of his films are classics that will always be popular with film lovers. He is probably most famous for his thrillers and mystery films including *Vertigo*, *Psycho*, and *The Birds*. If you watch his films carefully, you will usually be able to see him. That's because Hitchcock made a short appearance in all his films from 1938 onwards. Audiences love trying to find him!

2.32 **Read and listen. Then answer the questions in your notebook.**

1 Who was Hitchcock and when did he start his career?
2 Did he win any Oscars?
3 What awards did he win?
4 Did he appear in any of his films?

Reading text exercise

1 He was a film director. He started his career in 1925.
2 no
3 He won a Life Achievement Award from the American Film Institute and a special award from Queen Elizabeth II.
4 yes

Pronunciation

Sentence stress and weak forms

a 2.33 **Listen and repeat the sentences. Which words have the main stress? What happens to the words in blue?**

1 I'm going to watch a Hitchcock film tonight.
2 We're going to invite them to the party.
3 They aren't going to buy a house.

b 2.34 **Listen and repeat the sentences.**

Pronunciation exercise a

Words with main stress underlined:

1 I'm going to <u>watch</u> a <u>Hitchcock</u> <u>film</u> <u>tonight</u>.
2 We're going to <u>invite</u> them to the <u>party</u>.
3 They <u>aren't</u> going to <u>buy</u> a <u>house</u>.

The words in blue are not stressed and they are pronounced as weak forms.

Unit 7 Language Reference

Vocabulary Films

director • film a scene • film star • plot • producer • release a film • screen • script • soundtrack • special effects • star in a film • stunt • stuntman / stuntwoman • win an award

Suffixes

advertisement • argument • celebration • connection • decoration • development • education • enjoyment • equipment • excitement • movement • possession • prediction • suggestion

Grammar *will*

Affirmative	Negative	Interrogative	Short answers
I / You **will** change.	I / You **won't** change.	**Will** I / you change?	Yes, I / you **will**.
He / She / It **will** change.	He / She / It **won't** change.	**Will** he / she / it change?	No, he / she / it **won't**.
We / You / They **will** change.	We / You / They **won't** change.	**Will** we / you / they change?	Yes, we / you / they **will**.

be going to

Affirmative	Negative	Interrogative	Short answers
I **am going to** make a film.	I **am not going to** make a film.	**Am** I **going to** make a film?	Yes, I **am**.
You **are going to** make a film.	You **are not going to** make a film.	**Are** you **going to** make a film?	No, you **are not**.
He / She / It **is going to** make a film.	He / She / It **is not going to** make a film.	**Is** he / she / it **going to** make a film?	Yes, he / she / it **is**.
We / You / They **are going to** make a film.	We / You / They **are not going to** make a film.	**Are** we / you / they **going to** make a film?	No, we / you / they **are not**.

Present continuous

We use the present continuous for definite plans and arrangements in the future.
We use it with future time expressions, such as

- this evening
- tomorrow
- on Friday
- next week

First conditional

If clause	Consequence
If I **win**,	I'**ll go** to film school next year.
If I don't **win**,	I **will try** again.

Consequence	*If* clause
I'**ll go** to film school next year.	if I **win**.
I **will try** again	if I **don't win**.

Speaking Asking for and giving opinions

What did you think of *After Earth*?
What about the actors?
Did you like anything?

I thought it was rubbish.
They were awful and the script was really bad.
Yes, **I liked** the soundtrack.

Unit 7 Progress Check

Vocabulary Films

1 Complete the sentences with the words in the box.

script plot soundtrack
screen special effects

1 Can you move your head, please? I can't see the … .
2 Who wrote the … for that film? The dialogue is really funny.
3 The … of the film was confusing. It's a very complicated story.
4 The music in the film was great. I loved the … .
5 The scenes with the … were very realistic.

Exercise 1
1 screen
2 script
3 plot
4 soundtrack
5 special effects

Suffixes

2 Complete the sentences with the correct form of the words in brackets.

1 The wi-fi … (connect) is really bad here. I can't open any web pages.
2 What is your favourite … (advertise) on TV?
3 Scientists are working on the … (develop) of the new invention.
4 Has anyone got a good … (suggest) about where to go tonight?
5 There was great … (excite) when they announced the film's release.

Exercise 2
1 connection
2 advertisement
3 development
4 suggestion
5 excitement

Grammar Future forms

3 Complete the sentences with the correct form of *will* and the verbs in brackets.

1 Where do you think you … (live) in the future?
2 That film definitely … (not win) an award. It was terrible!
3 Do you think they … (make) another film together?
4 Perhaps they … (film) those scenes in Scotland. I'm not sure.
5 People … (not buy) the DVD. It's too expensive.

Exercise 3
1 'll live
2 won't win
3 'll make
4 'll film
5 won't buy

4 Order the words to make sentences and questions.

1 going / be / hot / It's / to / today / .
2 they / to England / Are / to / going / fly / ?
3 not / going / tonight / I'm / go out / to / .
4 you / What / next weekend / to / are / do / going / ?
5 going / stay / Where / you / to / on holiday / are / ?

Exercise 4
1 It's going to be hot today.
2 Are they going to fly to England?
3 I'm not going to go out tonight.
4 What are you going to do next weekend?
5 Where are you going to stay on holiday?

First conditional

5 Write the correct words in your notebook.

1 What do you say / will you say if they ask / 'll ask about your opinion of the film?
2 If I have / will have enough money, I buy / 'll buy the DVD.
3 Their parents don't be / won't be happy if they fail / 'll fail the exam.
4 If they don't leave / won't leave now, they are / 'll be late.
5 Do you go / Will you go to the concert if there are / will be any tickets?

Exercise 5
1 will you say; ask
2 have; 'll buy
3 won't be; fail
4 don't leave; 'll be
5 Will you go; are

Check your answers

Write your scores for exercises 1–5 in your notebook. What did you get for:

- films?
- suffixes?
- future forms?
- first conditional?

Extra Practice

If you need extra practice, go to:

- Unit 7 Grammar Reference
- Unit 7 Vocabulary Reference
- Unit 7 Grammar Exercises
- Unit 7 Vocabulary Exercises

Correct the activities with the class. Students who need extra revision and practice can go to:

Workbook
- Unit 7 Revision, page 48
- Grammar Reference and Practice, pages 78–9
- Vocabulary Reference, page 90

Student's Digital Material
www.allclear.macmillan.es

8 Our friends

Overview

Unit objectives and key competences

- Understand, memorize and correctly use vocabulary related to cultural conventions CLC
- Understand, memorize and correctly use verb and noun collocations CLC, L2L
- Identify the gist and main ideas in a travel guide about cultural differences CLC
- Learn about different cultural norms CAE, SCC
- Understand, contrast and correctly use modal verbs of obligation, prohibition and advice and the second conditional CLC, L2L
- Identify specific information through a listening activity about relationships CLC
- Use appropriate functional language to ask about a person and describe him or her CLC, SCC
- Write a formal letter using linkers of addition and contrast CLC, SIE, CAE
- Learn about the importance of overcoming adversity SIE
- Identify specific information in a text about Charles Rolls and Henry Royce CLC
- Learn about the origin of the Rolls-Royce car CAE
- Assimilate the All Clear Tips and Rules and study the Language Reference from the unit CLC, L2L, SIE
- Identify areas of language which need improvement and use ICT for extra practice DC, CLC, L2L

More information on Key Competences, page v

Linguistic content

Grammar

- Modal verbs of obligation, prohibition and advice: *must / mustn't, have to / don't have to, should / shouldn't*
- Second conditional

Recycled grammar

- Present simple (Unit 1)
- Comparatives (Unit 4)
- Present perfect (Unit 5)
- *will* and *be going to* (Unit 7)

Main vocabulary

- Making friends: *arrive early*, *be late*, etc
- Verb and noun collocations: *give advice*, *have an argument*, etc

Functional language

- Describing people / A party

Pronunciation

- The sounds /aɪ/ /ɪ/ /ʊ/ /ɔɪ/

Skills: learning outcomes

- **Reading** Understand specific information in a clearly structured travel guide about cultural differences. The student can re-read the more difficult parts, page 87
- **Listening** Extract the main ideas from a conversation about problems in relationships which is delivered in a clear, slow way, page 90
- **Speaking** Communicate effectively in an everyday situation, exchanging information about people, page 91
- **Writing** Write a formal letter in a conventional format with simple and relevant information set out in a logical order, page 92
- **Reading** Get the main ideas of short text about two famous friends. The student can re-read the more difficult parts, page 93

Lifelong learning skills and content-based learning

Life skills

- **Recognizing diversity** Acceptance of behaviour different from that usual in one's own culture, page 86
- **Communication** Acceptable rules of behaviour in relationships and friendships, page 90
- **Social development** The importance of recognizing achievement, page 92
- **Socio-cultural awareness** The origin of the Rolls-Royce brand, page 93

Learning strategies

- Awareness of verb and noun collocations, page 90

Cross-curricular content

- Language: verb and noun collocations, linking ideas: addition and contrast, conventions for opening and closing formal letters, pages 90 and 92
- Citizenship: respect for others, page 86

Further materials and evaluation

Digital material

- Student's and Teacher's Resource Centres
- Teacher's Presentation Kit
- Student's Digital Material: interactive vocabulary and grammar activities
- Video *Music* (Revision Units 7–9, page 108)

Student's website www.macmillansecondary.es

Workbook

- Vocabulary, pages 56–7
- Vocabulary Reference, page 92
- Grammar, pages 58–9
- Grammar Reference and Practice, pages 82–3
- Revision, page 60
- Culture: Reading and Listening, page 101
- Writing Guide, pages 118–9
- Speaking, page 128

Teacher's Resource File

Multi-level Materials Bank

- All Clear Basics, pages 36–40
- Vocabulary and Grammar Consolidation and Extension, pages 29–32
- Language Excellence, pages 15–6
- Translation and Dictation, pages 8 and 17

Lifelong Learning

- Digital Competence, pages 15–6
- Culture Video Material, pages 5–6
- Study Skills, pages 1–12

Evaluation and Key Competences

- Evaluation Rubrics, pages 1–7
- Key Competences, pages 15–6 and 33–4

Content-based Learning

- CLIL, pages 1–10
- Macmillan Readers, pages 1–7

Evaluation material

- Unit 8 end-of-unit test: Basic, Standard and Extra
- CEFR Skills Exam Generator

Web info

Tips to find extra information on: ways of appreciating different cultures, opinions about boyfriend–girlfriend problems, the Young Achievers Award, Rolls-Royce cars

Extra help for weaker students

Teacher's Resource File: All Clear Basics, pages 36–40

Material for fast finishers

Workbook: Grammar Extension, page 61
Teacher's Resource File: Vocabulary Extension, page 31
Teacher's Resource File: Grammar Extension, page 32
Teacher's Resource File: Language Excellence, pages 15–6

8 Our friends

Objectives

Vocabulary	Making friends; verb and noun collocations
Grammar	Modal verbs: obligation, prohibition and advice; second conditional
Speaking	Describing people
Writing	A formal letter

Vocabulary

Making friends

Exercise 1
1 interrupt a conversation
2 jump a queue
3 be polite
4 point
5 shake hands
6 arrive early
7 tell jokes
8 be late
9 click your fingers
10 be rude
11 bring a present
12 kiss a stranger
13 take off your shoes

1 2.35 **Listen and repeat the words. Match them with pictures 1–13.**

arrive early • be late • be polite • be rude • bring a present • click your fingers • interrupt a conversation • jump a queue • kiss a stranger • point • shake hands • take off your shoes • tell jokes

Exercise 2
Students' own answers

2 **Which of the actions in exercise 1 have you done today?**

Exercise 3
1 take off my shoes
2 shook hands with
3 told a joke
4 click your fingers at
5 jumped the queue

3 **Write the correct words in your notebook.**

1 He asked me to **tell a joke / take off my shoes / jump the queue** because they were dirty.
2 I **arrived early / shook hands with / was rude to** David Beckham. He was really friendly.
3 I **told a joke / kissed her / clicked my fingers**, but nobody laughed.
4 Don't **tell a joke to / click your fingers at / shake hands with** the waiter. It's very rude.
5 He **jumped the queue / told a joke / was late** because he wanted to get on the bus first.

Exercise 4
The Prime Minister

4 2.36 **Listen to Magda and Adam. Who has Adam shaken hands with?**

5 **In pairs, ask and answer the question.**

Have you ever shaken hands with someone famous?

Yes, I have. I met the king when he visited our school.

Vocabulary Reference

Lesson Aims:

Students learn and practise some phrases related to cultural conventions.
Students listen to a dialogue about meeting someone famous and identify specific information.

Vocabulary

Making friends

Warmer

Have a discussion with students about what is considered polite and rude behaviour in their country, eg is it rude not to say *please* and *thank you*, to talk with your mouth full, to talk loudly, to put your elbows on the table? What is the correct way to greet people? Highlight the fact that there are cultural differences in what is considered rude and polite. For example, in the UK it is considered rude not to say *please* and *thank you* whereas in other cultures it is not so important.

1 2.35

- Read out the words and check students understand the meanings.
- Play the audio. Students listen and repeat the words.
- Students look at the pictures and describe what is happening in one or two.
- Students match the pictures with the phrases.
- Check answers with the class.

Extra activity

In pairs, students classify the different actions as polite or rude. When they finish, get feedback and encourage debate if there is not agreement.

2
- Students compile a list of the actions they have done today.
- Conduct class feedback about the answers.

3
- Students read the sentences and choose the correct words to complete them.
- Check answers with the class.

4 2.36

- Students read the question and speculate about the answer. Elicit some suggestions and write them on the board, eg *king*, *president*, *famous footballer*, *politician*, etc.
- Play the audio. Students listen and find who Adam has shaken hands with.
- Check the answer with the class.

5

- Read the question and answer in speech bubbles and ask students to repeat them.
- Ask another student to ask you the question. Invent an answer if necessary.
- Students ask and answer the question in pairs.
- Ask some students to report their partner's answer.

Cultural note

In the past it was not common in the UK or USA to greet people by kissing. People would shake hands or just say hello without any physical contact. However, today it is much more common, especially between girls and women, though not so often between men.

Mixed-ability solutions

Students who need extra help: Exercise 5. Students write their answer first.

Fast finishers: Exercise 3. In pairs, one student covers the words in exercise 1. The other says the verb. Their partner has to complete the phrase, eg Student A: *interrupt*; Student B: *a conversation*. Then they change roles and repeat the exercise.

Self-study and extra practice

Workbook
- Vocabulary, page 50
- Vocabulary Reference, page 91

Teacher's Resource File
- All Clear Basics, page 36
- Vocabulary Consolidation, page 29
- Vocabulary Extension, page 31

Reading

A travel guide

Warmer

Find out who in the class has been abroad. Ask which countries they have been to and what cultural differences they noticed, eg with meal times, food, etc?

Word Check

Check students understand the new words: *cheek*, *burp*, *small talk*. Explain any they don't know.

1 2.37

- Students look at the pictures and read the headings in exercise 1.
- Play the audio. Students read and listen to the text and match the headings with the paragraphs.
- Check answers with the class.

2
- Students read the questions.
- Student read the text again and answer the questions.
- Check answers with the class.

Extra activity

Give students a minute to look in the text and find as many of the vocabulary expressions from exercise 1 on page 86 as possible.

3
- Read the question with the class.
- Students discuss the question in pairs.
- Get feedback from the class and write the main rules on the board.

All Clear Facts

Read the fact with the class.
Ask students if there are any gestures or particular body language in their country that have special significance.

Cultural note

In the United States and Canada, intermittent eye contact is extremely important in conveying interest and attention. In many Middle Eastern cultures, intense eye contact between people of the same gender is often a symbol of trust and sincerity; however, between people of the opposite gender, especially in Muslim cultures, anything more than brief eye contact is considered inappropriate. In Asian, African and Latin American cultures, extended eye contact is considered a 'challenge'. The Japanese tend to consider even brief eye contact uncomfortable.

Web info

Type these words in your search engine for information about ways of appreciating different cultures: 'Wikihow + understand admire culture differences'

Mixed-ability solutions

Students who need extra help: Exercise 2. Write the following options on the board.

1 *shake hands / bow your head*
2 *Mexico / China*
3 *Chile / Scotland*
4 *work / money*

Fast finishers: Exercise 2. Students write three things you should do in their country and three things you shouldn't. They can use the text for ideas.

Self-study and extra practice

Teacher's Resource File

- Key Competences: Reading, page 15

Reading

A travel guide

Word Check
cheek burp small talk

CULTURAL INTELLIGENCE

Home | News | Forum | Cultures | Travel | Accommodation | Top Locations | Forum | Sign up

Travel opens your mind to other cultures, but you should always learn about local customs before you go. Politeness is especially important. Here's our guide to being polite in different countries.

A
In France, men and women usually kiss each other on the **cheek**, but men shake hands. In the UK, Germany and the USA, kissing is common between friends but you should shake hands with strangers. In Russia, you shouldn't shake hands in the doorway of a house – it's bad luck.

Comment Like

B
In the UK, you don't have to bring a present, like flowers or chocolates, but people will be pleased if you do. In Germany, Japan or the UK you mustn't be late. It's very rude. In Mexico, you should be late – it's normal. In Japan, China and Scandinavia you must take your shoes off when you arrive, so you should wear clean socks!

Comment Like

C
In most European countries, if you **burped** after a meal, people would be offended. However, in China they would be pleased because it shows that you enjoyed the food. In India, you mustn't eat with your left hand because it's unclean. In Mexico, it's acceptable to eat with your hands, but in Chile it's the opposite! In France, you shouldn't divide a restaurant bill. You should pay the bill yourself (or wait for someone else to pay!).

Comment Like

D
In some countries, it's OK to interrupt someone in a conversation, but you shouldn't in Japan, the USA or the UK. Germans enjoy having serious conversations in social situations, but they aren't keen on **small talk**. In France, you mustn't talk about money at the table. It's very rude.

Comment Like

1 2.37 **Read and listen. Match headings 1–4 with paragraphs A–D. Write them in your notebook.**

1 Eating etiquette
2 Visiting people's homes
3 The art of conversation
4 Greetings

Exercise 1
1 C
2 B
3 D
4 A

All Clear Facts
In Bulgaria, you nod to say 'no' and shake your head to say 'yes'. In most other countries, it's the opposite.

2 **Read the text again. Answer the questions.**

1 What should you do when you meet someone for the first time in Germany?
2 In which country is it OK to be late?
3 Where mustn't you eat with your hands?
4 What topic of conversation is unacceptable at meals in France?

Exercise 2
1 shake hands
2 Mexico
3 Chile
4 money

3 **What other cultural rules do you know?**

Exercise 3
Students' own answers

Obligation, prohibition and advice

Obligation	She must / has to
No obligation	She **doesn't have to**
Prohibition	She **mustn't**
Advice	She **should** We **shouldn't** **Should** you …?

Language Reference p94

1 **Look at the table. Complete the rules with the words in the box.**

obligation | no obligation | prohibition

a) We use *must* or *have to* to show … . The speaker thinks something is very important.
b) We use *don't have to* to show there is … . The speaker thinks something isn't necessary.
c) We use *mustn't* to show … . The speaker thinks it is very important not to do something.

Exercise 1
a) obligation
b) no obligation
c) prohibition

2 **Write the correct words in your notebook.**

Rules for summer camp:

1 You **don't have to / must** be polite to the monitors.
2 You **mustn't / have to** take expensive gadgets. There isn't a safe place for them.
3 You **mustn't / don't have to** talk in bed. People need to sleep.
4 You **mustn't / don't have to** make your bed. You can choose.
5 You **have to / don't have to** look after the key to your room.
6 You **must / mustn't** be late. Classes start punctually at 8.30 am.

Exercise 2
1 must
2 mustn't
3 mustn't
4 don't have to
5 have to
6 mustn't

3 **Look at the question in the table. Do we use *have to* or *must* to ask questions about obligations?**

Obligation
Do I **have to** bring a present?
Yes, you do. / No, you don't.

Exercise 3
have to

4 **Write complete questions using *have to* in your notebook.**

young people / be / polite?
Do young people have to be polite?
1 you / be home / before midnight?
2 do / your homework / tonight?
3 your dad / get up early / on Saturday mornings?
4 visitors / bring presents / in your country?
5 you / take off your shoes / at home?

Exercise 4
1 Do you have to be home before midnight?
2 Do you have to do your homework tonight?
3 Does your dad have to get up early on Saturday mornings?
4 Do visitors have to bring presents in your country?
5 Do you have to take off your shoes at home?

5 **In pairs, ask and answer the questions in exercise 4.**

6 **Look at the sentences in the table. What is the difference between *should* and *must / have to*?**

Advice
You **should** shake hands, but you don't have to.
You **shouldn't** tell jokes at dinner, it's rude.

Exercise 6
Should expresses a recommendation whereas *must / have to* express an obligation.

7 **Write the correct words in your notebook.**

I'm really lucky because I (1)**shouldn't / don't have to** wait for school to talk to my best friend. My best friend is my sister, Karen, and we share a bedroom. However, we have some rules. I (2)**mustn't / don't have to** borrow her clothes and she (3)**has to / doesn't have to** ask me when she wants to listen to my music. We both (4)**mustn't / have to** keep our things tidy. We have one more rule. Because Karen's older than me, she (5)**doesn't have to / mustn't** go to bed when I do, but when she comes to bed, she (6)**doesn't have to / mustn't** wake me up if I'm asleep! Luckily she's really kind, so she never does. I (7)**should / don't have to** be more like her!

Exercise 7
1 don't have to
2 mustn't
3 has to
4 have to
5 doesn't have to
6 mustn't
7 should

Lesson Aims:

Students revise or learn and practise the modal verbs *must, mustn't, have to, don't have to* , *should* and *shouldn't* for obligation, prohibition and advice. (Continues on page 89.)

Grammar

Obligation, prohibition and advice

Warmer

Ask students about the rules in their school. Try to elicit some rules with *must* or *have to* (eg *You must / have to arrive by 9 o'clock.*), *mustn't* (eg *You mustn't copy in exams.*) and *don't have to* (eg *You don't have to wear a uniform.*). Write a sentence with an example of each structure on the board. Make sure that students understand the difference between *mustn't* and *don't have to.*

1
- Look at the table with the class. Ask students to translate the phrases.
- Students read and complete the rules in exercise 1 with the words in the box.
- Check answers with the class.

2
- Students choose the correct words to complete the sentences.
- Check answers with the class and clear up any confusion.

Extra activity

Book closed. Say the key word or words in each sentence in exercise 2 (eg *polite / monitors*) and elicit the complete sentence.

3
- Read the question and answers in the table with the class and ask students to translate them.
- Elicit whether we use *have to* or *must* to ask questions about obligations.

4
- Read the example with the class.
- Students write questions with *have to.*
- Check the questions with the class.

5
- The class repeat the questions in exercise 4 after you. Check for acceptable stress and intonation.
- Students ask and answer the questions in pairs.

6
- Check students understand the meaning of the word *advice.*
- Students look at the sentences. Elicit the translation of each sentence.
- Elicit the difference between *should* and *must / have to.*
- Make sure that students understand that that *should* and *shouldn't* are not as strong as *must, mustn't* and *have to.* They express a recommendation, not an obligation.

7
- Explain that in this exercise students need to choose between *should, have to* and *must* to complete a text. With a weaker class, do the first one with the class, asking why the answer is *don't have to* and not *shouldn't.*
- Check answers with the class.

Mixed-ability solutions

Students who need extra help: Exercise 5. Students write their answers first.

Fast finishers: Exercise 7. Students look at the reading text on page 87 and write four sentences with *must / have to, don't have to, should* and *shouldn't* to describe how you should act in different countries.

Lesson Aims:

Students revise or learn and practise the modal verbs *must*, *musn't*, *have to*, *don't have to*, *should* and *shouldn't* for obligation, prohibition and advice. (Continued from page 88.)
Students learn and practise the second conditional.

Grammar

8 • This exercise gives further practice in deciding when to use *should* and when to use *have to*, *don't have to* or *mustn't*.
- Students choose the correct words to complete the sentences.
- Check answers with the class.

Second conditional

Warmer

Write on the board:
If you interrupt people in a conversation in the USA, they … happy.
Elicit the missing verb (*won't be*). Then elicit what we call this type of sentence (*first conditional*).
Then write on the board:
If you interrupted people in a conversation in the USA, they wouldn't be happy.
Explain that this type of construction is called the second conditional, and that we use it to describe hypothetical or imaginary situations. Ask the class to translate the sentence.

9 • Look at the sentences in the grammar table with the class and elicit the tense that the verb in the *if* clause is in.
- Explain that in the second sentence, *I'd* is the contraction of *I would*.
- Elicit the translation of the sentences.

10 • Before students start, write on the board:
if clause: past simple
consequence: *would* + verb
- Students read the sentences and choose the correct words to complete them. With weaker classes, complete the first question with the class as an example.
- Check answers with the class and clear up any misunderstandings.

11 • Students complete the sentences with the correct form of the verbs in brackets to make second conditional sentences.
- Check answers with the class.

Extra activity

Students write three questions about hypothetical situations using *What would you do if … ?*. They then ask and answer their questions in pairs.

All Clear Grammar

12 • Tell students that this is a cumulative check of the grammar in Units 1 to 8.
- As this exercise is quite challenging, you may want students to do it in pairs.
- Students choose the correct words to complete the dialogue.

13 2.38
- Play the audio. Students listen and check their answers.
- Check answers with the class. This is a good moment to check they have understood the new grammar and to review the grammar from the previous units.

Mixed-ability solutions

Students who need extra help: Exercise 11. Give students the correct form of the first verb in each sentence.

Fast finishers: Exercise 11. Write the following sentence stems on the board. Students complete them.
If I won the lottery, …
If I saw Rafael Nadal in the street, …
If I saw a robbery, …
If I shook the King of Spain's hand, …
Students compare their sentences in pairs.

Self-study and extra practice

Workbook
- Grammar, pages 52–3
- Grammar Reference and Practice, pages 80–1

Teacher's Resource File
- All Clear Basics, pages 38–9
- Grammar Consolidation, page 30
- Grammar Extension, page 32
- Language Excellence, pages 15–6

Digital Activities
- Student's Digital Material

Exercise 8
1 mustn't
2 should
3 should
4 have to
5 don't have to

8 Complete the sentences with the words in the box.

should (x2) have to don't have to mustn't

1 You … walk on the grass. Look at the sign.
2 I think you … do your homework now so you can come to the cinema with me later on.
3 I want to look for a cheap flight to Italy. Which website … I use?
4 Do you … be 18 to join this gym?
5 We … go to school tomorrow – it's a public holiday!

Second conditional

If clause (imaginary situation)	Consequence
If he **told** a lie,	what **would** you **do**?
If he **told** a lie,	I'**d be** angry.

Consequence	*If* clause (imaginary situation)
What **would** you **do**	if he **told** a lie?
I'**d be** angry	if he **told** a lie.

9 Look at the sentences in the table. What tense is the verb in the *if* clause?

Exercise 9
past simple

10 Write the correct words in your notebook.

1 What **would / did** you say if your best friend **was / would be** late to meet you?
2 Dana **would go / went** out with Mike if he **wouldn't / didn't** play football all the time.
3 If he **told / would tell** me a lie, I **wouldn't be / wasn't** happy.
4 **Would you tell / Did you tell** the truth if you **didn't / wouldn't** like a friend's boyfriend?

Exercise 10
1 would; was
2 would go; didn't
3 told; wouldn't be
4 Would you tell; didn't

11 Complete the sentences using the second conditional.

1 I'm going to Paris this summer, but if I … (go) to London, I … (visit) Fatima.
2 If Mike … (not have) a lot of homework, he … (go) out.
3 If she … (have) more money, she … (buy) some new shoes.
4 If we … (go) to the pool instead of the cinema, we … (have) more fun.

Exercise 11
1 went; 'd visit
2 didn't have; 'd go
3 had; 'd buy
4 went; 'd have

All Clear Grammar
1 2 3 4 5 6 7 8 9

Exercise 12
1 are you going to have
2 must
3 have to
4 like
5 funnier
6 too
7 'd invite
8 knew

12 Write the correct words in your notebook.

Gabriella Hey, Mum says I can have a party.
Sadie Great! When (1)**will you have / are you going to have** it?
Gabriella In two weeks.
Sadie You (2)**must / mustn't** invite me. Please!
Gabriella Of course! Who else should I invite?
Sadie You (3)**have to / don't have to** invite Glyn. I really like him.
Gabriella But you (4)**have liked / like** Bob too.
Sadie No. Glyn's (5)**more funny / funnier** than Bob.
Gabriella OK. And I have to invite Chloe because I went to her party.
Sadie I didn't go. I was (6)**not enough / too** ill.
Gabriella It was a great party.
Sadie If it were my party, I (7)**'d invite / 'll invite** Brian. He's really good-looking.
Gabriella I'd ask Brian if I (8)**knew / know** him, but we've never met.

13 2.38 Listen and check your answers.

Vocabulary

Verb and noun collocations

Exercise 1
Students' own answers

1 2.39 **Listen and repeat the phrases. How do you say them in your language?**

give advice • give presents • get advice • get presents • have an argument • have fun • spend money • spend time (with friends) • tell lies • tell the truth

Exercise 2
1 have fun, spend time (with friends)
2 give presents, get presents
3 spend money
4 give advice, get advice
5 have an argument

2 **Match phrases from exercise 1 with the pictures. Some pictures show more than one phrase. Write them in your notebook.**

1

2

3

4

5

Exercise 3
1 time with; fun
2 advice
3 the truth
4 money
5 a lie; argument
6 a present

3 **Write the correct words in your notebook.**

1 I love spending **money on / time with** Sara. We always have **an argument / fun**.
2 I've tried to give my sister **presents / advice**, but she never listens to me.
3 My girlfriend always tells me **the truth / lies**. She's very honest.
4 John spent a lot of **money / time** on my birthday present. He's very generous.
5 My boyfriend told me **a lie / the truth** last night and we had **fun / an argument**.
6 He got **advice / a present** from his girlfriend – a leather jacket.

Listening

Exercise 4
1 present; an argument
2 isn't speaking; a lie

4 2.40 **Listen to the conversation and complete the sentences.**

1 Jack didn't buy his girlfriend a … and they had … .
2 Jess … to her boyfriend because he told her … .

Exercise 5
1 c
2 c
3 b
4 c

5 **Listen again and write the correct answers in your notebook.**

1 If Jack's girlfriend forgot his birthday, …
a) he'd go out with another girl.
b) he wouldn't mind.
c) he'd be angry.

2 The interviewer says Jack should …
a) say sorry.
b) forget her.
c) say sorry and buy her a present.

3 If Jess's boyfriend forgot her birthday, …
a) she'd do the same to him.
b) she'd find a new boyfriend.
c) she'd have an argument with him.

4 If Jack's girlfriend told him that lie, …
a) he'd find a new girlfriend.
b) he'd be angry.
c) he wouldn't mind.

Vocabulary Reference

Lesson Aims:

Students learn and practise some verb and noun collocations.
Students listen to an interview about relationship problems and identify specific information.

Vocabulary

Verb and noun collocations

Warmer

Write on the board: *football*, *a film*, *breakfast*. Ask students to think of verbs that can be used with these nouns, eg *play*, *watch*, *have*. Explain that a collocation is words that often go together and point out that it is very useful to learn common collocations.

1 2.39

- Play the audio. Students listen and repeat the phrases.
- Elicit the translation of the phrases.

2
- Students look at the pictures and match phrases from exercise 1 with them.
- Check answers with the class.

3
- Students read the sentences and choose the correct words to complete them.
- Check answers with the class.

Listening

Warmer

Brainstorm with the class why people sometimes have arguments with their boyfriend or girlfriend.

4 2.40

- Tell students that they are going to hear an interview about relationships.
- Students read the gapped sentences.
- Play the audio. Students listen and complete the sentences.
- Check answers with the class.

5
- Read the beginnings of the sentences and possible options to complete them with the class.
- Play the audio again. Students listen and choose the correct answers.
- Check answers with the class.

Web info

Type 'Yahoo answers + my boyfriend prefers to spend time with his friends' in your search engine for more information about boyfriend–girlfriend problems.

Mixed-ability solutions

Students who need extra help: Exercise 4.
Write the following options on the board.
1 *dress / present; an argument / problems*
2 *isn't speaking / is writing; some bad news / a lie*

Fast finishers: Exercise 3. Write the following words and expressions on the board.
lunch; the summer; €10; a joke; a letter
Ask students to decide in pairs which of the verbs in exercise 1 they could go with.

Self-study and extra practice

Workbook
- Vocabulary, page 51
- Vocabulary Reference, page 91

Teacher's Resource File
- All Clear Basics, page 37
- Vocabulary Consolidation, page 29
- Vocabulary Extension, page 31
- Key Competences: Listening, page 16

Digital Activities
- Student's Digital Material

Lesson Aims:

Students learn and practise functional language to describe people.

Speaking

Describing people / A party

Warmer

Quickly revise the character adjectives from Unit 1, page 12, eg by playing *Hangman* or writing the letters of each adjective on the board until students can guess the word. Then brainstorm with the class adjectives to describe people's physical appearance, eg *tall*, *short*, etc.

Model Dialogue

1 2.41

- Students read the question.
- Play the audio. Students listen to and read the dialogue.
- Elicit the answer to the question.

2

- Play the audio again. Students listen again and this time repeat the dialogue.
- Focus on the questions: *What's she like?*; *What does she look like?* and *What does she like doing?*. Elicit the translation of each one and elicit or explain the two different uses of *like*. Get the class to pay attention to stress and intonation.

Speaking Task

1 Talk about someone you met at a party

Students read the information and choose one of the people in the Student's Book. Alternatively, they invent a person.

2 Prepare a dialogue

Students look at the Model Dialogue and change the words in blue to make their own dialogue.

3 Speak

Students practise their dialogues in pairs.

Mixed-ability solutions

Students who need extra help: Speaking Task. Students write out their dialogue before they do step 3.

Fast finishers: Speaking Task. Students act out another dialogue about meeting a different person. If possible, they do this without looking at the Model Dialogue.

Self-study and extra practice

Workbook

- Speaking, page 127

Teacher's Resource File

- Key Competences: Speaking, pages 33–4

Digital Activities

- Student's Digital Material

Exercise 1
next weekend

Speaking

Describing people / A party

1 2.41 **Listen to the dialogue. When is Mike going to see Greta again?**

Model Dialogue

Abbie

Mike

Abbie: Hi Mike! What was the party like on Saturday?

Mike: It was great. I had a lot of fun and I met this girl called Greta.

Abbie: Greta? Where's she from?

Mike: She's Norwegian, but she's lived here for years.

Abbie: Oh yeah? So, what's she like?

Mike: She's friendly, funny and quite talkative.

Abbie: And what does she look like?

Mike: She's tall and she's got brown eyes and blonde hair. And we've got a lot in common.

Abbie: What does she like doing?

Mike: She likes playing tennis and watching films.

Abbie: You should call her.

Mike: I did. We're meeting next weekend.

2 **Listen again and repeat the dialogue.**

Speaking Task

1 Talk about someone you met at a party

First, choose one of the people below or invent a person.

NAME: Max
NATIONALITY: Australian
PERSONALITY: generous, quiet and quite shy
APPEARANCE: medium height, brown eyes, short brown hair, very good-looking
HOBBIES: surfing and playing computer games
6858785963248

NAME: Angela
NATIONALITY: German
PERSONALITY: very confident, lively and energetic
APPEARANCE: quite short, blue eyes, long black hair
HOBBIES: going to the gym and doing voluntary work
7851784963248

2 Prepare a dialogue

Look at the Model Dialogue and change the words in blue.

3 Speak

In pairs, practise your dialogue.

What was the party like?

It was fun and I met this girl called Angela.

Useful Language

Describing people

What's she like?
She's friendly, funny and quite talkative.

What does she look like?
She's tall and she's got brown eyes and blonde hair.

What does she like doing?
She likes playing tennis and watching films.

Writing

A formal letter

Exercise 1
See Extended answers on T92

1 2.42 **Read the Model Text and listen. Answer the question in your notebook.**

Why does Raj think Jo should receive the Young Achievers Award? Find three reasons.

Model Text

Young Achievers Award
50 Featherstone Street
London EC1Y 8RT

Dear Sir/Madam,

I am writing to nominate my friend Jo Henley for the Young Achievers Award.

Although Jo is only 16, she has achieved a lot. Her father is ill, so Jo looks after him while her mother is at work. She does the cooking as well as her homework every night. **Furthermore**, Jo has raised over £3,500 for charity by doing sponsored runs. **However**, she never complains and is always polite and cheerful.

In addition, she plays the drums in a band **and** always gets excellent marks at school. Most importantly, Jo is a fantastic friend. We always have fun together and we never have arguments.

For all these reasons I think you should give Jo the Young Achievers Award.

Yours faithfully,

Raj Tandon

2 **Look at the All Clear Tips and complete the rules with the words in bold.**

a) We use … and … to show contrast.
b) We use …, … and … to show addition.

Exercise 2
a) *although; however*
b) *furthermore; in addition; and*

All Clear Tips

Linkers of addition and contrast

Although Jo is only 16, she has achieved a lot.
However, she never complains.
Furthermore, Jo has raised £3,500 for charity.
In addition, she plays the drums **and** always gets excellent marks at school.

3 **Rewrite the sentences including the words in brackets.**

1 Mike is a bit shy. He's very friendly. (although)
2 Sophie is very talkative. She's not very confident. (however)
3 My brother is really good at sport. He's very clever. (furthermore)
4 Ava can already speak two languages. She's now learning Chinese. (in addition)

Writing Task

1 Plan

Make notes about a friend for a letter of recommendation and include:

Reason for writing: *Name of the person, name of the award*
Achievements: *special things that he / she does or has done*
What he / she is like: *character and personal qualities*
Other interesting information: *hobbies, free-time activities*

2 Write

Use the Model Text, your notes and this structure:

Paragraph 1: Reason for writing
Paragraph 2: Achievements; what he / she is like
Paragraph 3: Other interesting information
Paragraph 4: Conclusion

3 Check

☑ obligation, prohibition, advice
☑ making friends, verb and noun collocations
☑ linkers of addition and contrast

Exercise 3
1 Although Mike is a bit shy, he's very friendly. / Although Mike's very friendly, he's a bit shy.
2 Sophie is very talkative. However, she's not very confident.
3 My brother is really good at sport. Furthermore, he's very clever.
4 Ava can already speak two languages. In addition, she's now learning Chinese.

Lesson Aims:

Students practise using linkers of addition and contrast.
Students write a formal letter to propose a friend for a prize.

Writing

A formal letter

Warmer

Ask students if they have a friend who they admire a lot. Ask them to give reasons.

1 2.42

- Explain what a Young Achievers Award is (*a prize for young people who do something special*).
- Read the question with the class.
- Play the audio. Students read and listen to the text and answer the question.
- Check the answer with the class.
- Students look at the picture. Ask them which part of the letter it corresponds to.

Extended answers
Exercise 1

Possible answers:

Although Jo is only 16, she has achieved a lot.
She looks after her father while her mother is at work.
She does the shopping and the cooking as well as her homework every night.
She has raised over £3,500 for charity by doing sponsored runs.
She never complains and is always polite and cheerful.
She plays the drums in a band.
She always gets excellent marks at school.
She is a fantastic friend.

Extra activity

Explain or elicit various aspects of formal letters, eg the position of the two addresses and the date. Highlight the useful expressions for formal writing, eg *Dear … ; I am writing to …* ; etc; and *Yours faithfully,* when you don't use the name of the recipient and *Yours sincerely,* when you do.

All Clear Tips

2
- Read the All Clear Tips with the class.
- Elicit the translation of the sentences.
- Students complete the rules in exercise 2 with the words in bold.
- Check answers with the class.
- Elicit or explain the difference in use of *although* (to link two ideas or clauses) and *however, furthermore* and *in addition* (to introduce one idea).
- Elicit or explain how we can rewrite the first sentence in the All Clear Tips with *although* introducing the second clause (Although she has achieved a lot, Jo is only 16.).

3
- Students rewrite the sentences using the words in brackets. You may want to do the first sentence with the class as an example.
- Check answers with the class.

Writing Task

1 Plan

Read the notes with the class. Students make notes about a friend for a letter of recommendation. Tell them that they can invent a person.

2 Write

Look at the structure with the class. Students use their notes to write their letter. Emphasize that they should use some linkers of contrast and addition and that they should use appropriate language for a formal letter.

3 Check

Encourage students to check their work, paying particular attention to the points mentioned.

Web info

Type 'Young Achievers Award' in your search engine for information about the Young Achievers Award.

Mixed-ability solutions

Students who need extra help: Writing Task. Students just write the notes in step 1.

Fast finishers: Writing Task. In groups of three, students read each other's letters and decide which of the three friends most deserves the award.

Self-study and extra practice

Workbook
- Writing Guide, pages 116–7

Teacher's Resource File
- Key Competences: Writing, page 16

Lesson Aims:

Students learn about two famous friends.
Students practise the pronunciation of the /aɪ/ /ɪ/ /ʊ/ and /ɔɪ/ sounds.

Culture Reading

Famous friendships

Warmer

Ask students to think of some luxury car brands, eg Ferrari, Porsche, Lamborghini, etc. If they don't mention Rolls-Royce, write it on the board and see if they have heard of it. If you have internet access in the classroom, show the class some of the old Rolls-Royce models. Ask students why they think the company is called Rolls-Royce.
Students look at the heading of each paragraph in the reading text and tell you what they think the text is about.

2.43

- Students read the questions.
- Play the audio. Students read and listen to the article to find the answers to the questions.
- Check answers with the class.
- Help with any vocabulary problems, eg *successful*, *engineer*, *hot-air balloonist*, *realized*.

Extra activity

Ask students if they can think of any famous friends in their country. Tell them to think of the world of sport, entertainment, film, design and fashion, etc.
Write the answers to further questions from the text on the board and ask students to write the questions. For example, *1863 – When was Henry Royce born?; an engineering company – What sort of company did Henry Royce start?*

Pronunciation

/aɪ/ /ɪ/ /ʊ/ /ɔɪ/

a 2.44

- Play the audio. Students listen and repeat the words.

b 2.45

- Play the audio. Students listen and repeat the sentences.

Cultural note

Following financial problems in the 1970s and 1980s, Rolls-Royce split into different businesses. Today, Rolls-Royce Motor Cars Limited belongs to the German car manufacturer BMW. They currently make three Rolls-Royce models: the Phantom series, the Ghost series and the Wraith. Rolls-Royce plc is a British engineering company mainly making turbine engines for ships and aeroplanes.

Web info

Type these words in your search engine for more information about

- Rolls-Royce: 'rolls royce motor cars'
- the history of Rolls-Royce (video): 'youtube + history of Rolls Royce'

Mixed-ability solutions

Students who need extra help: Reading text. Write the following options on the board.

1 *10 / 18*
2 *driving cars / engineering*
3 *He was an adventurer and hot-air balloonist. / He was a pilot.*
4 *£395 / £593*

Fast finishers: Reading text. Students answer the following supplementary questions on the text. (Answers in brackets.)

1 *What was Royce's first company called?* (*F.H. Royce & Co.*)
2 *Where did Rolls study?* (*Cambridge University*)
3 *How did Rolls die?* (*in a plane accident*)
4 *How much does a modern Rolls-Royce cost?* (*€300,000*)

Self-study and extra practice

Workbook

- Culture: Reading and Listening, page 100

Culture Reading

EXTRA

Famous Friendships

Rolls-Royce

Rolls-Royce cars are famous all over the world. Rich celebrities drive them. Elvis Presley had one. David Beckham has one. Michael Jackson had five! But who were Rolls and Royce?

Henry Royce

Henry Royce was born in 1863. He was from a poor family and he started work when he was only 10 years old. He worked very hard and became a successful engineer. He started the engineering company F.H. Royce & Co. in Manchester in 1884. He died in 1933.

Charles Rolls

Charles Rolls was from a rich aristocratic family. He was born in 1877 and studied engineering at Cambridge University. He was a famous adventurer and a hot-air balloonist. He died in a plane accident in 1910.

Friends

Rolls and Royce met in 1904. Although they were very different, they became friends. Rolls knew that Royce was a brilliant engineer and thought his cars were the best in the world. Royce realized that Rolls was an excellent salesman and that he would make the cars successful. In 1906 they started the Rolls-Royce Company. The first Rolls-Royce cost £395. If you wanted a new Rolls-Royce today, you would have to be very rich because it would cost more than £200,000.

2.43 **Read and listen. Then answer the questions in your notebook.**

1 How old was Royce when he started work?
2 What was Royce's job?
3 What was Rolls famous for?
4 How much did the first Rolls-Royce car cost?

Reading text exercise

1 10 years old
2 He was a successful engineer.
3 He was an adventurer and hot-air balloonist.
4 £395

Pronunciation

/aɪ/ /ɪ/ /ʊ/ /ɔɪ/

a 2.44 **Listen and repeat the words.**

/aɪ/ drive, five, died
/ɪ/ click, rich, different, brilliant
/ʊ/ would, should, look
/ɔɪ/ Royce, point, coin

b 2.45 **Listen and repeat the sentences.**

Unit 8 Language Reference

Vocabulary Making friends

arrive early • be late • be polite • be rude • bring a present • click your fingers • interrupt a conversation • jump a queue • kiss a stranger • point • shake hands • take off your shoes • tell jokes

Verb and noun collocations

give advice • give presents • get advice • get presents • have an argument • have fun • spend money • spend time (with friends) • tell lies • tell the truth

Grammar Obligation

Affirmative
I / You **must** be polite. I / You **have to** be polite.
He / She / It **must** be polite. He / She / It **has to** be polite.
We / You / They **must** be polite. We / You / They **have to** be polite.

No obligation

Negative
I / You **don't have to** come.
He / She / It **doesn't have to** come.
We / You / They **don't have to** come.

Prohibition

Negative
I / You **must not** be late.
He / She / It **must not** be late.
We / You / They **must not** be late.

Interrogative	Short answers
Do I / you **have to** bring a present?	Yes, I / you **do**.
Does he / she / it **have to** bring a present?	No, he / she / it **does not**.
Do we / you / they **have to** bring a present?	Yes, we / you / they **do**.

Advice

Affirmative	Negative	Interrogative	Short answers
I / You **should** go.	I / You **should not** go.	**Should** I / you go?	Yes, I / you **should**.
He / She / It **should** go.	He / She / It **should not** go.	**Should** he / she / it go?	No, he / she / it **should not**.
We / You / They **should** go.	We / You / They **should not** go.	**Should** we / you / they go?	Yes, we / you / they **should**.

Second conditional

If clause	Consequence
If we **had** an argument,	I **would apologize**.
If you **did not like** him,	**would** you **tell** the truth?

Consequence	*If* clause
I **would apologize**	if we **had** an argument.
Would you **tell** the truth	if you **did not like** him?

Speaking Describing people

What's she like?	**She's** friendly, funny and quite talkative.
What does she look like?	**She's** tall and she's got brown eyes and blonde hair.
What does she like doing?	**She likes** playing tennis and watching films.

Unit 8 Progress Check

Vocabulary Making friends

1 Complete the text with the correct form of the verbs in the box.

bring	click	tell	shake	point

When you meet your British host family, remember this advice!

1 … hands with the parents.
2 You should … a present.
3 It's OK to … jokes to your host family.
4 When you're in a restaurant it is rude to … your fingers at the waiter.
5 It's also rude to … at people.

Exercise 1
1 Shake
2 bring
3 tell
4 click
5 point

Verb and noun collocations

2 Match verbs 1–5 with nouns a–e. Write them in your notebook.

1 give	a) an argument / fun
2 tell	b) advice / a present
3 spend	c) advice / a present
4 get	d) money / time
5 have	e) lies / the truth

Exercise 2
1 c
2 e
3 d
4 b
5 a

3 Complete the sentences with the correct form of collocations from exercise 2.

1 I … some lovely … for my birthday last week. The best was a new tablet!
2 My sister … me some good … about revising for my exams. She said I should be organized and start revising early.
3 My best friend is very honest and she never … .
4 I … with my girlfriend last week and we didn't talk for three days.
5 I'm going shopping to … the … that I received for my birthday. I might buy some new shoes.

Exercise 3
1 got (some lovely) presents
2 gave (me some good) advice
3 tells lies
4 had an argument
5 spend (the) money

Grammar Obligation, prohibition and advice

4 Write the correct words in your notebook.

1 A best friend **should / doesn't have to** always be honest and tell the truth.
2 John **doesn't have to / mustn't** do any homework tonight. He did it all last night.
3 You **don't have to / mustn't** talk in the library. You **have to / shouldn't** study quietly.
4 I **have to / don't have to** phone Jack. I talked to him at school today.
5 You **have to / don't have to** keep Monica's secret. She would be unhappy if you told anyone.

Exercise 4
1 should
2 doesn't have to
3 mustn't; have to
4 don't have to
5 have to

Second conditional

5 Correct the sentences in your notebook.

1 What do you do if you saw your best friend stealing?
2 If you have an argument with your best friend, would you apologize first?
3 If I see Steve today in school, I would ask him out.
4 I'd be very angry if my best friend wouldn't be honest with me.
5 If I will be famous, I'd still spend time with my friends.

Exercise 5
1 What ~~do~~ **would** you do if you saw your best friend stealing?
2 If you ~~have~~ **had** an argument with your best friend, would you apologize first?
3 If I ~~see~~ **saw** Steve today in school, I would ask him out.
4 I'd be very angry if my best friend ~~wouldn't be~~ **wasn't** honest with me.
5 If I ~~will be~~ **was** famous, I'd still spend time with my friends.

Check your answers

Write your scores for exercises 1–5 in your notebook. What did you get for:

- making friends?
- verb and noun collocations?
- obligation, prohibition and advice?
- second conditional?

Extra Practice

If you need extra practice, go to:

Unit 8 Grammar Reference
Unit 8 Vocabulary Reference
Unit 8 Grammar Exercises
Unit 8 Vocabulary Exercises

Correct the activities with the class. Students who need extra revision and practice can go to:

Workbook
- Unit 8 Revision, page 54
- Grammar Reference and Practice, pages 80–1
- Vocabulary Reference, page 91

Student's Digital Material
www.allclear.macmillan.es

9 Making music

Overview

Unit objectives and key competences

- Understand, memorize and correctly use vocabulary related to music CLC
- Understand, memorize and correctly use negative prefixes for adjectives CLC, L2L
- Identify the main ideas and specific detail in a text about streaming music over the internet CLC
- Learn about streaming music DC, SCC
- Understand, contrast and correctly use the present simple passive and the past simple passive CLC
- Differentiate between the use of the active and the passive CLC, L2L
- General tense revision CLC
- Identify specific information through a listening activity about a musician CLC
- Learn about a musician who has used YouTube to launch his career CAE, DC
- Use appropriate functional language to agree and disagree CLC, SCC
- Write about a musical hero using time expressions CLC, SIE
- Identify specific information in a text about two famous opera houses CLC
- Learn about two world-famous opera houses CAE
- Assimilate the All Clear Tips and Rules and study the Language Reference from the unit CLC, L2L
- Identify areas of language which need improvement and use ICT for extra practice DC, CLC, L2L

More information on Key Competences, page v

Linguistic content

Grammar

- Present simple passive and past simple passive
- Active and passive
- Tense revision

Recycled grammar

- Present simple (Unit 1)
- Past simple and past continuous (Unit 2)
- Present perfect (Unit 5)
- *will* (Unit 7)

Main vocabulary

- Music: *album cover*, *form a band*, etc
- Negative prefixes: *un-*, *im-*, *il-*: *unoriginal*, *impossible*, *illogical*, etc

Functional language

- Agreeing and disagreeing / A concert

Pronunciation

- Sentence stress and /ə/

Skills: learning outcomes

- **Reading** Understand specific information in a clearly structured news report about the pros and cons of streaming music online. The student can re-read the more difficult parts, page 97
- **Listening** Understand a radio programme about a musician who has used YouTube to launch his career. Delivered slowly and with clarity, page 100
- **Speaking** Participate effectively in a face-to-face informal dialogue, agreeing and disagreeing about bands and artists, page 101
- **Writing** Write a description of a musical hero with simple and relevant information set out in a logical order, page 102
- **Reading** Get the main ideas of a text about two famous opera houses. The student can re-read the more difficult parts, page 103

Lifelong learning skills and content-based learning

Life skills

- **Social development** The rights and wrongs of downloading music, page 97
- **Socio-cultural awareness** English-speaking musicians, pages 99, 100 and 102, world-famous opera houses in Australia and the USA, page 103
- **Communication** Agreeing and disagreeing, page 101

Learning strategies

- Use of different negative prefixes with adjectives, page 100

Cross-curricular content

- Music: technology-related issues, page 97; English-speaking musicians, pages 99, 100 and 102; famous opera houses, page 103
- Language: the use of prefixes to modify the meaning of adjectives (page 100)

Further materials and evaluation

Digital material

- Student's and Teacher's Resource Centres
- Teacher's Presentation Kit
- Student's Digital Material: interactive vocabulary and grammar activities
- Video *Music* (Revision Units 7–9, page 108)

Student's website www.macmillansecondary.es

Workbook

- Vocabulary, pages 56–7
- Vocabulary Reference, page 92
- Grammar, pages 58–9
- Grammar Reference and Practice, pages 82–3
- Revision, page 60
- Culture: Reading and Listening, page 101
- Writing Guide, pages 118–9
- Speaking, page 128

Teacher's Resource File

Multi-level Materials Bank

- All Clear Basics, pages 41–5
- Vocabulary and Grammar Consolidation and Extension, pages 33–6
- Language Excellence, pages 17–8
- Translation and Dictation, pages 9 and 18

Lifelong Learning

- Digital Competence, pages 17–8
- Culture Video Material, pages 5–6
- Study Skills, pages 1–12

Evaluation and Key Competences

- Evaluation Rubrics, pages 1–7
- Key Competences, pages 17–8 and 35–6

Content-based Learning

- CLIL, pages 1–10
- Macmillan Readers, pages 1–7

Evaluation material

- Unit 9 end-of-unit test: Basic, Standard and Extra
- End-of-term test, Units 7–9: Basic, Standard and Extra
- End-of-year test
- CEFR Skills Exam Generator

Web info

Tips to find extra information on: Spotify, Jessie J, the Sydney Opera House, the Met

Extra help for weaker students

Teacher's Resource File: All Clear Basics, pages 41–5

Material for fast finishers

Workbook: Grammar Extension, page 61
Teacher's Resource File: Vocabulary Extension, page 35
Teacher's Resource File: Grammar Extension, page 36
Teacher's Resource File: Language Excellence, pages 17–8

9 Making music

Objectives

Vocabulary	Music; negative prefixes
Grammar	The passive; active and passive; tense revision
Speaking	Agreeing and disagreeing
Writing	A description of a musical hero

Vocabulary

Music

1 2.46 **Listen and repeat the words. Match them with pictures 1–14.**

album cover • form a band • go on tour • go to number one • hit • music festival • playlist • play live at a concert • record • record a song • recording studio • release an album • single • song lyrics

Exercise 1
1 form a band
2 single
3 go to number one
4 hit
5 go on tour
6 recording studio
7 song lyrics
8 play live at a concert
9 release an album
10 music festival
11 record a song
12 record
13 album cover
14 playlist

2 **Write the correct words in your notebook.**

How do musicians become famous?
First, they (1)**form / release** a band, then they think of some good (2)**lyrics / playlists** and music for a song. After writing the song, they go to a (3)**recording studio / concert** to record the song. Then they release a (4)**single / cover**. If the song is a (5)**hit / record**, it could (6)**go / form** to number one and then they become famous. After that, the band should (7)**play / release** an album and go on tour so that they can (8)**record / play** live for their fans.

Exercise 2
1 form
2 lyrics
3 recording studio
4 single
5 hit
6 go
7 release
8 play

3 2.47 **Listen to Todd and Kate. Complete the sentence with the correct name.**

The last song that … downloaded was *The Monster* by Eminem.

Exercise 3
Todd

4 **In pairs, ask and answer questions about music.**

What was the last song you downloaded? Is it good?

It was *Que bonita la vida* by Dani Martín. It's OK.

Vocabulary Reference

Lesson Aims:

Students learn and practise vocabulary related to music.
Students listen a short conversation about songs and identify specific information.

Vocabulary

Music

Warmer

Ask students about their musical tastes and habits. What types of music do they like? When and where do they listen to music?

1 2.46

- Play the audio. Students listen and repeat the words.
- Elicit or explain the meaning of the words.
- Point out the different pronunciations of *record*, with the stress on the second syllable in the verb /rɪˈkɔː(r)d/ and on the first in the noun /ˈrekɔː(r)d/. Point out the pronunciation of *live* /laɪv/ in this context, as opposed to /lɪv/.
- Students match the words with the pictures.
- Check answers with the class.

2
- Students read the text and choose the correct words to complete it.
- Check answers with the class.

Extra activity

Ask students some questions to practise the vocabulary further, eg *Have you ever recorded a song?*; *Would you like to form a band?*; *Do you know the lyrics of many songs?*; *Can you think of any cool album covers?*

3 2.47

- Students read the gapped sentence.
- Play the audio. Students listen and complete the sentence with the correct name.
- Check the answer with the class.

4

- Read the example in the speech bubbles. Then tell students about the last song you downloaded.
- Elicit and write on the board other adjectives to give your opinion about songs, eg *fantastic* and *awful*.
- In pairs, students ask and answer the questions.

Mixed-ability solutions

Students who need extra help: Exercise 1. Write each expression in English and its corresponding translation on the board.

Fast finishers: Exercise 2. Students write three more sentences about what famous musicians do using some different expressions from exercise 1.

Self-study and extra practice

- Vocabulary, page 56
- Vocabulary Reference, page 92

Teacher's Resource File

- All Clear Basics, page 41
- Vocabulary Consolidation, page 33
- Vocabulary Extension, page 35

Lesson Aims:

Students read a news report about the pros and cons of streaming music over the internet for specific and general information.

Reading

A news report

Warmer

Ask students if they use the internet to listen to music and what applications they use. Try to elicit the concept of streaming (*listening in real time*). Use their answers to write the different ways the internet can be used to listen to music on the board.
Ask students to look at the pictures in the Student's Book and to tell you what they can see.

Word Check

Check students understand the new words: *piracy*, *subscription*, *music label*. Explain any they don't know.

1 2.48

- Read the headings with the class.
- Play the audio. Students read and listen to the text and match the headings with the paragraphs. Make it clear that they don't need to understand all of the text in order to do this.
- Check answers with the class.

2
- Students read the statements and ask you if there is anything they don't understand.
- Students read the text again and decide if each of the statements is true or false. Make it clear that they should copy the text that shows their answers.
- Check answers with the class.

Extended answers
Exercise 2

1 true – … the music business has had many problems over the last decade.
2 false – … you can listen to as many songs as you like for free.
3 false – The artists are then paid by the music labels.
4 true – It can also give publicity to new bands …
5 false – Streaming was criticized in the news recently by Thom Yorke … .

3
- Write two headings on the board: *Arguments in favour of streaming* and *Arguments against streaming*. Make sure that students understand what the headings mean.
- Students copy the headings and then refer back to the text to find the arguments mentioned and write them under the correct heading.
- Check answers with the class.

All Clear Facts

Read the fact with the class. Ask students if they know what a phonograph looked like. Show students a picture of one if you have access to the internet in the classroom. Alternatively, you could attempt to draw one.

Extra activity

Conduct a class discussion on the issue of streaming music based on the arguments presented in the text.

Cultural note

Spotify was launched in October 2008 by a small Swedish company. It now has over 40 million active users worldwide, over 20% of whom are paying subscribers. Over 1.5 billion playlists have been created using Spotify.

Web info

Type these words in your search engine for more information about Spotify: 'information spotify press figures'

Mixed-ability solutions

Students who need extra help: Exercise 2.
On the board, write the following key words from the text in order to help students find the answers.

1 *many problems*
2 *for free*
3 *music labels; artists*
4 *publicity; new bands*
5 *impossible; survive*

Fast finishers: Exercise 2. Students find five facts (not opinions) about Spotify that are mentioned in the text. (They are all contained in paragraph B.)

Self-study and extra practice

Teacher's Resource File

- Key Competences, Reading, page 17

Reading

A news report

Word Check
piracy subscription music label

To stream, or not to stream?

A **Piracy**, illegal downloads, and falling CD sales – the music business has had many problems over the last decade. But then along came streaming. For many people, it has saved the music industry. However, not everyone agrees.

B On streaming websites, such as Spotify, you can listen to as many songs as you like for free. If you pay a monthly **subscription**, you can also download individual songs and you don't get adverts. You can even make your own playlists. **Music labels** are paid each time a song is streamed or downloaded. The artists are then paid by the music labels.

C Companies such as Spotify say streaming is good for everyone. It's cheaper and more flexible for music fans. If you don't like a song or album, you just stream another one. Streaming has also reduced piracy. Why download music illegally when you can listen online for free? It can also give publicity to new bands, so more people go to their concerts.

D So, who is against streaming? Some artists say they aren't paid enough money. Millions are made by big music labels, but songwriters and musicians often receive a very small percentage of this money. Streaming was criticized in the news recently by Thom Yorke, lead singer of the band Radiohead. He thinks that it will be impossible for many bands to survive. But he has also said that streaming won't last and that new forms of listening to music will appear.

E What do you think? Is streaming positive or negative? Is it the future or is it just another chapter in the history of music?

1 2.48 **Read and listen. Match headings 1–5 with paragraphs A–E. Write them in your notebook.**

1 In favour of streaming
2 Against streaming
3 Is streaming the future?
4 How does streaming work?
5 Streaming to the rescue

Exercise 1
1 C
2 D
3 E
4 B
5 A

All Clear Facts
The first method of recording sound was invented in 1877 by Thomas Edison. It was called the phonograph.

2 **Read the text again. Write true or false in your notebook. Copy the text that shows your answers.**

1 The music industry had many difficulties before streaming.
2 You have to pay to listen to music on streaming sites.
3 Musicians aren't paid any money by music labels.
4 Musicians can get good publicity from music streaming services.
5 Thom Yorke has spoken in favour of streaming.

Exercise 2
See Extended answers on T97

3 **What arguments are mentioned in favour of streaming in the text? What arguments are mentioned against streaming?**

Exercise 3
In favour: It's cheaper and more flexible for music fans; it has reduced piracy; it can give publicity to new bands
Against: Artists (musicians and songwriters) aren't paid enough money; it will be impossible for many bands to survive (because they don't receive enough money)

Grammar

The passive

	Present simple passive	Past simple passive
Affirmative	Their song **is** play**ed** on the radio every day.	Their song **was** play**ed** on the radio yesterday.
Negative	Their songs **aren't** play**ed** on the radio every day.	Their songs **weren't** play**ed** on the radio yesterday.
Interrogative	**Are** their songs play**ed** on the radio every day?	**Were** their songs play**ed** on the radio yesterday?

Language Reference p104

Exercise 1
be + past participle

1 **Look at the sentences in the table. How do you form the passive?**

All Clear Rules

We use the passive when we want to stress the action, not the person who does it.
Active: *People **download** millions of songs every day.*
Passive: *Millions of songs **are downloaded** every day.*

2 **Complete the sentences with the affirmative and negative form of the present simple passive.**

1 Music … (record) in a studio.
2 Microphones … (positioned) in different parts of the studio.
3 Most new albums … (not released) on vinyl.
4 The recording … (divide) into many different tracks.
5 Cassettes … (not sell) in many music shops.

Exercise 2
1 is recorded
2 are positioned
3 aren't released
4 is divided
5 aren't sold

3 **Write complete questions using the present simple passive in your notebook.**

computers / use / at your school?
Are computers used at your school?
1 How / your bedroom / decorate?
2 dictionaries / allow / in your English class?
3 new music videos / upload / to YouTube every day?
4 How often / festivals / celebrate / in your region?

Exercise 3
1 How is your bedroom decorated?
2 Are dictionaries allowed in your English class?
3 Are new music videos uploaded to YouTube every day?
4 How often are festivals celebrated in your region?

4 **In pairs, ask and answer your questions in exercise 3.**

5 **Complete the sentences with the correct past simple passive form of the verbs.**

1 The cover of *Sergeant Pepper* … (design) by an artist called Peter Blake.
2 The pictures of the people … (made) of card.
3 The people … (choose) by The Beatles because they admired them.
4 At least three people from their original list … (not include) in the end.
5 The recording of the album … (complete) in April 1967.
6 The album … (not release) until June 1967.

Exercise 5
1 was designed
2 were made
3 were chosen
4 weren't included
5 was completed
6 wasn't released

6 **Write complete questions using the past simple passive in your notebook.**

1 Who / the cover / design / by?
2 What / the pictures of the people / make / of?
3 Who / the people / choose / by?
4 How many people / not include / on the final album cover?
5 When / the recording / complete?
6 the album / release / in April?

Exercise 6
1 Who was the cover designed by?
2 What were the pictures of the people made of?
3 Who were the people chosen by?
4 How many people weren't included on the final album cover?
5 When was the recording completed?
6 Was the album released in April?

Active and passive

Active	Passive
Millions of people **use** YouTube.	YouTube **is used by** millions of people.
Apple **invented** the iPod.	The iPod **was invented by** Apple.

Lesson Aims:

Students learn and practise the present simple passive and the past simple passive.

Grammar

The passive

Warmer

Write on the board the name of a song most of the class will know, eg *Happy*. Ask who sings it. Elicit the full answer, *Pharrell Williams sings it.*, and write it on the board. Then write on the board *It … by Pharrell Williams.* and elicit a different way of saying the same thing, ie *It is sung by Pharrell Williams.* Explain that this structure is called the passive. Elicit how it is formed. Ask students to find examples of the passive in the reading text on page 97.

All Clear Rules

Read the All Clear Rules with the class.

1
- Read the present simple affirmative and negative passive sentences in the grammar table with the class.
- Ask students to translate all the sentences and to compare them to their language.
- Elicit from the class how the passive is formed.

2
- Students read the gapped sentences and ask you about any words they don't understand.
- Complete the first sentence with the class as an example.
- Students complete the rest of the sentences with the affirmative or negative present simple passive form of the verbs in brackets.
- Check answers with the class.

3
- Ask the class to look again at the grammar table and elicit how we change the affirmative form of the present simple passive into the interrogative form.
- Look at the example with the class.
- Students write questions using the present simple passive.
- Check answers with the class.

4
- Practise the pronunciation of the questions in exercise 3. Insist on acceptable stress and intonation.
- Ask a student to ask you the example question and give your answer.
- Write the answer on the board. Elicit the other short answer and write it on the board.
- Students ask and answer the questions in pairs.

5
- Tell students to look at the past simple passive column of the table. Elicit how the past simple passive differs from the present simple passive.
- Complete the first sentence with the class as an example.
- Students complete the rest of the sentences with the past simple passive form of the verbs in brackets.
- Check answers with the class.

6
- Write the first question with the class.
- Students write the rest of the questions using the past simple passive.
- Check answers with the class.

Extra activity

Practise the pronunciation of the questions in exercise 6 and the answers in exercise 5. Insist on acceptable stress and intonation. Students ask and answer the questions in exercise 6 in pairs.

Mixed-ability solutions

Students who need extra help: Exercise 2.
Write the following options on the board.

1 *has recorded / is recorded*
2 *is positioned / are positioned*
3 *not released / aren't released*
4 *is dividing / is divided*
5 *haven't sold / aren't sold*

Fast finishers: Exercise 6. Books closed. Students remember as many details as they can about the album cover.

Lesson Aims:

Students develop an awareness of when the passive is used. Students learn and practise using *by* to introduce the agent. Students choose between using active and passive verbs. Students revise a variety of tenses.

Grammar

Active and passive

Warmer

Write on the board:
The artists are paid every month.
The music labels pay the artists every month.
Elicit which sentence contains the passive and which the active. Elicit whether we use the active or the passive when we start the sentence by talking about the person who does the action.

7
- Read the grammar table at the bottom of page 98 with the class.
- Students read and complete the rules in exercise 7 with *Active* or *Passive*.
- Check answers with the class.

All Clear Rules

Read the All Clear Rules with the class. Elicit how to say *by* in the students' language.

8
- Read the example with the class.
- Students rewrite the sentences using the passive. Emphasize that they should only use *by* when it is absolutely necessary to mention who does the action. In addition, tell the class they need to decide whether to use the present simple passive or the past simple passive.
- Check answers with the class.

Tense revision

9
- Students look at the picture. Ask if they recognize the singer in the picture (*Lorde*). Ask what they know about her.
- Make it clear that this exercise practises the present and past simple in both the active and the passive.
- Pre-teach any difficult vocabulary, eg *singer-songwriter*, *genres*, *hits* (on a website), *soundtrack* and *on tour*.
- As this exercise is quite challenging, you may want students to do it in pairs.
- Student read the text and choose the correct words to complete it.
- Check answers with the class.

Extra activity

Students study the text about Lorde for one or two minutes. Then they cover the text. Ask them questions using different tenses, eg *Where is she from?*; *When did she become famous?*.

All Clear Grammar

10
- Tell students that this is a cumulative check of the grammar in Units 1 to 9. Pre-teach any difficult vocabulary, eg *record-breaking*, *awards*, *starred*, *top film* and *what else*.
- As this exercise is quite challenging, you may want students to do it in pairs.
- Students choose the correct words to complete the text.

11 2.49
- Play the audio. Students listen and check their answers.
- Check answers with the class. This is a good moment to check they have understood the new grammar and to review the grammar from the previous units.

Mixed-ability solutions

Students who need extra help: Exercise 8. Write the present simple passive and the past simple passive forms of the verbs on the board. Students choose which form they need.

Fast finishers: Exercise 9. Students rewrite the following sentences with active verbs.
Bruno Mars' album, Unorthodox Jukebox, *was released in 2012. His songs are played all the time. He was given a Grammy.*

Self-study and extra practice

Workbook
- Grammar, pages 58–9
- Grammar Reference and Practice, pages 82–3

Teacher's Resource File
- All Clear Basics, pages 43–5
- Grammar Consolidation, page 34
- Grammar Extension, page 36
- Language Excellence, pages 17–8

Digital Activities
- Student's Digital Material

Exercise 7
a) Active
b) Passive

7 **Look at the sentences in the table on page 98 and complete the rules with *Active* or *Passive*.**

a) … sentences start with the person or thing that does the action.
b) … sentences start with the person or thing the action is done to.

All Clear Rules

We can use *by* to introduce the person who does or did the action in passive sentences.
Royals *was written* **by** *Lorde.*

Exercise 8
1 was written by Chris Martin.
2 are played (by radio stations) every day.
3 was released in 2001.
4 weren't given permission to go out.
5 is played (by DJs) all the time.
6 was invited to the concert (by Amy).

8 **Rewrite the sentences in your notebook using the correct form of the passive. Omit *by* where possible.**

They produce records in factories.
Records are produced in factories.

1 Chris Martin wrote *Viva la Vida*.
Viva la Vida …
2 Radio stations play a lot of songs every day.
A lot of songs …
3 They released their album in 2001.
Their album …
4 She didn't give us permission to go out.
We …
5 DJs play that song all the time.
That song …
6 Amy invited him to the concert.
He …

Tense revision

9 **Read the text about Lorde and write the correct words in your notebook.**

Lorde (1)**is / was** a singer-songwriter. She (2)**was / is** born in New Zealand in 1996. She (3)**is influenced / influences** by different musical genres as well as literature and poetry and she started writing songs at the age of 14. Lorde (4)**became / was become** famous in 2013 when her first EP (5)**was released / released** for download via SoundCloud. Her first album *Pure Heroine* was a Number 1 all around the world and the most well-known song from that album, *Royals,* (6)**received / was received** over 750,000 hits on YouTube. In fact, her songs (7)**download / are downloaded** by thousands of people every day! Another one of her songs (8)**included / was included** on the soundtrack to the second *Hunger Games* film. We hope she goes on tour in the UK soon.

Exercise 9
1 is
2 was
3 is influenced
4 became
5 was released
6 received
7 are downloaded
8 was included

All Clear Grammar

1 2 3 4 5 6 7 8 9

Exercise 10
1 is usually known
2 is
3 became
4 was released
5 became
6 won
7 has won
8 are played
9 has starred
10 will he do

10 **Write the correct words in your notebook.**

Marshall Bruce Mathers III (1)**usually knows / is usually known** as Eminem. He (2)**is / was** a rapper, record producer and actor. He first (3)**became / was becoming** popular in 1999 when his album *The Slim Shady LP* (4)**released / was released**. The album (5)**became / was become** a record-breaking best-seller and it (6)**won / was winning** a Grammy for Best Rap Album. Since then, Eminem (7)**won / has won** many other awards. His songs (8)**played / are played** all the time. Furthermore, he (9)**was starring / has starred** in a top film. What else (10)**does he do / will he do** in the future?

11 2.49 **Listen and check your answers.**

Grammar Reference

Vocabulary

Negative prefixes

Exercise 1
Students' own answers

1 (2.50) **Listen and repeat the words. How do you say them in your language?**

adventurous • friendly • happy • imaginative • legal • logical • necessary • original • patient • perfect • possible • practical • reliable • supportive • trustworthy

She loves wearing impractical shoes.

Exercise 2
1 *un-*
2 *il-*
3 *im-*

2 **Read sentences 1–3 and find three negative prefixes.**

1 The song doesn't sound new – it's really unoriginal.
2 That doesn't make sense – it's completely illogical.
3 It's impossible to use this website – it doesn't work very well.

3 **Copy and complete the table with the negative form of the words in exercise 1.**

un-	im-	il-
unoriginal	*impossible*	*illogical*

Exercise 3
un-: unadventurous, unfriendly, unhappy, unimaginative, unnecessary, unoriginal (example), unreliable, unsupportive, untrustworthy
im-: impatient, imperfect, impossible (example), impractical
il-: illegal, illogical (example)

4 **Complete the sentences with the negative adjectives in exercise 3.**

She never helps her friends – she's really *unsupportive*.
1 I don't understand what the question means, so it's … to answer.
2 They are very … and hate waiting!
3 You don't have to do that – it's … .
4 That is against the law. It's … .
5 Don't tell him your secrets. He's … and he'll tell everyone!
6 He never likes visiting new places or doing exciting things. He's so … .
7 I saw her crying this morning. She looked really … .
8 They never have any new ideas. They're so … .

Exercise 4
1 impossible
2 impatient
3 unnecessary
4 illegal
5 untrustworthy
6 unadventurous
7 unhappy
8 unoriginal

Listening

Exercise 5
It is changing how some artists become famous and how they relate to their fans.

5 (2.51) **Listen to the programme. Why is the new music trend important in the music industry?**

6 **Listen again. Write true or false in your notebook.**

1 The new musicians aren't very successful in the music charts.
2 The artists don't have managers or record labels.
3 According to Luke, digital music is more popular than physical music.
4 Luke believes that the music industry hasn't changed in the last 15 years.
5 Saida is going to watch one of the new artists play live.

Exercise 6
1 false
2 true
3 true
4 false
5 false

Vocabulary Reference

Lesson Aims:

Students learn and practise negative prefixes.
Students listen to an interview about a pop star who became famous thanks to YouTube and identify specific information.

Vocabulary

Negative prefixes

Warmer

Write the words *possible*, *legal* and *happy* on the board. Ask students what the opposite of the words are, and introduce the concept of prefixes to convey the opposite meaning. You may also want to draw parallels to the use of prefixes in the students' own language.

1 2.50

- Play the audio. Students listen and repeat the words. Make sure that they stress them correctly.
- Read the words with the class and elicit the translation when possible, or give it in the case of unknown words, eg *reliable*, *supportive* and *trustworthy*.

2
- Students read the sentences and identify the negative prefixes.
- Compare with the words in their language and ask the class if the prefixes are the same.

3
- Read the examples in the table with the class. Explain that, as a general rule, words which start with *p* take the prefix *im-* and words that start with the letter *l* take *il-*; *un-* is often used with the other letters.
- Students copy and complete the table with the negative form of the adjectives in exercise 1.
- Check answers with the class.

4
- Read the example with the class.
- Students read and complete the sentences with words from exercise 3.
- Check answers with the class.

Extra activity

Students choose five of the adjectives, either positive or negative, which they think describe their character. They then compare answers in pairs.

Listening

Warmer

Ask the class if they can think of any musicians who have had millions of hits on YouTube, eg Lady Gaga, Psy, etc.

5 2.51

- Tell the class that they are going to listen to a programme about a new trend in the music industry.
- Read the question with the class.
- Play the audio. Students listen and answer the question.
- Check the answer with the class.

6
- Students read the statements.
- They try to decide if they are true or false from the first time they listened.
- Play the audio again. Students listen again and decide if each statement is true or false.
- Check answers with the class.

Mixed-ability solutions

Students who need extra help: Exercise 4. Write two options for each sentence on the board.

Fast finishers: Exercise 3. Students work in pairs. Students take turns to say an adjective. Their partner must say the opposite adjective with the correct prefix and stress.

Self-study and extra practice

Workbook
- Vocabulary, page 57
- Vocabulary Reference, page 92

Teacher's Resource File
- All Clear Basics, page 42
- Vocabulary Consolidation, page 33
- Vocabulary Extension, page 35
- Key Competences: Listening, page 18

Digital Activities
- Student's Digital Material

Lesson Aims:

Students learn and practise functional language to give opinions about musicians and going to a concert.

Speaking

Agreeing and disagreeing / A concert

Warmer

Ask students what bands and artists they would like to see live in concert.

Model Dialogue

1 2.52

- Students read the question.
- Play the audio. Students listen to and read the dialogue.
- Elicit the answer to the question.

2

- Play the audio again. Students listen again and this time repeat the dialogue.
- Focus on the expressions *I think so too.*; *Me too.*; *Me neither.*; *I totally disagree; I'm not sure.* and *I see what you mean*. Get the class to pay attention to stress and intonation.

Speaking Task

1 Talk about a concert

Students look at the names and the pictures and choose one of the bands or artists. Alternatively, they use their own ideas.

2 Prepare a dialogue

Students look at the Model Dialogue and change the words in blue to make their own dialogue.

3 Speak

Students practise their dialogues in groups of three.

Mixed-ability solutions

Students who need extra help: Speaking Task. Students write out their dialogue before they do step 3.

Fast finishers: Speaking Task. Students act out another dialogue using other bands and artists. If possible, they do this without looking at the Model Dialogue.

Self-study and extra practice

Workbook

- Speaking, page 128

Teacher's Resource File

- Key Competences: Speaking, pages 35–6

Digital Activities

- Student's Digital Material

Speaking

Agreeing and disagreeing / A concert

Exercise 1
Mia wants to go to the Lady Gaga concert.

1 2.52 Listen to the dialogue. Which concert does Mia want to go to?

Model Dialogue

Kristina: I really want to get a ticket for the Lady Gaga concert.

Mia: Me too. Her live shows are amazing.

Kristina: Have you heard her new album? It's her best.

Mia: I totally disagree. I think her last album had much better songs.

Kristina: I see what you mean, but I think the concert will be great anyway.

Mia: Yeah, I think so too. Can you come, Louis?

Louis: No, I can't. I've got a ticket for the Katy Perry concert. Why don't you come with me instead?

Mia: No, thanks! I don't like Katy Perry.

Kristina: Me neither, but have fun!

2 Listen again and repeat the dialogue.

Speaking Task

1 Talk about a concert

Choose one of the bands or artists below or choose others.

Rihanna

Bruno Mars

The Arctic Monkeys

2 Prepare a dialogue

Look at the Model Dialogue and change the words in blue.

3 Speak

In pairs, practise your dialogue.

I really want to get a ticket for the Bruno Mars concert.

Me too. His live shows are really good.

Useful Language

Agreeing and disagreeing

I think so too.	I totally disagree.
Me too.	I see what you mean.
Me neither.	

Exercise 1
1 1988
2 She's a songer-songwriter.
3 in 2011 / at the age of 23
4 Her first album went to number one in the UK Charts and millions of copies were sold around the world. She has performed live at concerts and festivals all over the world. She gave a spectacular performance at the London Olympics. She has released her second album and is planning a tour now.
5 She does lots of amazing charity work.
6 for her fantastic music and her work to help others

Writing

A description of a musical hero

1 2.53 **Read the Model Text and listen. Answer the questions in your notebook.**

1 When was Jessie J born?
2 What does she do?
3 When did she become famous?
4 What are her main musical achievements?
5 What else does she do?
6 Why does the writer admire her?

Model Text

Jessica Cornish was born in London in 1988. She is usually known by her artistic name, Jessie J. She is an English singer-songwriter.

She became famous at the age of 23 when her first album, *Who You Are*, was released in 2011. It went to number one in the UK Charts and millions of copies were sold around the world. Since then, she has performed live at concerts and festivals all over the world. In 2012, she gave a spectacular performance at the London Olympics. Recently, she has released her second album, *Alive*, and is planning a tour now.

Incredibly, she has also found time to do lots of amazing charity work. In 2013, she shaved off all her hair on live TV to raise money for different charities.

I admire Jessie J for her fantastic music and her work to help others.

Exercise 2
Students' own answers

2 **Look at the All Clear Tips. Translate the time expressions in bold.**

All Clear Tips

Time expressions

Taylor Swift was born **in** 1989. She released her first single **at the age of** 17 and her second album came out a year **later**. It was number one **for** 11 weeks. Two years **ago** she won a Grammy and **since then** she has won other awards. **Last year**, she went on tour. **Recently**, she has appeared in her first film. She is planning a new album **now**.

3 **Write the correct words in your notebook.**

1 Kid Cudi was born **in** / **at** 1984.
2 He became famous **in** / **at** the age of 25.
3 **Last** / **Recently**, he sang with Lady Gaga.
4 A year **ago** / **last** he starred in a TV series.
5 He is thinking about doing a film **now** / **since**.

Exercise 3
1 in
2 at
3 Recently
4 just
5 ago
6 now

Writing Task

1 Plan

Make notes about the person you are going to write about and include:

Personal details: *name, when and where they were born, what they do*
Musical achievements: *hits, albums, sales, awards, performances, plans*
Other achievements: *charity work, other achievements*
Conclusion: *why you admire this person*

2 Write

Use the Model Text, your notes and this structure:

Paragraph 1: Personal details
Paragraph 2: Musical achievements
Paragraph 3: Other achievements
Paragraph 4: Conclusion

3 Check

☑ music
☑ the passive, different tenses
☑ time expressions

Lesson Aims:

Students practise using time expressions.
Students write a description of a musical hero.

Writing

A description of a musical hero

Warmer

Ask students if they have a musical hero. If so, ask who it is it and why they like or admire that person.

1 2.53

- Students look at the picture. Ask them if they know who the person is and what they know about her.
- Ask students to read the first paragraph of the text and say or confirm who it is about.
- Students read the questions. Clear up any possible vocabulary problems, eg *main musical achievements*.
- Play the audio. Students read and listen to the text and answer the questions.
- Check answers with the class.

Extra activity

Students choose the correct option for the heading of each paragraph in the text.

1 *Personal details / Early life*
2 *Concerts given / Musical achievements*
3 *Hobbies / Other achievements*
4 *Conclusion / Her future career*

All Clear Tips

2
- Read the All Clear Tips with the class.
- Students translate the time expressions in bold.
- Point out that these expressions are important when you want to write a biography because you can use them to sequence the events in the person's life.
- Ask students to find the all time expressions in the Model Text.

3
- Students read the sentences and choose the correct words to complete them.
- Check answers with the class.

Writing Task

1 Plan
Read the notes with the class. Make it clear that the first thing they need to do is to decide who they want to write about. Students make notes about their musical hero. They may need help to find some of the information.

2 Write
Look at the structure with the class. Students use their notes to write a description of their musical hero. Emphasize that they should use some of the time expressions to order the events in their hero's life.

3 Check
Encourage students to check their work, paying particular attention to the points mentioned.

Web info

Type these words in your search engine for more information about Jessie J: 'Mail online + fragile bullied girl'

Mixed-ability solutions

Students who need extra help: Writing Task. Students just complete the notes in step 1.

Fast finishers: Writing Task. Students read their description to their partner but they say *X* instead of the name of the person. Their partner has to guess who they are describing.

Self-study and extra practice

Workbook
- Writing Guide, pages 118–9

Teacher's Resource File
- Key Competences: Writing, page 18

Lesson Aims:

Students learn about two world-famous opera houses.
Students practise sentence stress and the pronunciation of the /ə/ sound.

Culture Reading

Famous music venues

Warmer

Ask students if they like classical music, whether they have ever been to a classical music concert, whether they know the names of any famous composers or opera singers and whether they know any world famous concert halls or opera houses.

2.54

- Read the questions with the class.
- Play the audio. Students read and listen to the text and answer the questions.
- Check answers with the class.

Extra activity

Brainstorm with the class famous places where music is performed in their country, either classical or pop music.

Pronunciation

Sentence stress and /ə/

a 2.55

- Play the audio. Students listen and repeat the sentences.
- Ask students which words have the main stress in the sentence (*the words with the key information*). Then ask how the words in blue are pronounced (*they are unstressed and have the /ə/ sound*).
- Play the audio again. Students listen and repeat the sentences again.

b 2.56

- Play the audio. Students listen and repeat the words and phrases with the /ə/ sound.

Web info

Type these words in your search engine for more information about

- the Sydney Opera House: 'Sydney Opera House'
- the Met: 'Metropolitan Opera House'

Mixed-ability solutions

Students who need extra help: Reading text. Explain the meaning of the following words and phrases: *performances*; *venues*; *one of the busiest performing arts centres*; *attended*; *performed*; *develop their careers*; *broadcasted live performances*.

Fast-finishers: Reading text. Write some more questions about the texts on the board, eg

Sydney Opera House
How many performances are there each year?
What famous people have performed there?
The Met
What does the Met do for young singers?
What has the Met started to do recently?

Self-study and extra practice

Workbook

- Culture: Reading and Listening, page 101

Culture Reading

EXTRA

Famous music venues

THE SYDNEY OPERA HOUSE

The Sydney Opera House, in Australia, is one of the great iconic buildings of the 20th century. It was opened in 1973 by Queen Elizabeth II. It is famous for music concerts and theatre performances in the six separate venues inside. It is the home of the Sydney Symphony Orchestra and Opera Australia. It is one of the busiest performing arts centres in the world. Every year, more than 1,500 performances are attended by about two million people. Many famous pop stars and singers have performed at the Opera House. There's something for everyone.

THE MET

The Metropolitan Opera House, or 'The Met', is in New York. It is the home of The Metropolitan Opera, America's biggest classical music organization. It has a young artists programme to help young singers develop their careers. Luciano Pavarotti became famous after singing there. Other famous singers such as Plácido Domingo regularly sing there. The Met has broadcast live performances on the radio since 1931 and now they are streamed directly to smartphones.

2.54 **Read and listen. Then answer the questions in your notebook.**

1 What can you see at the Sydney Opera House apart from opera?
2 How many people go to performances at the Sydney Opera House every year?
3 Where is The Met?
4 What can you watch on your smartphone?

Reading text exercise
1 music concerts and theatre performances
2 about two million people
3 New York
4 live performances at the Met

Pronunciation exercise a
Words with main stress underlined:
1 Sydney Opera House was opened by the Queen.
2 Performances are attended by about two million people.
3 It is the home of The Metropolitan Opera.
4 Are plays performed at your school?
The words in blue are not stressed and the vowel is pronounced /ə/.

Pronunciation

Sentence stress and /ə/

a 2.55 **Listen and repeat the sentences. Which words have the main stress in each sentence? What happens to the words in blue?**

1 Sydney Opera House was opened by the Queen.
2 Performances are attended by about two million people.
3 It is the home of The Metropolitan Opera.
4 Are plays performed at your school?

b 2.56 **Listen and repeat the words and phrases with the /ə/ sound.**

Unit 9 Language Reference

Vocabulary Music

album cover • form a band • go on tour • go to number one • hit • music festival • playlist • play live at a concert • record • record a song • recording studio • release an album • single • song lyrics

Negative prefixes

illegal • illogical • impatient • imperfect • impossible • impractical • unadventurous • unfriendly • unhappy • unimaginative • unnecessary • unoriginal • unreliable • unsupportive • untrustworthy

Grammar The passive: present simple

Affirmative	Negative	Interrogative	Short answers
I **am** invited.	I **am not** invited.	**Am** I invited?	Yes, I **am**.
You **are** invited.	You **are not** invited.	**Are** you invited?	No, you **are not**.
He / She / It **is** invited.	He / She / It **is not** invited.	**Is** he / she / it invited?	Yes, he / she / it **is**.
We / You / They **are** invited.	We / You / They **are not** invited.	**Are** we / you / they invited?	No, we / you / they **are not**.

The passive: past simple

Affirmative	Negative	Interrogative	Short answers
I **was** invited.	I **was not** invited.	**Was** I invited?	Yes, I **was**.
You **were** invited.	You **were not** invited.	**Were** you invited?	No, you **were not**.
He / She / It **was** invited.	He / She / It **was not** invited.	**Was** he / she / it invited?	Yes, he / she / it **was**.
We / You / They **were** invited.	We / You / They **were not** invited.	**Were** we / you / they invited?	No, we / you / they **were not**.

Active and passive

Active	Passive
Millions of people **use** YouTube.	YouTube **is used** by millions of people.
Apple **invented** the iPod.	The iPod **was invented** by Apple.

by

by
We can use *by* to introduce the person who does or did the action in passive sentences.
Royals was written ***by*** Lorde.

Speaking Agreeing and disagreeing

I think so too.
Me too.
Me neither.
I totally disagree.
I see what you mean.

Unit 9 Progress Check

Vocabulary Music

1 **Match 1–5 with a–e to make phrases. Write them in your notebook.**

1 release	**a)** at a concert
2 record	**b)** a band
3 play live	**c)** a song in the studio
4 go	**d)** a new album
5 form	**e)** on tour

Exercise 1
1 d
2 c
3 a
4 e
5 b

Negative prefixes

2 **Complete the sentences with the negative forms of the words in brackets. Use *un-*, *il-* and *im-*.**

1 Kate is not very creative at all. She's really .... (imaginative)
2 Peter hates waiting. He's very .... (patient)
3 They are very .... They never want to try anything new. (adventurous)
4 Those children never say 'hello'. They're .... (friendly)
5 That doesn't make sense. It's .... (logical)

Exercise 2
1 unimaginative
2 impatient
3 unadventurous
4 unfriendly
5 illogical

Grammar Active and passive

3 **Write complete sentences and questions using the present simple passive.**

1 CDs / use / to store music.
2 How many / CDs / sell / every year?
3 That song / play / a lot on the radio.
4 That song / not listen to / very often nowadays.
5 DVDs / not sell / in that shop.

Exercise 3
1 CDs are used to store music.
2 How many CDs are sold every year?
3 That song is played a lot on the radio.
4 That song is not listened to very often nowadays.
5 DVDs are not sold in that shop.

4 **Complete the sentences and questions with the past simple passive form of the verbs in brackets.**

1 That record ... (release) last year.
2 When ... (the band / form)?
3 Who ... (those covers / design) by?
4 Millions of music videos ... (download) last year.
5 That song ... (not write) by Eminem.

Exercise 4
1 was released
2 was the band formed
3 were those covers designed
4 were downloaded
5 wasn't written

Tense revision

5 **Complete the sentences with the correct form of the verbs in brackets.**

1 We ... (visit) the museum last year.
2 Jane ... (play) tennis every summer.
3 I live in Oxford now, but I think I ... (live) in London when I'm older.
4 They ... (watch) a DVD when I arrived.
5 I ... (do) this exercise at the moment.

Exercise 5
1 visited
2 plays
3 'll live
4 were watching
5 'm doing

All Clear Self-C...

Check your answers

Write your scores for exercises 1–5 in your notebook. What did you get for:

- music?
- negative prefixes?
- active and passive?
- tense revision?

Extra Practice

If you need extra practice, go to:

- Unit 9 Grammar Reference
- Unit 9 Vocabulary Reference
- Unit 9 Grammar Exercises
- Unit 9 Vocabulary Exercises

Correct the activities with the class. Students who need extra revision and practice can go to:

Workbook
- Unit 9 Revision, page 60
- Grammar Reference and Practice, pages 82–3
- Vocabulary Reference, page 92

Student's Digital Material
www.allclear.macmillan.es

Revision Units 7–9

Vocabulary

- Films
- Suffixes
- Making friends
- Verb and noun collocations
- Music
- Negative prefixes

Work with a partner. Read the clues and write the words. Make sure you spell the words correctly! Who finishes first?

START

Which 'P' do you give and receive? (7)

Which 'A' can a film win? (5)

Which 'A' is a disagreement? (8)

Which 'B' is a group of musicians? (4)

Which 'F' is Benicassim? (8)

Which 'I' means not patient? (9)

Which 'J' can you tell to make someone laugh? (4)

Which 'S' is the words of a film? (6)

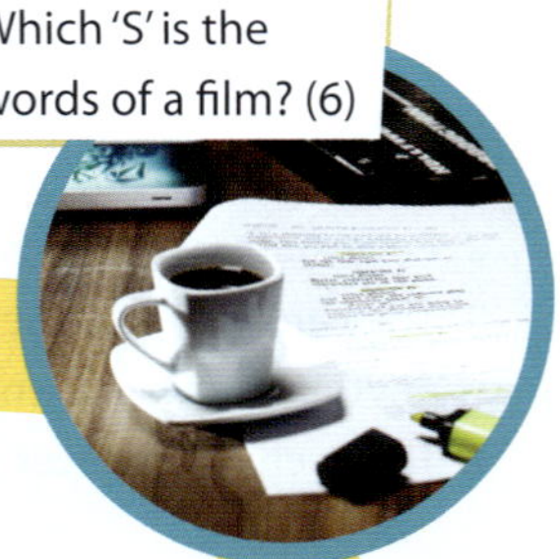

Which 'U' means not happy? (7)

Which 'P' are your ideas for the future? (11)

FINISH

Revision Units 7–9
Vocabulary

present
award
argument
band
festival
impatient
joke
script
unhappy
predictions

Lesson Aims:

Students revise and practise vocabulary from Units 7 to 9.

Revision Units 7–9

Vocabulary

Warmer

Students look through Units 7 to 9 and tell you what vocabulary areas they have seen. Alternatively, you could get the class to do this from memory and then to check by looking in the Student's Book.

- Do the board game as a competition. Explain these rules to the class before you start.
- Students work in pairs. They identify the words for each picture. The numbers in brackets show the number of letters in each word.
- When they have finished, they shout *Stop!* All the other teams must stop writing.
- Check answers with the class and write them on the board.
- Teams get two points for each correct answer and minus one point for each wrong answer. For a blank, they get zero points.
- Ask how many points the teams have, starting at 20 (the maximum) and working down.

Extra activity

In pairs, students write similar clues to other vocabulary seen in Units 7 to 9. They then swap with another pair and identify the words.

Lesson Aims:

Students revise and practise the grammar from Units 7 to 9.

Revision Units 7–9

Grammar

Future forms

Warmer

Write on the board:

1 *I think that one day we will all work from home.*
2 *I'm going to learn to drive next year.*
3 *Take an umbrella! It's going to rain. Look at the sky!*
4 *I'm meeting my friends at 7 pm.*

Students translate the sentences and identify the tenses used.

Then write on the board:

a *a definite future arrangement*
b *a future plan or intention*
c *a prediction when there is clear evidence that something is going to happen.*
d *a prediction*

Students match the uses a–d with the sentences 1–4.

1 • Students choose the correct alternatives to complete the sentences.
• Check answers with the class.
• If you detect any major problems, you might want to read through the grammar section of the Language Reference on page 84 with the class.

Modal verbs

Warmer

Write on the board:

I must / have to / mustn't / don't have to / should / shouldn't tidy my room tonight.

Students translate the different possibilities and then to decide which one(s) are true for them.

2 • Students write sentences using the modal verbs in brackets.
• Check answers with the class.
• If you detect any major problems, you might want to read through the grammar section of the Language Reference on page 94 with the class.

First and second conditionals

Warmer

Write on the board:

If I pass all my exams this year, I'll be very happy.
If I passed all my exams this year, I'd be very happy.

Students translate the sentences. Ask them which sentence is a first conditional sentence and which is a second conditional sentence.

3 • Students complete the sentences with the correct form of the verbs in brackets to make conditional sentences.
• Check answers with the class.
• If you detect any major problems, you might want to read through the grammar section of the Language Reference on pages 84 and 94 with the class.

Active and passive

Warmer

Write on the board:

Jenny ate all the cakes.
All the cakes were eaten by Jenny.

Elicit which sentence is an example of the active and which is an example of the passive.

Students translate the sentences. Elicit how we form the passive in general (*be* + past participle).

4 • Students complete the sentences with the active or passive form of the verbs in brackets.
• Check answers with the class.
• If you detect any major problems, you might want to read through the grammar section of the Language Reference on page 104 with the class.

Grammar check

5 • Tell students that this exercise revises all the grammar they have seen in Units 7 to 9 and it will give them a good idea of how well they have learnt it.
• Explain any potentially difficult vocabulary in the text, eg *straightaway*, *notice* and *soundtracks*.
• Students choose the correct words to complete the text.
• Check answers with the class.

Grammar

- Future forms: *will, be going to,* present continuous
- First conditional
- Obligation, prohibition and advice
- Second conditional
- The passive
- Active and passive
- Tense review

Future forms

1 **Write the correct words in your notebook.**

1 I think the film will win / is winning an award tomorrow.
2 They aren't going / don't go to go on holiday next summer.
3 Will cinemas change / Are cinemas changing a lot in the future?
4 I don't think he will / won't be in the film.
5 Be quiet! The film is going to / will start.

Exercise 1
1 will win
2 aren't going
3 Will cinemas change
4 will
5 is going to

Modal verbs

2 **Write complete sentences using the modal verbs in brackets in your notebook.**

1 you / be home at 11 pm? (have to)
2 my cousins / study English in their school. (don't have to)
3 you / shake hands when you meet someone new. (should)
4 students / be late for class. (mustn't)
5 you / invite me to your barbecue next weekend. (must)

Exercise 2
1 Do you have to be home at 11 pm?
2 My cousins don't have to study English in their school.
3 You should shake hands when you meet someone new.
4 Students mustn't be late for class.
5 You must invite me to your barbecue next weekend.

First and second conditionals

3 **Complete the conditional sentences with the correct form of the verbs in brackets.**

1 If you work hard, you … (pass) your exams.
2 If my friend … (tell) me a lie, I would be very unhappy.
3 What … (you / do) if you had an argument with your best friend?
4 I will come to the cinema if you … (buy) me a ticket.
5 If I won a million euros, I … (not spend) the money – I … (save) it.

Exercise 3
1 'll pass
2 told
3 would you do
4 buy
5 wouldn't spend; 'd save

Active and passive

4 **Complete the sentences with the active or passive form of the verbs in brackets.**

1 The film … (direct) by Ridley Scott last year.
2 The song … (download) by 10,000 people on the first day of release.
3 People often … (celebrate) local festivals with fireworks in the main square.
4 Coldplay … (release) their sixth studio album in 2014.
5 CDs … (not buy) by many people nowadays.

Exercise 4
1 was directed
2 was downloaded
3 celebrate
4 released
5 aren't bought

Grammar check

5 **Write the correct words in your notebook.**

If you (1) watch / watched a silent film, you'd know straightaway that there was something different about the film. But, would you notice if the film (2) has / had no music? Yes, you probably would. The music is a very important part of a film and influences your emotions. If it is a horror film, the music (3) would / will make you feel more frightened.
Films had music before they had words. In the 1920s, music (4) wrote / was written for silent movies. The music (5) is played / was played live in the cinema while people were watching the film. Nowadays, film soundtracks are big business. Many composers (6) collaborate / are collaborated with directors and producers to create music for their films. For example, a lot of the music for Steven Spielberg's films (7) was composed / were composed by John Williams.
Many films (8) use / are used different tunes for important characters. Can you imagine Darth Vader or James Bond on screen without their famous tunes? It's impossible. You (9) mustn't / must hear the music too.

Exercise 5
1 watched
2 had
3 will
4 was written
5 was played
6 collaborate
7 was composed
8 use
9 must

Cultural Awareness: Music

Multimedia

1 How much do you know about music in Britain? Do the quiz.

Exercise 1
1 c
2 b
3 b
4 a
5 c
6 a

1 What instruments can be heard in traditional English folk music?
a organs b panpipes c violins

2 Bagpipes are from …
a Northern Ireland. b Scotland. c Wales.

3 Which one of the Beatles continues to be successful today?
a Ringo Starr b Paul McCartney c John Lennon

4 How do most people in Britain listen to their music these days?
a on mp3 players b on the radio c on vinyl

5 What is the name of the classical concerts held at the Royal Albert Hall in the summer?
a The Prawns b The Bombs c The Proms

6 There are hundreds of music festivals in Britain – the most famous is Glastonbury, which is held in …
a June. b July. c August.

WATCH

2 **Watch the documentary about music and answer the questions.**

Exercise 2
1 classical and rock
2 the O2 Arena
3 musicals

1 What sort of music do students at school often play?
2 What is the name of the venue in London which hosts concerts by world famous artists such as Coldplay?
3 What kind of shows are *Cats* and *Les Misérables*?

Lesson Aims:

Students do a quiz to see how much they know about music in Britain.
Students watch a video about music in Britain.

Cultural Awareness:

Music

Warmer

Brainstorm the names of famous British pop groups and artists with the class.

1
- Tell students they are going to do a quiz about music in Britain. Pre-teach *bagpipes* (question 2) using the picture.
- Students do the quiz individually.
- Students compare answers in pairs.
- Check answers with the class.

Extra activity

Books closed. Read out the questions in the quiz without the options. Students try to answer from memory.

2
- Tell students that they are going to watch a documentary about music in Britain.
- Read through the questions with the class, clearing up any vocabulary problems, eg *venue*, *hosts* and *shows*.
- Play the video. Students watch and listen and find the answers to the questions.
- Check answers with the class.

Web info

Type these words in your search engine for more information about the Beatles: 'youtube + history of the Beatles okibeachpeach'

Culture Video: *Music*

This Culture video and accompanying worksheet, teaching notes, videoscript and answer key are in the Teacher's Resource Centre.
The worksheet, teaching notes, videoscript and answer key can also be found in the Teacher's Resource File.

Lesson Aims:

Students prepare and give a presentation about a type of music.

Digital Competence:

Presentations

Warmer

Ask the class if they have ever prepared a presentation. If so, ask what equipment they used and if they found it easy or difficult to prepare it. Students look at the digital presentation and identify what it is about.

Extra activity

Ask students if they think that this is a good presentation and why they think that. Elicit whether they think it is easy to follow, whether they think it is attractive and whether there is any information about rap music that they would like to know that it is missing.

Task

Explain to students that they are going to prepare and give a presentation in groups about a type of music they are interested in.

Step 1 Divide the class into groups of four or five.

Explain that students first need to decide which kind of music they are going to do the presentation about.

Each group chooses the type of music they want to do their presentation about and finds information, videos and photos about it.

If appropriate, make it clear that students will need to do their research and prepare their presentation out of the classroom. You can suggest that different people in the group look for different types of information, eg basic facts, audio, video, photos, newspaper cuttings, etc.

Step 2 Students pool their resources and prepare their presentation. Make it clear that the presentation should be easy to follow, attractive and contain all the essential information about the type of music they have chosen.

Step 3 Students practise giving their presentation. Tell students that they should time their presentation to make sure that is neither very long nor very short. They also need to decide which member of the group is going to present which part of the presentation.

Step 4 Each group gives their presentation to the class. They end by asking for feedback.

The rest of the class gives feedback.

Web info

Type these words in your search engine for tips on how to give a presentation: 'wikihow + how to do a presentation in class'

Term Project

For a different type of project, see the Life Skills Collaborative Project in the Workbook, pages 134–5.

Digital Competence: Presentations

Multimedia

Give a presentation about a type of music or a singer.

Rap music

Look at the digital presentation. What is it about?

HOME SHOWS NEWS PICTURES VIDEOS search

RAP MUSIC

- Rapping is speaking or chanting lyrics, often with a beat.
- Many people think rap is like poetry.
- Rap songs are often about social or political themes.
- Rapping first started in America in the 1970s, especially among young African Americans, but it didn't become popular until 1979. In 1979, the Sugarhill Gang released their single *Rapper's Delight*. It was a big hit! Suddenly, record producers noticed this new musical genre.
- After that, many rap acts started, for example Run-DMC and N.W.A. At first, most rap artists were African-American men.
- In the 1980s, female rap bands such as Salt-n-Pepa, and white rap bands such as the Beastie Boys, had big hits.
- Nowadays, rappers such as Eminem and Tinie Tempah are very popular.

SOCIAL MEDIA FEED HELP ABOUT US CONTACT US

TASK **Prepare a presentation about a different kind of music. Follow the steps below.**

Step 1 Decide which kind of music you are going to do the presentation about and find information, videos and photos about that kind of music.

Step 2 Prepare your presentation together. Write the text and prepare any video clips, sound, or photos that you want to include.

Step 3 Practise giving your presentation.

Step 4 Give your presentation to the class. Ask your classmates for feedback!

Irregular verbs

Infinitive	Past simple	Past participle
be /biː/	was / were /wɒz/, /wɜːr/	been /biːn/
begin /bɪˈɡɪn/	began /bɪˈɡæn/	begun /bɪˈɡʌn/
break /breɪk/	broke /brəʊk/	broken /ˈbrəʊkən/
bring /brɪŋ/	brought /brɔːt/	brought /brɔːt/
build /bɪld/	built /bɪlt/	built /bɪlt/
buy /baɪ/	bought /bɔːt/	bought /bɔːt/
choose /tʃuːz/	chose /tʃəʊz/	chosen /ˈtʃəʊzn/
come /kʌm/	came /keɪm/	come /kʌm/
do /duː/	did /dɪd/	done /dʌn/
drink /drɪŋk/	drank /dræŋk/	drunk /drʌŋk/
drive /draɪv/	drove /drəʊv/	driven /ˈdrɪvən/
eat /iːt/	ate /eɪt/	eaten /ˈiːtən/
fall /fɔːl/	fell /fel/	fallen /ˈfɔːlən/
find /faɪnd/	found /faʊnd/	found /faʊnd/
fly /flaɪ/	flew /fluː/	flown /fləʊn/
forget /fərˈget/	forgot /fərˈgɒt/	forgotten /fərˈgɒtən/
get /get/	got /gɒt/	got /gɒt/
give /gɪv/	gave /geɪv/	given /ˈgɪvən/
go /gəʊ/	went /went/	gone /gɒn/
have /hæv/	had /hæd/	had /hæd/
hear /hɪər/	heard /hɜːrd/	heard /hɜːrd/
know /nəʊ/	knew /njuː/	known /nəʊn/
learn /lɜːrn/	learnt / learned /lɜːrnt/, /lɜːrnd/	learnt / learned /lɜːrnt/, /lɜːrnd/
leave /liːv/	left /left/	left /left/
lose /luːz/	lost /lɒst/	lost /lɒst/
make /meɪk/	made /meɪd/	made /meɪd/
meet /miːt/	met /met/	met /met/
pay /peɪ/	paid /peɪd/	paid /peɪd/
put /pʊt/	put /pʊt/	put /pʊt/
read /riːd/	read /red/	read /red/
run /rʌn/	ran /ræn/	run /rʌn/
say /seɪ/	said /sed/	said /sed/
see /siː/	saw /sɔː/	seen /siːn/
sell /sel/	sold /səʊld/	sold /səʊld/
sing /sɪŋ/	sang /sæŋ/	sung /sʌŋ/
sit /sɪt/	sat /sæt/	sat /sæt/
speak /spiːk/	spoke /spəʊk/	spoken /ˈspəʊkən/
take /teɪk/	took /tʊk/	taken /ˈteɪkən/
teach /tiːtʃ/	taught /tɔːt/	taught /tɔːt/
tell /tel/	told /təʊld/	told /təʊld/
think /θɪŋk/	thought /θɔːt/	thought /θɔːt/
wear /weər/	wore /wɔːr/	worn /wɔːrn/
win /wɪn/	won /wʌn/	won /wʌn/
write /raɪt/	wrote /rəʊt/	written /ˈrɪtən/

Starter unit

Vocabulary

1

safari park, cathedral, monument, aquarium, castle, statue, market

2

1 *b* 2 e 3 d 4 a 5 c

3

1 cathedral
2 castle
3 town square
4 statue
5 market
6 safari park
7 art gallery

4

life events: *get a job*, get married, leave home
computers: keyboard, mouse, webcam
character adjectives: brave, cruel, loyal
natural disasters: drought, famine, tornado

5

1 *say*
2 mean
3 lend
4 pronounce
5 got

6

a 4 b 5 c *1* d 3 e 2

Grammar

1

1 Has
2 is
3 goes
4 doesn't
5 live
6 my
7 are
8 study

2

1 C 2 C 3 U
4 U 5 C 6 U
7 C 8 U 9 U

3

1 there is some
2 there is some
3 there are some; there aren't any
4 there is some; there isn't any
5 there is some; there isn't any
6 there are some; there aren't any

4

1 *What*
2 How
3 Where
4 Who
5 Why
6 Where

5

a 2 b *1* c 5 d 6 e 4 f 3

6

Students' own answers

7

1 Does
2 Have
3 Is
4 Has
5 Is

8

Students' own answers

Speaking

1

1 *What*
2 Are
3 Can
4 What
5 Can
6 Would

2

a 5 b 3 c 4 d 6 e *1* f 2

3

1 *lost*
2 music room
3 big
4 subjects
5 Science and music
6 guitar
7 drummer
8 audition

Unit 1: My interests

Vocabulary

1

1 relax
2 play tennis
3 go dancing
4 go to the gym
5 go to the cinema
6 play an instrument
7 go out for a meal

2

1 *d* 2 f 3 e 4 b 5 a 6 c

3

1 *b* 2 e 3 c 4 d 5 f 6 a

4

E	U	F	C	A	U	T	I	O	U	S
N	N	R	S	E	L	F	I	S	H	T
E	S	I	T	W	J	C	A	Y	S	O
R	O	E	E	Y	U	O	U	Q	V	S
G	C	N	F	U	N	N	Y	U	M	E
E	I	D	C	L	O	F	Q	I	O	R
T	A	L	K	A	T	I	V	E	N	I
I	B	Y	M	Z	U	D	K	T	J	O
C	L	E	I	Y	Q	E	O	A	C	U
P	E	F	C	A	I	N	D	W	I	S
H	O	N	E	S	T	T	E	S	H	Y

5

1 Talkative; Quiet
2 Unsociable; Friendly
3 Serious; Funny
4 Honest; Dishonest
5 Selfish; Generous
6 Cautious; Adventurous

6

1 lazy
2 energetic
3 friendly
4 generous
5 talkative

7

Students' own answers

Grammar

1

1 play
2 relaxes
3 doesn't go
4 don't have

2

1 Does (your sister) like; she does
2 Does (your brother) play; he doesn't
3 Do (your friends) go; they don't
4 Do (we) have; we do

3

1 never go
2 usually do
3 is hardly ever
4 are often
5 sometimes goes

4

1 usually go
2 are hardly ever
3 always does
4 often go
5 never make
6 sometimes arrive

5

Students' own answers

6

1 are going
2 isn't working
3 is drawing
4 aren't watching
5 aren't eating

7

1 goes
2 meet
3 often goes
4 'm wearing
5 usually gives
6 're drawing

8

1 's wearing; wears
2 talk; 're talking
3 're chatting; chat
4 watches; 's watching
5 'm writing; write
6 feels; 's feeling

9

1 Everyone enjoys getting presents.
2 My sister is bad at singing.
3 Millie is keen on learning English.
4 I love taking photos of my friends.
5 My parents are interested in visiting museums.

10

1 swimming
2 singing
3 playing
4 relaxing
5 drawing

11

Students' own answers

Revision

1

1 I hate walking in the rain.
2 Why are you wearing that funny hat?
3 My parents love looking at old photos.

2

1 You're always late for your guitar lessons.
2 Excuse me, I'm looking for the train station.
3 I love dancing at parties.

4

Students' own answers

5

1 B *'m staying*
2 C 'm having
3 C being
4 B drives
5 A take
6 C are sitting
7 A isn't chatting
8 B 's playing
9 A love relaxing
10 A are you doing

Extension

1

1 *are you talking*
2 'm practising
3 acting
4 am
5 singing
6 always feel
7 hardly ever go
8 fall
9 Is your phone ringing
10 is

Unit 2: Connected

Vocabulary

1

post a comment, go online, store data, upload a video clip, scan a document, take a photo, write a blog, send an email

2

1 read an e-book
2 print a document
3 take a photo
4 charge a mobile phone
5 plug in a memory stick

3

1 scan
2 send
3 charge
4 play
5 make

4

1 comment
2 blog
3 memory stick
4 online
5 document
6 e-book

5

1 *e*	2 g	3 c	4 h
5 d	6 a	7 f	8 b

6

1 *c*	2 a	3 d	4 b

7

1 doctor
2 lab technician
3 artist
4 lawyer
5 scientist
6 postal worker

Grammar

1

1 was
2 wasn't
3 were
4 was
5 weren't

2 and 3

1 built; I
2 used; R
3 realized; R
4 saw; I
5 took; I
6 thought; I
7 wanted; R

4

1 Was; it wasn't
2 Were; I wasn't
3 Were; there were
4 Were; they weren't
5 Was; she was

5

1 wrote
2 offered
3 posted
4 found
5 started

6

1 Callum didn't write his blog last year.
2 My uncle didn't offer me free guitar lessons.
3 I didn't post any comments on your blog yesterday.
4 My mum didn't find the car keys in the kitchen.
5 The lesson didn't start at 10 am.

7

1 *bought*
2 arrived
3 was
4 learnt
5 uploaded
6 sent
7 played

8

1 *did* (you) *buy*
2 bought
3 Did (you) know
4 taught
5 did (you) do
6 sold
7 did (he) want
8 lost

9

1 were
2 was
3 were
4 were
5 was

10

1 *was working*
2 was reading
3 were watching
4 was downloading
5 was looking
6 were talking

11

1 Where were you at ten o'clock last night?
2 Did you live here five years ago?
3 What were you wearing yesterday?

12

1 Katy wasn't reading a blog. She was posting comments on a blog.
2 Kyle and Carrie weren't watching DVDs. They were doing their homework.
3 Dan wasn't downloading music. He was uploading photos.
4 My mum wasn't looking at photos. She was watching TV.
5 You weren't talking on your mobile. You were sending a text.

13

Students' own answers

Revision

1

1 How long were we chatting online last night?
2 Did anyone post any comments on your blog?
3 My grandmother travelled around America on a motorbike.

2

1 We didn't meet our friends at the match.
2 Did you see the programme last night?
3 I was charging my mobile when Max arrived.

4

Students' own answers

5

1 C *joined*
2 B did
3 C have
4 C decided
5 A chose
6 C Did
7 A did
8 C were
9 B was doing
10 A jumped

Extension

1

1 *do*
2 always ask
3 don't
4 was
5 like
6 always happy
7 doing
8 found
9 drew
10 I'm designing

Unit 3: Incredible stories

Vocabulary

1

1 down
2 into
3 out of
4 over
5 under
6 towards
7 away from
8 round
9 along
10 through
11 across

2

1 into
2 up
3 out of
4 towards
5 under
6 over

3

1 frightened
2 worried
3 surprised
4 annoying
5 tired

4

1 interesting
2 excited
3 stressed
4 surprised
5 frightening

5

1 tiring
2 annoyed
3 bored
4 tired
5 exciting
6 frightened
7 boring

Grammar

1

1 While
2 when
3 when
4 while

2

1 found; was cleaning
2 fell; was picking
3 was doing; cut

3

1 didn't answer; was having
2 Did you see; were walking
3 was he wearing; saw
4 didn't hear; was listening
5 was writing; stopped

4

1 My cat jumped into my bag while I was packing it.
2 He crashed into a car because he was talking on his phone.
3 Who was driving when they had the accident?
4 Where were you sitting when you saw the spaceship?

5

1 *was surfing*
2 attacked
3 was lying
4 appeared
5 didn't hurt
6 came
7 made
8 saw
9 went
10 took

6

1 *b* 2 a 3 c 4 d

7

1 present continuous
2 past simple
3 past continuous

8

1 *d* 2 b 3 e 4 a 5 c

9

1 did you do
2 dropped
3 wears
4 are smiling

10

1 *was sitting*
2 was holding
3 's trying
4 ran
5 didn't come
6 jumped
7 was lying
8 pulled
9 told
10 wear

Revision

1

1 We saw dolphins when we were sailing around the island.
2 While I was swimming in the river, somebody took my clothes.
3 What do you usually wear when you go running?

2

1 We met your cousin yesterday while we were walking to school.
2 They always go to the mountains every summer.
3 What are you thinking about at the moment?

4

Students' own answers

5

1 *B look*
2 C goes
3 C was having
4 B didn't run
5 C had
6 A stood
7 B fell
8 C got
9 C is writing
10 A doesn't work

Extension

1

1 *was staying*
2 were
3 playing
4 played
5 were playing
6 found
7 was
8 is studying
9 said
10 did

Unit 4: A wonderful world

Vocabulary

1

1 *f* 2 c 3 e 4 b 5 a 6 d

2

1 *ruin*
2 lighthouse
3 tomb
4 cave
5 coastline
6 reef

3

1 ruin
2 castle
3 opera house
4 tomb
5 lighthouse

4

1 noisily
2 badly
3 quietly
4 easily
5 carefully
6 angrily
7 happily
8 hard
9 fast
10 well

5

add *-ly*: *quickly*, badly, quietly, carefully
remove *y*, add *-ily*: noisily, easily, angrily, happily
irregular: hard, fast, well

6

1 good
2 carefully
3 bad
4 quick
5 happy
6 angrily

7

1 You always work hard.
2 She walked up the hill easily.
3 I shut the door quietly.
4 We opened the window quickly.
5 She's talking happily to her friends.
6 He put it carefully on the table.

8

1 quickly
2 good
3 careful
4 well
5 quick

Grammar

1

1 smaller, the smallest
2 bigger, the biggest
3 earlier, the earliest
4 larger, the largest
5 more interesting, the most interesting
6 more beautiful, the most beautiful
7 better, the best
8 worse, the worst

2

1 older
2 better
3 more popular
4 easier
5 more important
6 worse

3

1 The longest
2 the oldest
3 The tallest
4 the most dangerous
5 The heaviest
6 the most beautiful

4

1 shorter
2 the biggest
3 bigger
4 the smallest
5 smaller

5

1 aren't
2 was
3 isn't
4 is
5 isn't

6

1 isn't as old as the Parthenon
2 isn't as hot as Egypt
3 aren't as interesting as castles
4 isn't as noisy as Delhi

7

1 *the biggest*
2 as quiet
3 more interesting
4 better
5 the largest
6 warmer
7 fresher
8 the most unusual

8

1 too
2 enough
3 too
4 enough

9

1 enough vegetables
2 too high
3 not sweet enough
4 big enough

10

1 *n't near enough*
2 too cold
3 not big enough
4 too small
5 too dark
6 n't old enough

Revision

1

1 It's the biggest lighthouse in the world.
2 The caves aren't as famous as the ruins.
3 Have you got enough money to pay for the tickets?

2

1 The castle was more interesting than the lighthouse.
2 The pyramids in Peru are not as old as the pyramids in Egypt.
3 We haven't got enough time to visit the castle.

4

Students' own answers

5

1 *B best*
2 C cleaner
3 A warm
4 C to swim
5 B the most
6 A too
7 C too cold
8 C the most
9 B as
10 A than
11 B too dangerous

Extension

1

1 *travelling*
2 went
3 flew
4 most
5 were driving
6 put
7 ride
8 rode
9 as good as
10 better
11 am thinking
12 long enough

Unit 5: Real-life heroes

Vocabulary

1

1 collect money
2 wash cars
3 have a barbecue
4 have a bring and buy sale
5 sell badges
6 do a sponsored swim
7 sell cakes
8 organize a jumble sale
9 make a charity CD

2

1 make a charity CD
2 wash cars
3 collect money
4 do a sponsored swim
5 sell badges
6 sell raffle tickets

3

1 make
2 do
3 make
4 do
5 do
6 make
7 do
8 make
9 do
10 make
11 do

4

1 make a mistake
2 do homework
3 do exercise
4 do your best
5 do someone a favour

5

1 make a decision
2 make … laugh
3 make friends
4 make … money
5 do charity work

Grammar

1

1 bought
2 done
3 gone
4 had
5 learnt
6 made
7 met
8 sold

2

1 have
2 has
3 has
4 have
5 have

3

1 You haven't made a mistake.
2 The film hasn't started.
3 She hasn't found her keys.
4 They haven't done their homework.
5 We haven't had lunch.

4

1 has taught
2 haven't sold
3 has spent
4 have done
5 hasn't organized
6 has raised

5

1 Have (they) seen; haven't
2 Has (your mum) washed; hasn't
3 Has (your dad) made; has
4 Have (we) raised; have

6

1 *Have you heard*
2 has raised
3 has helped
4 have decided
5 have sold
6 Have (you) had

7

1 ever
2 never
3 ever
4 ever
5 never

8

1 Have you ever played
2 Have you ever cleaned
3 Have you ever organized
4 Have you ever sung
5 Have you ever sold

9

Students' own answers

10

1 since
2 since
3 for
4 since
5 for
6 for

11

1 *haven't written*
2 for
3 have been
4 have joined
5 haven't played
6 since
7 haven't had
8 haven't seen
9 for
10 Have (you) heard

12

1 How long has she worked for that charity?
She's worked for that charity since 2008.
2 How long has that restaurant been open?
It's been open for two weeks.
3 How long have you had that laptop?
I've had it since March.
4 How long has Luis worn glasses?
He's worn glasses for two years.

Revision

1

1 How long have you worked for this charity?
2 We've made her really happy with that present.
3 They haven't collected any money yet.

2

1 She's worked for a charity since January.
2 I've done two sponsored swims.
3 I've never done a sponsored run.

4

Students' own answers

5

1 *B 've raised*
2 A have
3 C has
4 A haven't
5 B 've collected
6 A have done
7 C never made
8 B since
9 C for
10 B Have you ever done

Extension

1

1 *for*
2 organizing
3 made
4 sold
5 was
6 funniest
7 was showing
8 got
9 are organizing
10 since
11 never done
12 interesting

Unit 6: Amazing journeys

Vocabulary

1

T	P	O	S	T	C	A	R	D	S	Y
R	A	C	Z	I	R	D	Z	H	Q	O
A	E	B	X	Q	F	V	U	R	S	G
I	Q	G	U	I	D	E	B	O	O	K
N	G	N	G	J	O	N	M	A	U	B
A	R	R	I	V	E	T	B	S	V	M
P	A	C	K	O	P	U	B	E	E	X
O	V	S	T	T	Z	R	W	T	N	E
K	I	U	S	L	T	E	P	O	I	S
S	U	I	T	C	A	S	E	F	R	X
J	L	T	R	I	P	Y	L	F	S	K

2

1 a guidebook
2 home
3 a train
4 adventures
5 people
6 a suitcase
7 a trip

3

1 set off
2 plan a trip
3 buy souvenirs
4 get on a train
5 arrive

4

1 bad
2 hot
3 happy
4 big
5 tired
6 cold
7 frightening
8 small

5

1 terrifying
2 freezing
3 delighted
4 boiling
5 exhausted
6 amazing

6

1 delighted
2 tiny
3 freezing
4 enormous
5 awful
6 terrifying

7

1 freezing
2 enormous
3 terrifying
4 tiny

Grammar

1

1 PS
2 PS
3 PP
4 PP
5 PS

2

1 present perfect
2 past simple

3

1 have had
2 's worked
3 saw
4 have never tried
5 Have you ever been
6 passed

4

1 ✗ I was in Brighton two weeks ago.
2 ✗ I've never tried Japanese food.
3 ✓
4 ✗ Holly has been in Italy since August.
5 ✗ She didn't speak to me last week.

5

1 have changed
2 bought
3 have painted
4 has been

6

1 Has Lucy ever been to New York?
2 Where did you buy those amazing shoes?
3 How long have you known your best friend?
4 How much money have they raised since March?

7

1 *Have you ever been*
2 had
3 Did you fly
4 drove
5 Have you seen
6 went
7 haven't seen

8

Students' own answers

9

Countable: cat, idea, people, seat, sock
Uncountable: *bread*, information, money, noise, water

10

1 many
2 much
3 many
4 many
5 much

11

1 many
2 a few
3 a lot of
4 many

12

1 a little
2 a few
3 many
4 a few
5 much
6 a little

Revision

1

1 You haven't done much exercise this week.
2 I've only brought a little money with me.
3 Has there been any news from your friend?

2

1 Mel hasn't spoken to me since she got back.
2 We bought lots of souvenirs when we were in Mexico.
3 It doesn't take much time to get there.

4

Students' own answers

5

1 *C 've been*
2 A went
3 B learnt
4 C a lot of
5 B visited
6 A some
7 A watched
8 A a few
9 C much
10 B did you do

Extension

1

1 *started*
2 walking
3 has already walked
4 ever
5 became
6 often attack
7 has got
8 more
9 spending
10 many
11 a lot
12 isn't
13 want
14 says

Unit 7: Films

Vocabulary

1

1 producer
2 film star
3 screen
4 special effects

2

plot, stunt, script, soundtrack, stuntwoman

3

1 stunt
2 soundtrack
3 plot
4 stuntwoman

4

1 release
2 star
3 win

5

1 soundtrack
2 screen
3 special effects
4 film star
5 stuntman

6

1 scene
2 award
3 star
4 release

7

	verb	noun
	advertise	*advertisement*
1	decorate	decoration
2	enjoy	enjoyment
3	equip	equipment
4	excite	excitement
5	possess	possession
6	suggest	suggestion

8

1 argument
2 celebration
3 connection
4 development
5 movement
6 prediction

9

1 celebration
2 move
3 equipment

10

1 connection
2 possession
3 decoration
4 enjoyment
5 excitement

11

1 advertisement
2 prediction
3 suggestion
4 education
5 development

Grammar

1

1 definitely
2 probably
3 after
4 before

2

1 You will definitely find it amazing.
2 You definitely won't be bored.
3 The actor will probably become famous.
4 The audience definitely won't forget the castle scene.

3

1 definitely won't like
2 will probably make
3 probably won't go
4 will definitely be able to

4

1 In 2200, will people take holidays on Mars?
Yes, they will. / No, they won't.
2 In 2100, will the sea cover half of Europe?
Yes, it will. / No, it won't.
3 Will the world's climate get hotter?
Yes, it will. / No, it won't.

5

1 future; intentions
2 present; future

6

1 'm going to train
2 Are you going to make
3 isn't going to win
4 'm not going to see
5 're going to travel

7

1 is he playing, is playing
2 is he taking, is taking

8

1 change
2 first; comma

9

1 give
2 win
3 'll go
4 will
5 do

10

1 help
2 tell
3 will give
4 will she stay

11

1 If we have enough money, we'll buy ice creams.
2 Your mum will be angry if you get home late.
3 If my friends are free tonight, we'll watch a film.

12

Students' own answers

Revision

1

1 I don't think this film will win many awards.
2 If they make a CD of the soundtrack, I'll definitely buy it.
3 I'm going to make a suggestion about that scene.

2

1 I'll tell you the plot of the film.
2 Are you going to join the school film club?
3 If Stella enters the competition, she'll win.

4

Students' own answers

5

1 *C I'll*
2 A 'm going
3 B get
4 C I'll try
5 B 'm going to
6 C it's
7 A I'll
8 C I'm going to spend
9 B is going to come
10 A 're going to have

Extension

1

1 *watching*
2 since
3 often stay
4 watched
5 funnier
6 enough time
7 I'm going
8 have
9 I'll watch
10 I've seen
11 best
12 I'm going
13 I'll spend
14 many

Unit 8: Our friends

Vocabulary

1

1 jump
2 arrive
3 interrupt
4 kiss
5 be
6 be

2

1 *f* 2 c 3 e 4 a 5 d 6 b

3

1 kiss
2 jump
3 shake
4 take off
5 click

4

1 bring a present
2 tell jokes
3 point at someone
4 be late
5 arrive early

5

P	R	E	S	E	N	T	S	O	A
E	I	F	B	I	X	C	Y	J	G
A	R	G	U	M	E	N	T	O	Q
B	N	A	F	R	X	Y	N	Q	P
A	D	V	I	C	E	Y	T	P	A
Q	S	E	U	Z	R	O	I	S	T
W	N	T	Q	V	T	I	M	Z	R
A	H	N	A	T	F	U	E	F	U
V	W	E	E	L	I	E	S	U	T
O	J	K	M	O	N	E	Y	N	H

6

1 *presents*, advice
2 time, money
3 argument
4 lies
5 truth
6 fun
7 advice, presents

7

1 spend
2 spend
3 tell
4 get
5 give

8

1 argument
2 fun
3 get
4 presents

9

Students' own answers

Grammar

1

1 *b* 2 d 3 a 4 c

2

1 must
2 mustn't
3 must
4 mustn't

3

1 have to
2 don't have to
3 has to
4 don't have to
5 has to

4

1 don't have to
2 don't have to
3 mustn't
4 doesn't have to
5 don't have to
6 mustn't

5

1 Do you have to pay
2 do young people have to do
3 do you have to be
4 Do students have to wear
5 do you have to do
6 Do your friends have to learn

6

Students' own answers

7

1 should eat
2 should drink
3 shouldn't sleep
4 should do
5 shouldn't go out

8

1 should
2 mustn't
3 should
4 shouldn't
5 mustn't

9

1 *mustn't*
2 mustn't
3 has to
4 don't have to
5 should

10

1 had
2 would phone
3 would tell
4 were

11

1 would let
2 wouldn't be
3 needed
4 'd go

12

1 I wouldn't ask Lulu for help if I were you.
2 He would have more time if he didn't watch TV all day.
3 If people didn't drive so much, this town would be cleaner.
4 I wouldn't have to do the washing-up if we had a dishwasher.

Revision

1

1 Should I give them some advice about travelling?
2 I would apologize if I had an argument with my best friend.
3 They don't have to take off their shoes.

2

1 They don't have to dress up for the party, but they can if they want to.
2 You shouldn't tell lies to your best friend.
3 If I knew the answer, I would tell you.

4

Students' own answers

5

1 A *would prefer*
2 B have to
3 B should
4 C mustn't
5 B has to
6 B mustn't
7 A mustn't
8 C didn't
9 A don't have to
10 C should

Extension

1

1 *for*
2 met
3 have been
4 play
5 than
6 best
7 should
8 are practising
9 were playing
10 work
11 a few
12 see
13 I'll
14 paid
15 don't have to
16 I'm

Unit 9: Making music

Vocabulary

1

1 go on
2 form
3 play
4 record
5 release

2

1 *c* 2 e 3 b 4 a 5 d

3

1 a playlist
2 a single
3 a hit
4 a record

4

1 live
2 album
3 went to
4 single
5 lyrics
6 recorded
7 went on
8 studio
9 festivals

5

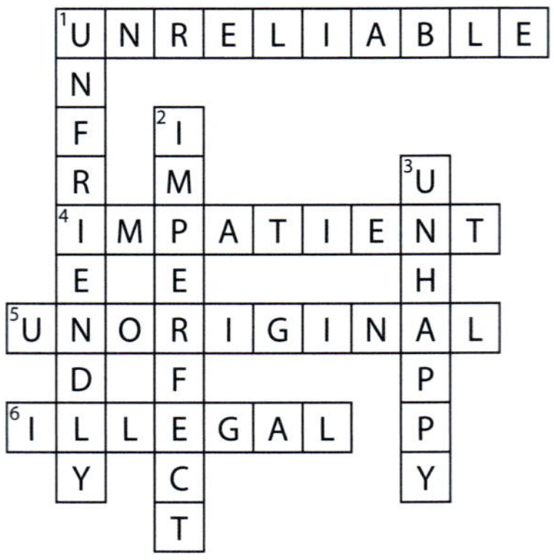

6

1 impossible
2 illogical
3 impractical
4 unsupportive
5 unnecessary
6 unadventurous
7 unimaginative

7

1 unfriendly
2 untrustworthy
3 unnecessary
4 impractical
5 unsupportive

8

1 unadventurous
2 illegal
3 unhappy
4 impossible
5 unoriginal

9

Students' own answers

Grammar

1

1 are
2 are
3 is
4 are

2

1 is produced
2 aren't allowed
3 are spoken
4 aren't released

3

1 What is the British flag called?
2 Where are kimonos worn?
3 How is 'Leicester' pronounced?
4 How often are the Olympic games held?

4

1 It's called
2 They're worn
3 It's pronounced
4 They're held

5

1 was
2 were
3 was
4 were

6

1 *were taken*
2 weren't allowed
3 were shown
4 was photographed
5 were recorded

7

1 Who were these books written by?
2 Who was this table chosen by?
3 When were these CDs bought?

8

1 P 2 A 3 A 4 A 5 P

9

1 wasn't released in 2008
2 were written three years ago
3 aren't recorded at Abbey Road Studios
4 were used in these songs
5 weren't created with a computer

10

1 past simple
2 present continuous
3 present perfect
4 past continuous

11

1 *was given*
2 bought
3 exists
4 wanted
5 were living
6 was working
7 was played
8 is called
9 has become
10 visit
11 are planning
12 will visit

Revision

1

1 Where were these songs recorded?
2 Some album covers are designed by famous artists.
3 This playlist was made for my sister's party.

2

1 Are these shoes made of plastic?
2 This album wasn't released last year.
3 How long have you been in this band?

4

Students' own answers

5

1 *A is known*
2 B is
3 A became
4 C sang
5 A was
6 C became
7 A was followed
8 B has been
9 C began
10 A has

Extension

1

1 most
2 have disappeared
3 gave
4 are still playing
5 for
6 A lot of
7 the best
8 were playing
9 had
10 weren't
11 as
12 are still arguing
13 are bought
14 was copied

Grammar Practice

Unit 1

1

1 relaxes
2 does
3 don't eat
4 doesn't speak

2

1 Do you and Tom like football?
2 Does Eduardo draw cartoons?
3 Do your grandparents play computer games?
4 Does your mum speak French?

3

1 Yes, we do.
2 No, he doesn't.
3 No, they don't.
4 Yes, she does.

4

1 I always walk to school.
2 They hardly ever go to a youth centre.
3 Clara is sometimes unsociable.
4 We usually chat online.

5

1 's
2 are
3 is
4 'm
5 are

6

1 She isn't listening to music now.
2 You aren't playing the violin.
3 At the moment Joe isn't sleeping.
4 I'm not having lunch right now.
5 Max and I aren't doing our homework.

7

1 isn't
2 they
3 Is
4 not
5 Are

8

1 making
2 learning
3 drawing
4 going
5 chatting

Unit 2

1

1 *was*
2 wasn't
3 were
4 wasn't
5 were
6 Was
7 was

2

1 printed R
2 read I
3 sent I
4 wrote I
5 worked R
6 became I

3

1 took
2 posted
3 arrived
4 did
5 went

4

1 Marc didn't take a photo of us.
2 He didn't post his comment.
3 My mum didn't arrive home.
4 I didn't do my homework every day.
5 They didn't go online to find a website.

5

1 Did (you) want; Yes, I did.
2 Did (they) take; Yes, they did.
3 Did (your sister) work; No, she didn't.
4 Did (you) make; No, I didn't.

6

1 was using
2 wasn't doing
3 was playing
4 was waiting

7

1 Was it raining at six o'clock?; it
2 Were Simon and Jen working as teachers?; were
3 Were the students downloading documents?; weren't

Unit 3

1

1 ran
2 saw
3 was trying
4 were sitting
5 phoned

2

1 was skiing; broke
2 was walking; found
3 were chatting; came
4 took; were diving
5 were having; started

3

1 while
2 while
3 When
4 when

4

1 goes
2 'm dancing
3 does (your mum) do
4 stay
5 's watching

5

1 *was doing*
2 didn't know
3 was sitting
4 switched
5 were playing
6 watched

6

1 *c*
2 e
3 b
4 f
5 a
6 d

Unit 4

1

1 easier; the easiest
2 better; the best
3 angrier; the angriest
4 more famous; the most famous
5 more beautiful; the most beautiful

2

1 the noisiest
2 worse
3 more tiring
4 the largest
5 further

3

1 I'm bigger than you.
2 It's the most exciting city in the world.
3 Is David more famous than Victoria?
4 You're happier than me.
5 That exercise was the hardest.

4

1 not as luxurious as
2 as large as
3 not as expensive as
4 not as close to the sea as

5

1 too difficult
2 too slow
3 tall enough
4 n't cold enough

Unit 5

1

1 collected
2 learnt
3 met
4 organized
5 raised

2

1 have
2 has
3 have
4 have
5 has

3

1 I haven't made a mistake.
2 Gemma hasn't bought a new bag.
3 The students haven't done voluntary work.
4 We haven't had a good time today.
5 My brother hasn't visited the Tower of London.

4

1 Have your parents sold their house?
2 Has Miss Martinez given you any homework?
3 Have you ever eaten shark?
4 Has Rory washed his dad's car?

5

1 Yes, they have.
2 No, she hasn't.
3 No, I haven't.
4 Yes, he has.

6

for: a few minutes, a long time, a year, eight months, hours
since: *2009*, nine o'clock, February, last year, the beginning of the century

7

1 for
2 since
3 since
4 for
5 since

Unit 6

1

1 *'ve seen*
2 've been
3 stayed
4 didn't stay
5 've met
6 has bought

2

1 got
2 've been
3 felt
4 has worked
5 haven't travelled

3

1 *Have* (*you ever*) *been*
2 've visited
3 did (you) go
4 went
5 've lived
6 've (ever) had
7 took

4

1 many
2 a little
3 a few
4 any
5 a lot of

5

1 any
2 many
3 much
4 much
5 any

6

1 She drinks a little water every 30 minutes.
2 I've got a lot of friends in the USA.
3 It's empty – there aren't any books in it.
4 There's a little food, but not much.

Unit 7

1

1 My brother will definitely be a film star.
2 Pia definitely won't pass the exam.
3 Schoolchildren probably won't use books.
4 My parents will probably let me have a party.

2

1 Will you and your friends make a charity CD?
2 Will you go out for a meal on Saturday?
3 Will your school be open tomorrow?
Students' own answers

3

1 'm not going to buy
2 's going to fall
3 Is … going to work
4 isn't going to study

4

1 *'s playing tennis*
2 are going out for a pizza
3 are coming
4 is doing a sponsored swim

5

1 won't be
2 work
3 doesn't rain
4 'll send

6

1 If you don't pass your exam, will you take it again?
2 We'll miss the bus if we don't leave now.
3 If Tom has enough money, will he come?
4 I'll go out tonight if I have time.

Unit 8

1

1 have to stand up
2 Do you have to wear
3 don't have to have
4 doesn't have to walk

2

1 must
2 have to
3 doesn't
4 don't have to
5 Do we have to

3

1 mustn't forget
2 mustn't play
3 mustn't tell
4 mustn't interrupt

4

1 should
2 should
3 should
4 shouldn't
5 shouldn't

5

1 moved
2 would be
3 had
4 would

6

1 would (you) say; kissed
2 had; wouldn't be
3 didn't know; 'd ask
4 would complain; didn't like

Unit 9

1

1 is downloaded
2 isn't spoken
3 aren't sold

2

1 Are the lyrics written in Spanish?
Yes, they are.
2 Are saxophones played on the soundtrack?
No, they aren't.
3 Are CDs made in that factory?
Yes, they are.

3

1 *was built*
2 was bought
3 were converted
4 wasn't recorded
5 were recorded
6 was used

4

1 Was it designed as a recording studio?
2 What kind of music was played there at first?
3 When were The Beatles' songs recorded?
4 What was recorded there recently?

5

1 No, it wasn't.
2 At first, classical music was played there.
3 They were recorded there between 1962 and 1970.
4 The soundtracks for *Skyfall* and *Gravity* were recorded there recently.

6

1 sell tickets to the music festival online.
2 is watched by millions of people.
3 released their first album last year.
4 are recorded at Abbey Road.
5 downloaded the single.
6 was written by Pablo Alborán.

Vocabulary Reference

Unit 1

1

voluntary work
to the cinema
tennis
cartoons
out for a meal
to a youth centre
models
computer games

1 voluntary work; models
2 to the cinema; out for a meal (in either order)
3 tennis; computer games (in either order)
4 cartoons; to a youth centre

2

L	F	R	I	E	N	D	L	Y	F	F	D	A
S	H	G	E	N	E	R	O	U	S	U	I	D
T	H	Y	N	Y	S	S	E	L	F	I	S	H
A	D	V	E	N	T	U	R	O	U	S	H	O
L	A	U	R	I	O	U	S	U	N	B	O	N
K	U	T	G	E	L	F	I	S	N	H	N	E
A	E	O	E	E	A	T	S	H	Y	O	E	S
T	N	G	T	E	Z	M	M	V	O	E	S	T
I	H	Y	I	E	Y	O	M	R	M	O	T	U
V	F	I	C	O	N	F	I	D	E	N	T	E
E	U	N	S	O	C	I	A	B	L	E	O	S

Unit 2

1

1 post a comment
2 take a photo
3 send an email
4 play a video game
Mystery word: technology

2

1 actor
2 firefighter
3 lab technician
4 police officer
5 postal worker
6 electrician

3

researcher
scientist
artist
journalist
politician
builder
doctor
lawyer

Unit 3

1

towards
along
into
through
round
up
out of
down
across
over
away from
under

2

annoying
surprising
frightening
exciting
tiring
boring

3

1 frightened
2 excited
3 tired
4 worried
5 boring
6 annoying
7 surprised

Unit 4

1

1 lighthouse
2 temple
3 castle
4 rainforest
5 opera house
6 pyramid

2

happily
hard
noisily
fast
easily
angrily
quietly
quickly

Unit 5

1

do a sponsored swim
have a bring and buy sale
make a charity CD
sell badges
wash cars
sell cakes

2

1 exercise
2 friends
3 homework
4 nothing
5 charity work
6 mistake
7 best
8 decision
9 favour
10 money
11 happy
12 laugh

Unit 6

1

plan a trip
get on a train
buy a guidebook
pack a suitcase
send postcards
come back home

2

arrive, meet people, come back home, set off, have adventures, get off a train, buy souvenirs

3

1 freezing
2 awful
3 terrifying
4 exhausted
5 amazing
6 enormous

Unit 7

1

1 release a film
2 director
3 film a scene
4 special effects
5 star in a film
6 win an award

2

P	E	R	D	N	B	E	D	U	C	A	T	I	O	N
M	O	V	E	M	E	N	T	L	S	D	Y	A	M	D
O	S	R	C	O	A	Y	U	T	Z	V	E	A	W	D
P	O	P	O	E	N	J	O	Y	M	E	N	T	C	E
O	N	S	R	I	P	M	K	F	A	R	E	L	O	V
S	E	O	A	S	U	G	G	E	S	T	I	O	N	E
S	K	L	T	R	E	D	D	Y	R	I	N	C	N	L
E	X	C	I	T	E	M	E	N	T	S	E	B	E	O
S	E	J	O	M	A	R	G	U	M	E	N	T	C	P
S	I	M	N	U	E	Q	U	I	P	M	E	N	T	M
I	S	H	D	G	J	P	O	W	U	E	S	N	I	E
O	P	R	E	D	I	C	T	I	O	N	C	V	O	N
N	X	H	C	E	L	E	B	R	A	T	I	O	N	T

Unit 8

1

1 take off your shoes
2 bring a present
3 be polite
4 shake hands
5 be rude
6 tell jokes
7 click your fingers
8 jump a queue
8 interrupt a conversation

2

1 advice
2 time
3 present
4 lies
5 truth
6 argument
7 fun
8 money

Unit 9

1

playlist
record
hit
single
music festivals
lyrics
recording studio
to number one

1 playlist; music festivals
2 record; lyrics
3 hit; recording studio
4 single; to number one

2

1 go on tour
2 form a band
3 go to number one
4 play live at a concert
5 record a song
6 release an album

3

impossible
unadventurous
unsupportive
impatient
unreliable
unimaginative
untrustworthy
unoriginal

Culture: Reading & Listening

Unit 1

1

1 London, UK
2 light blue and dark blue

2

1 T 2 T 3 F 4 T 5 F

3

1 About 250,000 people
2 6.8 km
3 16–20 minutes
4 The cox steers the boat and shouts at the crew to make them go faster.

4

1 T 2 F 3 F 4 T

Unit 2

1

1 in a coal mine
2 a steam engine

2

1 T 2 F 3 F 4 T 5 F

3

1 *e* 2 b 3 c 4 a 5 d

4

1 F 2 F 3 F 4 T

Unit 3

1

1 Jack
2 Ralph
3 Simon
4 Piggy

2

1 F 2 T 3 F 4 T 5 F

3

1 *d* 2 a 3 b 4 e 5 c

4

1 F 3 T
2 T 4 F

Unit 4

1

1 1933–1937
2 Everyone – cyclists, pedestrians and cars

2

1 F 2 T 3 F 4 T 5 T

3

1 *e* 2 b 3 d 4 a 5 c

4

1 F 2 F 3 F 4 T

Unit 5

1

1 C 2 D 3 B 4 A

2

1 T 2 F 3 F 4 T 5 F

3

1 *b* 2 d 3 c 4 a

4

1 F 2 F 3 T 4 F

Unit 6

1

Many places including New Zealand, Australia, South Africa, Brazil, Chile and Ecuador

2

1 a 2 b 3 a 4 b

3

1 slavery
2 shells
3 environment

4

1 *c* 2 a 3 d 4 e 5 b

Unit 7

1

Jaws, *Raiders of the Lost Ark*, *Schindler's List*

2

1 F 2 T 3 T 4 F 5 F

3

1 *d* 2 b 3 c 4 a

4

1 T 2 F 3 F 4 T

Unit 8

1

1 at a church festival in 1957
2 in New York in 1980

2

a 7 b 2 c 4 d 3
e 5 f *1* g 6

3

1 *e* 2 b 3 d 4 c 5 a

4

1 T 2 F 3 T 4 F

Unit 9

1

1 cultural events (classical and pop concerts, opera, ballet, circus, poetry, award ceremonies, tennis matches and boxing contests)
2 (classical music) concerts

2

1 b 2 a 3 a 4 a 5 b

3

1 *e* 2 b 3 a 4 c 5 d

4

1 F
2 T
3 T
4 F

Writing Guide

Unit 1

Step 1

1

She is sometimes lazy, she doesn't like cleaning or washing-up and her room is always untidy.

2

1, 3 and 4

3

1 to Katie's flat
2 She's friendly, funny and energetic.
3 maths, art and music
4 She's painting trees and flowers on the walls of her room.
5 talking about films and clothes, listening to music, spending time together, doing homework

Step 2

Students' own answers

Unit 2

Step 1

1

some sunglasses, a T-shirt, a DVD and a cap

2

1 F 2 T 3 F 4 T

3

1 a 2 b 3 b 4 a 5 b

Step 2

1 *15th birthday present*
2 at Auntie Ann's house
3 mp4 player
4 exactly what I wanted
5 all the time
6 **a** won a BMX competition
  b passed her driving test
7 new science teacher
8 school holiday

Unit 3

Step 1

1

b) Accidents can happen

2

The correct order is *c*, e, b, d, a.

3

1 T 2 F 3 T 4 T 5 F

Step 2

1 *was going to school*
2 late for school
3 was raining
4 ran into the road
5 **a** stopped too fast
  b didn't want to hit the cat
6 two teenagers
7 **a** helped Hayley move
  b phone for help

Unit 4

Step 1

1

in Paris

2

1 T 2 F 3 T 4 F 5 F

3

1 *b* 2 d 3 a 4 f 5 c 6 e

Step 2

1 *West London*
2 a really long street with shops on both sides
3 antiques and jewellery
4 Saturday
5 **a** fruit and vegetables
  b retro and vintage clothes
6 traditional British cooking
7 The Electric Cinema

Unit 5

Step 1

1

He was delighted.

2

1 *b* 2 a 3 d 4 c

3

1 Students at Riverside school.
2 People in Africa.
3 Student Anna Kemp.
4 Head teacher Tom Black.

Step 2

1 *Oakwood Academy*
2 £8,000
3 a sponsored swim and a bring and buy sale and we sold raffle tickets
4 Greenpeace
5 many students have studied environmental problems at school
6 a big success
7 raise £10,000 for Oxfam

Unit 6

Step 1

1

She's happy.

2

1 T 2 F 3 F 4 F 5 T

3

The correct order is *c*, b, e, a, d.

Step 2

1 *Chinchón*
2 **a** First
  b took a bus to Heathrow airport
3 **a** an accident on the road and the bus was late
  b two hours
4 plane to Madrid
5 **a** for three hours to get on the plane
  b Then
6 **a** Next
  b Chinchón by car
7 **a** there was a lot of traffic
  b two hours
  c finally
8 my aunt and uncle are having a big family dinner with all my cousins

Unit 7

Step 1

1

Good – it is one of his favourite films

2

1 F **2** T **3** T **4** F **5** F

3

1 Steven Spielberg
2 There are several: Henry Thomas, Robert MacNaughton, Drew Barrymore and Dee Wallace
3 The powerful emotion
4 Adults, teenagers and children

Step 2

Students' own answers

Unit 8

Step 1

1

The student exchange

2

1 b **2** a **3** b

Step 2

Students' own answers except:

4 a Although
5 b Furthermore
6 c In addition

Unit 9

Step 1

1

c) gives information about Katy Perry's life.

2

1 23
2 *One of the Boys*
3 She appeared in the MTV Europe Music Awards.
4 She's performed in her *Prismatic* tour.
5 She has helped children's charities. She's a goodwill ambassador for UNICEF.
6 Because her music is good and she helps other people.

Step 2

Students' own answers except:

7 b Since
8 a Last

Speaking

Unit 1

1

1 They are in a restaurant.
2 They are eating and chatting.
3 Students' own answers

2

Students' own answers

Unit 2

1

1 He's an artist.
2 He was painting a picture.
3 Students' own answers

2

Students' own answers

Unit 3

1

1 The people are in the air. They are jumping out of a plane.
2 Students' own answers
3 Students' own answers

2

Students' own answers

Unit 4

1

1 The picture shows ruins of a temple in Greece.
2 Students' own answers
3 Students' own answers

2

Students' own answers

Unit 5

1

1 The people are in a race. They are raising money for charity.
2 Students' own answers
3 Students' own answers

2

Students' own answers

Unit 6

1

1 The people are in Rome. The girl on the right is looking at a guidebook. The other two people are taking a photo.
2 Students' own answers
3 It looks like they have been to the Colosseum.

2

Students' own answers

Unit 7

1

1 The person in the foreground is the director. The people in the background are actors.
2 It looks like they are filming a scene.
3 Students' own answers

2

Students' own answers

Unit 8

1

Students' own answers

2

Students' own answers

Unit 9

1

1 The people are playing live at a concert.
2 drums and guitars
3 Students' own answers

2

Students' own answers

Student's Book Audioscripts

Starter unit, Listening, Introductions, page 6, exercises 1 and 2, track 1.02

Mia Hi, I'm Mia. I'm 15. I live in London. I like going to the cinema with friends. I like watching science-fiction films but I don't like horror films. When I'm at home, I like watching cartoons on TV like *Family Guy* and *The Simpsons*.

Max Hello. I'm Max. I'm 14 and I'm English, but I live In Scotland. I don't like going to the cinema because it's very expensive. I like watching films at home on DVD. My favourite films are fantasy films, but I can't stand romantic comedies – they're so boring! I love watching reality shows on TV.

Ruby Hi. I'm Ruby. I'm also 14 and I live in Manchester in the north-west of England. I'm like Max – I hardly ever go to the cinema. I like downloading films and watching them on my laptop at home. I like adventure films, but I don't like animated films. I love watching sports programmes on TV because I play football.

Unit 1, Vocabulary, page 8, exercise 3, track 1.05

Emma What are your favourite free-time activities, Danny?

Danny I like playing computer games and playing tennis, but my favourite activity is playing football. What about you?

Emma I like doing artistic things like making models of animals or drawing cartoons. My favourite activity is going to the youth centre. We always do a lot of different fun things there.

Unit 1, Listening, Celebrity hobbies, page 12, exercises 5 and 6, track 1.09

We usually only see celebrities when they are performing or in the public eye. But stars need to relax too and when they have some free time, they enjoy their hobbies just like you and me.

Heart-throb actor Robert Pattinson is really musical and loves playing the piano. In fact, he even plays on the soundtrack of some of his films. He's also keen on reading.

We all know that Fernando Alonso is a Formula 1 racing magician, but he also does magic in his free time. Yes, really! When the world champion driver is not racing cars, he enjoys doing magic tricks for his friends.

Another sports star, footballer Cristiano Ronaldo, also has a surprising free-time activity. He loves playing bingo. 'It can be very exciting,' he says.

Many celebrities like collecting things. Leonardo DiCaprio, star of blockbusters like *The Wolf of Wall Street* and *Django Unchained*, collects toy action figures. His favourites are his massive collection of *Star Wars* characters.

And finally, Spanish actress Penelope Cruz has a musical hobby. That's right, she loves singing karaoke! The Oscar-winning actress sings rap songs, especially Eminem songs, when she wants to relax! Maybe we'll see her in the Top 40 sometime soon.

Unit 1, Pronunciation, page 15, exercise b, track 1.14

1 There are two bottles of juice in the fridge.
2 I often draw cartoons online.
3 The local shop is very close.

Unit 2, Vocabulary, page 18, exercise 3, track 1.16

Sophie How many hours do you use a computer every week?

Chen A computer? About three. I spend about one hour chatting online and about two hours playing computer games.

Sophie How many hours do you watch TV every week?

Chen About four or five.

Sophie And how many hours do you spend listening to music on your mp3 player?

Chen A lot! Probably about eight hours.

Unit 2, Listening, A miracle – thanks to technology, page 22, exercises 5 and 6, track 1.20

When most people use the phrase 'the miracle of technology' they're talking about the latest smartphone, tablet or app, but not a human being. For Martin Jones, however, technology worked a real-life miracle.

Martin was working as a builder when he had a terrible accident. As a result of the accident, Martin went totally blind and for 12 years he couldn't see at all.

Then doctors told him about a new technology. It used a special optical lens to help blind people see again. At first, scientists couldn't use the technology because the patient's immune system rejected the plastic lens. Then they discovered that they could implant the lens into a tooth! First, doctors took out one of Martin's teeth. Then they put the optical lens into the tooth. Then they implanted the tooth into his eye.

Martin was blind when he met his wife, Gill. When he opened his eyes after the operation, she was standing by his bed. She was the first person he saw. 'It was incredible to see her for the first time,' said Martin. Now, he laughs about his 'science-fiction eye' and he's happy he isn't blind.

Scientists say the new technology can help more people in the future. They are already planning more operations.

Unit 3, Vocabulary, page 28, exercise 4, track 1.27

William Hey, Fatima, have you got any funny superstitions?

Fatima What do you mean?

William Well, for example, Charlotte never walks under ladders. She thinks it's bad luck.

Fatima Well, I usually jump over lines in the road, I don't walk on them. What about you?

William Me? I don't have any superstitions, I …

Charlotte That's not true! You always walk away from black cats.

Unit 3, Listening, Tree couple get home safely, page 32, exercises 4 and 5, track 1.31

And finally, some good news. The missing couple, Keith and Jennifer Lee, are safely back at home with their four children after spending two days trapped in the mountains.
Keith and Jennifer went up to the mountains last Tuesday to get a tree for Christmas just like they do every year. They found a tree, cut it down and put it onto the roof of their car. They were driving home on a remote mountain road in the middle of the forest when they got trapped by snow. Their phones weren't working because they were so high up. It was a worrying situation.
A family friend, Sophie Smith, was looking after the children. When the Lees didn't return, Sophie became worried. She called the police and they started a search. Dozens of people walked along the roads and through the trees looking for the Lees' car, and a helicopter flew over the area.
Two days and two nights later, Keith finally put rocks under the wheels and he was able to move the car. They were very tired but excited because their car was working again. They were driving home when they heard about the search for them on the radio. They phoned the police and they phoned Sophie. Everyone was delighted, especially their children.
Keith is planning to go back to the mountains again next year, but Jennifer doesn't want to go. It was a frightening experience for her – she thinks they should buy a tree next year!

Unit 3, Pronunciation, page 35, exercise b, track 1.36

1 They were hiding in the trees.
2 She wasn't alone.
3 Was he talking to David?
4 He was running away when the bear attacked.

Unit 4, Vocabulary, page 42, exercise 3, track 1.38

Emma What's Mérida famous for?
Ryan Um, I don't know. Give me a clue.
Emma Who lived in Spain around two thousand years ago?
Ryan Oh! The Romans. Oh yeah, Mérida is famous for its Roman ruins.

Unit 4, Listening, A trip to New York, page 46, exercises 5 and 6, track 1.42

Michela Hi Ben, you're back! How was your trip to New York?
Ben It was really cool! We had a great time.
Michela Yeah? What did you do?
Ben Loads of stuff. We did a lot of sightseeing. You know, we visited all the most famous places, like the Statue of Liberty, Brooklyn Bridge, …
Michela Did you go up the Empire State Building?
Ben Yeah, yeah, we did that too.
Michela What about … Did you go to any museums?
Ben Well, my dad really wanted to visit the Metropolitan Museum of Art. It's the biggest museum in New York. We were having a coffee in a diner when we realized that it was late. We ran really quickly to the museum, but we were too late and it was already closing.
Michela Oh, that's a shame.
Ben Well, it was for my mum and dad. I didn't really want to go anyway. Museums are a bit too boring for me.
Michela What about the food? Everyone says that it's one of the best places in the world for eating out.
Ben Oh, yeah, the food was great. We had waffles for breakfast, burgers, amazing pizza, Thai food, Mexican food, incredible.
Michela Did you buy anything?
Ben Yes, we went shopping one day. I bought some jeans and …
Michela … and those cool new trainers, right?
Ben Actually, I had these already … but … look … I got this for you. Here.
Michela Oh … an 'I love NYC' baseball cap … wow, thanks Ben … just what I need.
Ben Go on. Try it on.
Michela Oh … it … isn't really big enough … never mind. Why don't you give it to your cousin?
Ben Right, I'll do that … 'cause your head's just too big, isn't it?
Michela Oi! Just 'cause you've been to New York!

Unit 4, Pronunciation, page 49, exercise b, track 1.47

1 Slaves built the Taj Mahal.
2 It was a beautiful, dark cave.
3 The ruins are in a rainforest.

Unit 5, Vocabulary, page 52, exercise 3, track 2.02

Alex Which fundraising idea do you think is best Lucy?
Lucy I think selling cakes is a good idea because everyone can participate.
Alex I think making a charity CD is a good idea because everyone can buy one.
Lucy Why don't we have a bring and buy sale, then we can sell cakes and CDs?
Alex Good idea!

Unit 5, Listening, Selena Gomez, Goodwill Ambassador, page 56, exercises 5 and 6, track 2.06

Selena Gomez is an actress and a pop singer. She has been famous since she was a child. She's starred in a hit TV series and she's been very successful with her band, Selena Gomez and the Scene.
But not everyone knows about the work that Selena does for charity. She supports Island Dog, a charity that helps dogs in Puerto Rico, and RAISE Hope for Congo, a charity that campaigns to end violence against Congolese women.
In August 2009, at the age of 18, Selena became the youngest UNICEF Goodwill ambassador. She started working on the Trick-or-Treat for UNICEF campaign, which raises money at Halloween when children go from door to door collecting money.
Her first official visit with UNICEF was to Ghana where she saw children living without enough food, clean water or medicines. She realized that by visiting Ghana she was publicizing their problems. This is what being a Goodwill Ambassador is all about – making people aware of the world's problems and encouraging them to help.
During her first visit, she met a 14-year-old boy. He really wanted to go to school but couldn't. When Selena was at school many children didn't like school or homework, but this boy was different. That visit to Ghana had a huge impact on her and she has never forgotten the boy who wanted to go to school.

Unit 5, Pronunciation, page 59, exercise b, track 2.11

1 We haven't seen many films in English.
2 She hasn't collected money.
3 He's written lots of emails.
4 He's bought a charity CD.

Unit 6, Vocabulary, page 62, exercise 3, track 2.13

Zoe I like your T-shirt, Chas. Where did you get it?
Chas I bought it in Rome. It was a souvenir.
Zoe A souvenir T-shirt, what a good idea.
Chas I buy a T-shirt in every place I visit. Have you ever bought any souvenirs?
Zoe Yes, I have. I bought this baseball cap in New York.

Unit 6, Listening, Solo sailor, page 66, exercises 5 and 6, track 2.17

David What are you reading, Bhav?
Bhav It's an article about Mike Perham.
David Mike Perham? Who's he?
Bhav Well, he was the youngest person to sail around the world alone. He's an interesting guy.
David Oh, yeah? How old was he when he did it?
Bhav Only 17. In fact, he celebrated his 17th birthday in the middle of the Indian Ocean.
David When did he do it?
Bhav In 2009. It took him nine months and he sailed over 30,000 miles on his yacht, called totallymoney.com!
David Funny name.
Bhav Yeah, it is a bit. It's an interesting story. He had a lot of adventures on his trip. He had good conditions in the Indian Ocean, but there were awful storms in the South Pacific. He didn't have many problems with his boat. However, he had to stop in the Canary Islands, Portugal and Cape Town to repair his auto-pilot, the machine that sailed the boat while he was sleeping.
David Did he meet any whales or sharks?
Bhav No, fortunately he didn't.
David So what's he doing now?
Bhav Well, he wants to be the first person to travel around the world by sea, land and air. Since his sailing trip, he's already driven around the world. At the moment, he's taking flying lessons to prepare for the third and final part.

Unit 6, Pronunciation, page 69, exercise b, track 2.22

1 I've heard about *The World on Wheels*.
2 I've drunk green tea.
3 I've just been to the countryside.

Unit 7, Vocabulary, page 76, exercise 4, track 2.24

Isabel So, Xavi, what's your favourite film?
Xavi *Gravity*.
Isabel Why do you like it?
Xavi I like the script and the special effects. What's your favourite film?
Isabel *The Hobbit*.
Xavi Why do you like it?
Isabel Because I love fantasy films.

Unit 7, Listening, Teenage film-makers, page 80, exercises 5 and 6, track 2.29

Presenter Welcome to our weekly look at the world of cinema. First, we're going to hear from our entertainment reporter, Holly Thomson, about a special film programme for teenagers. Holly, can you tell us a bit about Fresh Films?

Reporter Yes, Fresh Films is a programme which started over ten years ago to give teenagers experience in film-making. It gives access to training, equipment and connections to help make their dreams come true. Their mission is to develop teenagers' talent and potential.

Presenter So, I imagine that teenagers watch professional film-makers working on a film set.

Reporter The professionals guide and lead the teenagers on the film set, but it's the teenagers themselves who are responsible for all aspects of the film production. It's a hands-on, practical programme.

Presenter How exciting! How do you get a place on the programme?

Reporter Well, it's open to anyone aged 13–18. All you have to do is explain to the organizers why they should choose you. If they choose you, you'll spend a week working with a team of teenage film-makers to make a real short film. Some of the past participants now have careers in film. Some teenage film-makers even got to work with Hollywood celebrities.

Presenter And do you need experience to enter the programme?

Reporter No, absolutely no experience is necessary. You just need to love films and film-making. You will also like working in a team.

Presenter Tell me about *The Stream*.

Reporter After a decade of making short films, Fresh Films decided to do something different and they created a feature-length film …

Presenter That's a full-length film, isn't it?

Reporter Yes, that's right. Groups of teenage film-makers worked together to film and produce scenes from a full-length feature film. The result was *The Stream*.

Presenter And the film was released on iTunes as well as in the cinema.

Reporter Yes, and all the money raised from ticket sales and downloads was donated to charity.

Presenter Thanks Holly. Maybe we'll see more feature-length films from Fresh Films in the future. And now …

Unit 7, Pronunciation, page 83, exercise b, track 2.34

1 I'm going to buy a ticket.
2 The filming is going to start.
3 They aren't going to do the stunts.

Unit 8, Vocabulary, page 86, exercise 4, track 2.36

Magda Have you ever shaken hands with someone famous Adam?

Adam Yes. I shook hands with the Prime Minister when he visited my town. And you?

Magda No, I've never met anyone famous.

Unit 8, Listening, Relationship advice, page 90, exercises 4 and 5, track 2.40

Interviewer So, your best friend is Harry, is that right?

Jack I don't really have one best friend. I have a group of good friends. We all like the same things: football, computer games, going to parties, … meeting girls!

Interviewer And have you got a girlfriend?

Jack Well, yes, I think so.

Interviewer You think so?

Jack Well, I'm going out with a girl called Gina, but we had an argument yesterday.

Interviewer What was it about?

Jack Well, it was her birthday last Monday and, well, I forgot and I didn't buy her a present, so she got a bit angry.

Interviewer I'm not surprised. If she forgot your birthday, how would you feel?

Jack I'd be angry I suppose. What do you think I should do?

Interviewer Well, if I were you, I'd apologize and give her a present. What do you think, Jess? If you were Jack's girlfriend, what would you do?

Jess Me? Jack's girlfriend? You're joking, aren't you?

Interviewer OK, but just imagine you were. What would you do?

Jess Well, I wouldn't be his girlfriend anymore. I'd find a new boyfriend.

Interviewer Really?

Jess Yeah, definitely.

Interviewer And have you got a boyfriend now?

Jess Err, well, yes, but I'm not speaking to him at the moment,

Interviewer Why not?

Jess He told me a lie. He said he couldn't see me because he was studying, but really he was watching football with his friends.

Interviewer Jack, what do you think Jess should do?

Jack I don't think it was a big lie. If my girlfriend did that, I wouldn't mind too much.

Jess Well, I don't care what Jack thinks. For me, people must be honest. That's the most important quality in a person I think. A friend, a boyfriend or a girlfriend should always tell you the truth.

Unit 8, Pronunciation, page 93, exercise b, track 2.45

1 You shouldn't write in books.
2 Click your fingers.
3 He died in a plane crash.
4 Point at her boyfriend.

Unit 9, Vocabulary, page 96, exercise 3, track 2.47

Kate So, Todd, what was the last song you downloaded? Was it good?

Todd It was *The Monster* by Eminem. Yeah, it's not bad, I like it. What was the last song you downloaded? Was it good?

Kate It was *Wrecking Ball* by Miley Cyrus. It's fantastic! I play it all the time.

Unit 9, Listening, A new trend in the music world, page 100, exercises 5 and 6, track 2.50

Saida And on today's programme we have a report about a new trend in the music industry that everyone is talking about. Luke Harrison is here with the details. Luke, what can you tell us?

Luke Hi Saida. Well, it's safe to say that this new trend in music distribution is breaking all the rules of how some artists find fame and the leaders of this trend are a new generation of musicians who are reinventing how music is released to the public. They are video bloggers, writers, songwriters, musicians and most importantly, they've had hits in the official music charts.

Saida That's impressive! Which record labels are they signed to?

Luke Well Saida, that's the amazing thing. These artists have had all this success without the support of a record label or a manager.

Saida How amazing! What's the secret, apart from great music and lyrics?

Luke Well, think about how much the music industry has changed. A recent survey said that nowadays more digital music is sold than music in the shops …

Saida You mean people buy more music online than on CDs or records?

Luke Yes, that's correct. But we're not simply talking about music sales here. Over the last 15 years we've seen the change from CDs to music downloads to music streaming websites and many young consumers now prefer to access music online.

Saida So do you think that these new artists are successful because of changes in the music industry?

Luke It's one reason, yes, but there are other reasons too. Some of these new artists have created a style of releasing and distributing music by using YouTube. They have their own YouTube channels and many of them have thousands of subscribers and receive millions of views.

Saida That's incredible. Can I go and see any of them play live?

Luke I'm afraid not Saida. Most of these artists don't go on tour or play in music festivals. They connect with fans online rather than in a concert or on stage and some post video diaries every week sharing stories with fans. In fact, this generation of musicians was called 'the future of music' by some music experts.

Saida It sounds fascinating. Can you send me a link …

Unit 9, Pronunciation, page 103, exercise b, track 2.56

1 I'm going to buy another one.
2 My brother's living in America.
3 The computer was made in China.

Workbook Audioscripts

Unit 1, Culture: Listening, page 93, exercise 4, track 30

Interviewer Welcome to *Do Something*. Today, we're asking about hobbies. I'm here with Caleb. Hi. Where are you from?
Caleb I'm from Windsor, near London.
Interviewer OK. And what's your favourite free-time activity?
Caleb I like rowing. I go three times a week, before school.
Interviewer Before school? What time do you get up?
Caleb Well, I usually get up at seven o'clock, but on rowing days I always get up at six o'clock.
Interviewer And what do you like about rowing?
Caleb I love being on the river. It's quiet and relaxing. But I don't enjoy getting up early. In fact, I hate it – especially in the winter!
Interviewer Caleb, thank you.

Unit 2, Culture: Listening, page 94, exercise 4, track 32

Hedy Lamarr was a famous Hollywood actress. She was in more than 30 films in the 1930s and 1940s. But she was also an inventor. She was born in Austria in 1914, but she moved to the USA to be an actress. In Hollywood, Lamarr didn't like parties. She was interested in new ideas. In 1942, during the Second World War, Lamarr and her friend George Antheil talked about radio signals to torpedoes, or bombs used in the sea. They thought of a way to make sure the enemy didn't stop the torpedoes. Their idea was a way of changing the frequency of the radio signals controlling the torpedoes so that the enemy could not jam, or break, them. But the American government didn't use their idea at the time. Years later, their idea helped develop the wireless technology in modern mobile phones and wi-fi.

Unit 3, Culture: Listening, page 95, exercise 4, track 34

Ada Blackjack lived on a deserted island for two years. In 1921, she got a job as a cook for some explorers. They travelled to Wrangel Island in the Arctic Ocean, but the weather was bad and they couldn't leave the island. They ate all their food and couldn't hunt enough animals for meat. Some of the explorers went to get help, but a man called Lorne Knight was too ill to travel, so he and Ada stayed on the island. After Knight died, Ada was alone. She hunted birds and other animals. After a few more months, a ship arrived and an explorer rescued Ada. She went home, but she returned to the Arctic later and lived there until the age of 85.

Unit 4, Culture: Listening, page 96, exercise 4, track 36

Hi. I'm Madison and I'm from San Francisco in the USA. I think San Francisco is the best city in the world! What's San Francisco famous for? Well, the Golden Gate Bridge, of course, but there are other things, too. The city's cable cars are probably as famous as the bridge. Tickets cost around $5 – and riding in a cable car is a great way to see the city! There's Chinatown, too. It's on Grant Avenue, the oldest street in the city. There are lots of shops and restaurants, and it's really fun. If you want to visit a famous old prison, you can take a boat to Alcatraz. Alcatraz is a small rocky island out in San Francisco Bay. The prison closed in 1963, so there aren't any prisoners there now.

Unit 5, Culture: Listening, page 97, exercise 4, track 38

Rosa Parks was born in Alabama in 1913. From a young age, Rosa was interested in equality for African-American people and she and her husband worked as volunteers in a civil rights organization. Rosa worked in a department store and she took the bus there and back every day. On 1st December 1955, the bus driver asked her to give up her seat to a white person and Rosa refused. This wasn't the first time Rosa refused and the police arrested her. A bus boycott followed and, after 13 months, segregation ended. Rosa paid a high price for her courage. She lost her job and had to move to Detroit because white people attacked her home. But she continued working for civil rights and dedicated her life to helping African-American people. Many people called her the 'mother of the Civil Rights Movement'. She died on 24th October 2005.

Unit 6, Culture: Listening, page 98, exercise 4, track 40

And now, the news. A 16-year-old boy has become the youngest person to walk to the North Pole. Lewis Clarke, from Bristol in England, has spent nearly 50 days in freezing temperatures and winds of 190 kilometres an hour. Lewis started his 1,100-kilometre journey on 2nd December, just two weeks after his 16th birthday. During the trip, Lewis travelled an average of eight hours a day on skis, and covered around 29 kilometres a day. Now, Lewis is coming back home to study for his GCSE exams at school. He has raised more than £3,000 for charity.

Unit 7, Culture: Listening, page 99, exercise 4, track 42

Interviewer I'm Katy Simpson, reporting for London Radio. I'm outside the Roxy Cinema for the first night of the new *Hunger Games* film, *Mockingjay*. It's just been released. Excuse me? Hi! What's your name?
Bethany Bethany.
Interviewer Can I ask you what you thought of the film, Bethany?
Bethany Amazing! The plot is really clever and the stunts were brilliant. So exciting! And Jennifer Lawrence is wonderful. Perfect. I think she'll get an Oscar for this – best actress. It's her best film ever.
Interviewer And you're her friend? Boyfriend, maybe?
Josh Er, well …
Interviewer OK! What's your name?
Josh Josh. Er, yeah, I thought it was really good. Philip Seymour Hoffman also stars in the film and he's fantastic. There are some great special effects with some animals in the forest, too.
Bethany You'll love it!
Interviewer Bethany, Josh, thank you. And, you, can I ask you … ?

Unit 8, Culture: Listening, page 100, exercise 4, track 44

Hi. I'm Lydia and my best friend is Natalie. How did we meet? Well, we first met at primary school, actually. We started on the same day. I found lunchtime very noisy and I was crying. Natalie was really kind. She came up to me and took my hand. She sat with me and I didn't feel sad any more. We've been best friends since that day. She was much braver than me at school – she still is! – and more confident. I love spending time with her. What do I like about her? Well, she's always telling jokes and she makes me laugh. She's always generous, too. And If I was ever in trouble, I know Natalie would help me without asking any questions. She'll always be there for me.

Unit 9, Culture: Listening, page 101, exercise 4, track 46

The Arctic Monkeys are from Sheffield, a city in the north of England. They are Alex Turner (vocals), Jamie Cook (guitar), Nick O'Malley (bass) and Matt Helders (drums). The band was formed in 2002 when they were at school. One of the reasons the Arctic Monkeys became successful is that fans of the band used the internet to share music and information. The fans filmed the band and put the videos on a website. Their first single, *I bet you look good on the dance floor*, was released in October 2005. It went straight to number one and became an instant hit.
Since those early days, the Arctic Monkeys have released five studio albums and one live album and are famous all over the world. If you want to see them in concert, you should get tickets as soon as possible because they sell out fast!